CW01084506

ILLUSTRATED FLORA OF MALLORCA

ELSPETH BECKETT

ILLUSTRATED FLORA OF MALLORCA

Illustrations by the author

EDITORIAL MOLL
MALLORCA
2008

First edition: July 1993
Second edition: January 2008

© Elspeth Beckett
© Editorial Moll
Can Valero, 25
07011 Palma (Mallorca)
E-mail:info@editorialmoll.cat
http://www.editorialmoll.cat

ISBN: 978-84-273-0895-4
Depòsit Legal: PM-3.057-2007

Imprès a Gràfiques Mallorca — Inca

CONTENTS

PREFACE
from the First Edition

This book is intended to be an easily accessible guide to the flowering plants of Mallorca. It is modelled on W. Keble Martin: *The Concise British Flora in Colour*, Ebury Press and Michael Joseph 1965.

It falls short of the model in many ways. One is unavoidable. Not all the illustrations here are from Mallorcan specimens. Keble Martin lived mainly in industrial parishes, and his 'patch' was much larger, but it was more accessible than mine, and some of it could be reached for short excursions as well as longer holidays. My visits to Mallorca totalled 1-3 weeks a year until I retired recently and could go rather more. He also started when he was younger and spread his efforts over 60 years.

This does mean that some plants may look 'not quite right' to people who live in Mallorca. I have made it clear in the text when a non-Mallorcan specimen was used, usually for rarer plants. Occasionally I found something in Mallorca after painting it from a specimen from elsewhere. If it looked very different I repainted the page, otherwise I added a small supplementary illustration or a note in the text.

Like Keble-Martin I was engaged for much of the time I was working on this project in another occupation. He was a parson, I was a GP. My first trip to Mallorca in 1976 was to take some of my children for a cheap sunny holiday. A lot of people go for the same reason. Some, sadly, never venture beyond the beaches, and so miss the best things -wild rugged mountains with spectacular rock formations, stony paths without a house in sight, nightingales singing, frogs croaking, and flowers everywhere.

Visitors to Mallorca cannot always depend on the sun. It can rain heavily there at almost any time of the year, particularly in the spring. It is because of this that flowers can be found in plenty at almost any time, and the countryside may remain green and lush much later in the year than in other parts of the Mediterranean area.

The list of plants known to occur in Mallorca is derived from:

F. Barceló: *Flora de las Islas Baleares*. Palma de Mallorca 1879-1881

F. Bonafè: *Flora de Mallorca*. Palma de Mallorca 1977-80

J. Duvigneaud: *Catalogue Provisoire de la Flore des Baléares*, Liège, 2nd Edition 1979

Alfred Hansen: *Additions and Corrections to J. Duvigneaud Catalogue Provisoire de la Flore des Baléares, 2. Edition*. Copenhagen 1985 (privately circulated): also correspondence with Dr Hansen.

H. Knoche: *Flora Balearica*. Montpellier 1921-23

Lleonard Llorens et al. (1991) (unpublished at time of writing).

Tutin et al.: *Flora Europaea*. Cambridge 1964-80

And various papers mentioned in the text and in the bibliography.

A few were added from specimens and photos from members of the Botanical Society of the British Isles, and from my own 'finds' in Mallorca. I have tried to illustrate most of the flowering plants likely to be found now, excepting hybrids, and usually only including one subspecies if there is more than one. I had hoped at one time to include *all* the flowering plants ever recorded for Mallorca, but this was a hope only a very inexperienced botanist could entertain. Gradually I came to realise that there was, as in other areas, a body of well-established plants that fluctuates very little over the years, including some rare ones. But there are too records over 200 years or so of about the same number of marginally established species which come and go. These include some escaping from cultivation as crops or for ornament and some arriving as impurities in seed for cultivation, or carried by birds and other agencies (including botanists' socks?). There are some very doubtful records where one plant has been recorded for another (for example *Hypericum elodes* for *H. tomentosum*). Because of my initial optimism some of the plates completed first include plants which have not been seen in Mallorca recently if ever (for example *Moluccella spinosa*). Their status should be clear from the text.

The illustrations are pen drawings coloured in watercolour. A sample of each plant is included, but not usually the whole plant. For most grasses I have shown only the flowering part. Live specimens or close-up photographs were used when possible, but some were done from herbarium specimens. I have tried to avoid numbering of details as much as possible as this tends to clutter up the page -the main number is usually placed between the main illustration and the corresponding details. Usually the main illustration is x 1 or slightly reduced, and the details more or less enlarged. Hairs were drawn in sepia ink like the main outline: this does not mean that they were this colour.

Each plant illustrated is described in a correspondingly numbered entry in the text. The descriptions are largely based on those in the Flora Europaea, to which a page reference is added whenever possible. I have given an English name when I know a genuine one, but not when the only name is one recently contrived from the Latin.

The description is followed by the flowering time, usually after Knoche or from my own observation, and some indication of habitat and/or rarity.

ACKNOWLEDGEMENTS

I am much indebted to the authors and publishers of sources listed in the Bibliography, especially those listed in the Preface, and to Mr Anthony Bonner, whose *Plants of the Balearic Islands* (Palma de Mallorca 1982) with its excellent bibliography put me on the right track for many plants and nearly all the sources of information.

Others who have helped me include first and foremost Dr Stephen Jury, Curator of the Herbarium of Reading University and Dr Humphrey Bowen, until recently unofficial doyen of the same department.

Next I would like to thank the Botanical Society of the British Isles, particularly the then General Secretary Mrs Mary Briggs, but for whose encouragement in the early stages I might have given up. An advertisement in *BSBI News* produced many species I could not find, and I am indebted to the following for photographs and specimens: Mr Rodney Burton, Mr Chris Burkinshaw (who produced *on the spot* a live plant of *Damasonium alisma* at a BSBI meeting in the British Museum of Natural History), Mrs A.A.Butcher, Mr Eric J. Clement, Dr Susan Eden (many photographs, specimens and general encouragement), Mr John Hooper, Mr David Nicolle, Mr John Ounsted (who gave me growing plants of *Veronica verna* and *Trifolium dubium*), Mr Alan Outen, Mr R.M.Payne, Mr Mervyn Southam, Mrs R. Strickland, Mr W.F.Taylor, Mr Mark Thompson, Dr R.M. Veall and Mr J.J.Zawadski.

In the later stages I received much help from Professor Lleonard Llorens of the Universitat de les Illes Balears, who went through the whole text and suggested some alterations, particularly to do with distribution of plants in Mallorca. He also lent me a copy of his new list of Balearic plants before publication. Dr Juan Rita of the same department helped with specimens of plants I had failed to find, and specimens and photos of a new endemic he had recently discovered. Dr Irene Ridge and Mr Fred Rumsey came to Mallorca with me, adding their professional skills to my inexpertise. Mrs Pat Bishop of the RSPB in Mallorca encouraged with her characteristic kindness, and she and her late husband, Mr Dennis Bishop introduced me to other naturalists who shared their warm hospitality, including Professor Palmer Newbould, Mrs Jo Newbould and Mrs Dinah McLennan, all working for Earthwatch in the Albufera, who helped find several missing species.

Dr S.M.Walters kindly allowed me to take live specimens from Cambridge University Botanic Garden. These include most of the species I have noted 'from garden specimen', though a few were from photographs taken at the Royal Botanic Gardens at Kew and the Oxford University Botanic Garden, and some from my own garden, grown from commercial sources. Mr Alan Cook's enthusiastic help in finding live specimens of some of the grasses at the Royal Botanic Gardens at Kew was particularly appreciated. Mr A.R.Vickery, the Keeper, kindly loaned some specimens from the British Museum Herbarium.

Others I thank for expert opinions on difficult species: Dr John Akeroyd, Dr R.R.Baum, Mr P.M.Benoit, Dr P.F.Cannon, Professor C.D.K.Cook, Dr Matthias Erben, Dr Alfred Hansen, Dr A.C.Jermy, Professor D.M.Moore, Dr J.R.Press, Dr Juan Rita, Dr T.C.G.Rich, Mr Fred Rumsey, M/s Fatima Sales, Mme Odette and M. André Sotiaux, Professor Clive A. Stace, Mr P.D.Sell, Dr P.J.O.Trist, Dr Sara Webster, Dr Frank White and Mr Jeffery Wood.

My thanks too to Señor Francesc Moll, the publisher, for his friendly co-operation and for bringing the whole endeavour to fruition. His personal knowledge of the plants of Mallorca and the out-of-the-way places where they grow was an added bonus. And finally, family and friends, many of whom came to Mallorca with me and helped in the search, and the people of Mallorca whose hospitality so adds to the many pleasures to be experienced in their beautiful island.

PREFACE to the second edition

In this edition many mistakes to which the reviewers or others have drawn attention have been corrected. I have visited Mallorca again, and all names are now given with an authority. As far as possible I have used names from the first edition of the FE. I felt that this was more likely to be available (usually in the larger Public Libraries) to the interested amateur than local Flora and monographs, and though the constant revision and updating of botanical names may be desirable for professional botanists, for amateurs it is much less confusing to stick as far as possible to a readily available standard work.

SIGNS and ABBREVIATIONS: HOW TO USE THIS BOOK

Ma, Mi, and I indicate records from Mallorca, Minorca and Ibiza respectively. Reference to smaller islands (mainly Formentera off the coast of Ibiza and Dragonera and Cabrera off the coast of Mallorca) is made only when one of these is the only station for a particular plant in the Balearic Islands.

It seems important that those compiling lists of plants occurring in an area indicate whether they have personally seen it alive in the area. Plants become extinct, and the presence of a nineteenth century specimen of a plant from Mallorca in a herbarium does not prove that it is part of the current Flora. I have seen live specimens of all the **ILLUSTRATED** plants from Mallorca except those with **NS** (Not Seen). I have not seen those not illustrated.

In cases where I have not seen the plant I have indicated when Duvigneaud records having seen it, his list being comparatively recent. Knoche (1921-23) indicates when he has seen a plant in the Balearic Islands, but does not always make it clear whether he has seen it in Mallorca. Other lists, including Professor Llorens' list, do not distinguish between recent records and herbarium specimens. Plants not recorded as having been seen recently may in fact have been seen, and the finding not published or published in a publication unseen by me. Some of these plants are rare, some very like a commoner plant and therefore overlooked. Sometimes plants are under-recorded because they flower when not many people are looking for them, or because they are too dull for much consideration.

Where the FE does not record a plant as occurring in the Balearic Islands I have added 'Not BI in FE'. 'BI in FE' is only added where there seems some doubt about the occurrence of a plant here. The FE, though a reference work of truly monumental importance, is not always right (and it is inconceivable that a work with such an enormous range of factual information should ever be so).

At the end of each page of text opposite the illustrations there is a list of plants occurring only in the other Balearic Islands. This is to help people who may use the Flora in Minorca or Ibiza. These records are listed without reference to the source or any critical evaluation of it, apart from a ? when I know the record to be doubtful. These islands are strictly outside the scope of this book.

Other abbreviations:

cf .... compare
subsp. .... subspecies
x .... multiplied by (degree of linear magnification or reduction)

NOTES ON THE MALLORCAN FLORA

Islands well separated from the mainland tend to have an interesting flora which has evolved in isolation. There may also be relics of an older flora whose survival has somehow been facilitated, for instance by the non-occurrence of a competitor. *Hypericum balearicum*, the endemic St John's Wort, is such a survivor from a group which has disappeared from the mainland. There are 30 -40 species and subspecies endemic to Mallorca (and others endemic to the Balearic Islands as a group), and many plants here show the beginning of speciation in minor but significant variation from mainland populations.

There is at least one monotypic genus on the island which is confined to Mallorca and Corsica, the minute umbellifer *Naufraga balearica*. *Centaurea balearica*, an endemic of Minorca once (dubiously) recorded from Mallorca has recently been separated from *Centaurea* because of its distinctive features and is now named *Femeniasia balearica* (Rodr. Fem.) Susanna.

Other plants here are outposts of the African flora. *Silene pseudatocion* seems to be increasing in Mallorca, its only station in Europe. *Helianthemum caput-felis* and *Tamarix boveana*, also African species, have a local foothold on mainland Spain too.

Some of the absences are interesting too. They include *Juniperus communis, Urtica dioica, Pastinaca sativa, Bellis perennis* and probably *Sagina procumbens* and *Cerastium fontanum*, all of which are very widespread in Europe outside these islands. Some people eat *Urtica dioica*, and butterflies like it too, but for me any place without it deserves extra points, not because it stings (so does the remarkable *Urtica atrovirens* subsp. *bianorii*), but because it has displaced so many more attractive plants in the British hedgerows.

Some of the plant communities in Mallorca

Pinewoods

Many areas of the coast and lower slopes of the mountains are covered in woods of *Pinus halepensis*. Except where these are too dense there is an understorey of shrubs such as *Pistacia lentiscus, Cistus monspeliensis, Fumana thymifolia, Phillyrea angustifolia, Smilax aspera* and *Ruscus aculeatus*. Occasionally the spectacular purplish spikes of the Orchid *Limodorum abortivum* may be found here.

Where the wood is thinner or recently burnt *Cistus salvifolius* may replace *Cistus monspeliensis*, with some *Cistus albidus*. Herbaceous plants here may include *Lotus tetraphyllus, Linum trigynum, Rubia peregrina, Dorycnium pentaphyllum* and *Blackstonia perfoliata*.

Dry open habitats not under trees

These are often dominated by a Pampas-like grass, *Ampelodesmos mauritanica*, sometimes with *Rosmarinus officinalis, Hypericum balearicum, Astragalus balearicus* and *Cneorum tricoccon*. In other places broom-like shrubs predominate, *Calicotome spinosa* (mainly in the north and west), and *Genista lucida* (mainly in the east). Other shrubs occurring locally in dry open scrub are *Chamaerops humilis* (the Mediterranean Dwarf Palm), *Arbutus unedo* (the Strawberry tree) and *Euphorbia dendroides*.

Herbaceous plants which often grow here are *Orchis pyramidalis, Rumex intermedius, Ferula communis,* and *Thapsia gymnesica* Rosselló & Pujadas, *Ruta* species, *Coris monspeliensis,* the pinkish form of *Centaurea maritima, Ajuga iva, Teucrium chamaedrys, Teucrium botrys, Micromeria filiformis* and, flowering in the autumn, *Urginea maritima*.

In open areas in the higher parts of the mountains a high proportion of the plants are endemic to the Balearic Islands or to Mallorca. *Hypericum balearicum, Phlomis italica* and the 'hedgehog plants' *Teucrium subspinosum* and *Astragalus balearicus* (hedgehog-sized lower down, but up to 1m high nearer the peaks) may be dominant over large areas, with other shrubby species locally such as *Rhamnus lycioides, Buxus balearica, Acer granatense, Santolina chamaecyparissus* and Whitebeam, Yew and Holly (all three rather rare here). Herbaceous plants include *Helleborus foetidus* and *H. lividus, Linaria aeruginea* subsp. *pruinosa, Pastinaca lucida, Arenaria grandiflora, Vincetoxicum hirundinaria* and, flowering later in the year, *Merendera filifolia* and *Crocus cambessedesii*.

Roadsides and fields

One of Mallorca's main attractions (one I have never seen mentioned in tour operators' brochures) is the country lanes, winding between orchards of almond, fig, carob and olive carpeted with *Calendula officinalis* or *Bellis annua,* and crops of broad beans and other vegetables with *Allium nigrum, Anchusa azurea* and *Gladiolus illyricus* sticking out above them and *Adonis annua* and *Nigella damascena* hiding beneath them. On either side are walls covered in *Clematis cirrhosa* subsp. *balearica,* and *Rosa sempervirens,* or hedgerows of Sloe, Blackberry and wild Olive as a backing to a herbaceous border of Poppies, *Kundmannia sicula, Echium plantagineum, Urospermum dalechampii, Allium roseum* and, later, Fennel and *Dittrichia viscosa.* A walk along such a lane is full of surprises, including people picking the tender young shoots of *Asparagus acutifolius* to eat à la beurre.

Where the walls are of traditional stone (many now, alas, are of concrete blocks) they may support *Polypodium australe, Sedum dasyphyllum, S. stellatum, S. sediforme, Umbilicus* species, *Saxifraga tridactylites, Anagallis arvensis, Centranthus calcitrapae,* several species of *Valerianella, Campanula erinus, Muscari neglectum,* and *Ophrys speculum* -and many other plants.

Oakwoods

Woods of *Quercus ilex,* the Holm Oak, dominate much of the lower slopes of the mountains. They are often too dense to be hospitable to other plants. In the most shaded parts there may be saprophytic plants not dependant on light such as the yellow bird's nest, *Monotropa hypopitys,* and the orchids *Neottia nidus-avis* and *Limodorum abortivum. Epipactis microphylla* also tolerates quite heavy shade. Where a little less shady most of the shrubs found in Pinewoods will grow, especially *Cistus monspeliensis,* which seems to tolerate shade well, with Bracken and the orchids *Cephalanthera damasonium* and *C. longifolia.*

Selaginella denticulata, Asplenium trichomanes, Ceterach officinarum, Polypodium australe, Sibthorpia africana, Erodium reichardii and *Arenaria balearica* are all common on moist overhung surfaces of walls and rocks in the woods.

Sandy habitats, including coastal dunes and the higher parts of sandy shores

Larger shrubs in sandy coastal areas not covered by trees include the almost ubiquitous *Pistacia lentiscus*, also *Juniperus oxycedrus* and *J. phoenicea*. Locally *Halimium halimifolium, Solanum sodomeum, Myrtus communis, Phillyrea angustifolia*, and *Cistus clusii* may also be found. Where not over trampled there may be a nearly continuous cover between these of smaller shrubs, including small plants of *Cistus salvifolius*, with *Teucrium polium, Helichrysum stoechas, Fumana thymifolia, Limonium echioides, Scrophularia ramosissima* and *Crucianella maritima*.

Herbaceous plants here include *Rumex bucephalophorus, Medicago littoralis, Lotus cytisoides, Centaurium tenuiflorum*, many species and hybrids of *Limonium, Erodium cicutarium, Frankenia* species, *Euphorbia terracina, Eryngium maritimum, Ononis reclinata, Convolvulus cantabrica, C. althaeoides, Orchis coriophora, Ophrys* species, and more locally *Asteriscus maritimus, Matthiola sinuata, Medicago marina, Thesium humile, Petrorhagia nanteuilii, Ajuga iva* and *Tuberaria guttata*.

Saltmarshes

Some of these have disappeared under coastal development, but saltmarsh species survive behind the hotels of Can Pastilla and S'Arenal. Small areas remain in many places, including Port de Pollença, the Albufereta and Port d'Andratx. All these have their own peculiar plants with a limited distribution elsewhere, including *Gynandiris sisyrhinchium, Cressa cretica*, and *Sphenopus divaricatus*.

The main saltmarsh areas are the Albufera (including the area outside the Nature Reserve), and the Salines of Campos. The Albufera has areas of dune as well as saltmarsh, though parts of the dunes outside the nature reserve are being bulldozed away to make artificial beaches (perhaps these areas will become new areas of saltmarsh). Large areas of the marsh are dominated by *Phragmites australis, Cladium mariscus, Scirpus maritimus, Arundo donax, Juncus maritimus, J. subulatus, Inula crithmoides, Arthrocnemum fruticosum* and *A. glaucum*.

Other species in the wetter parts of the marsh include *Aster tripolium, Salsola soda, Euphorbia pubescens, Apium nodiflorum, Pulicaria odora, Sonchus maritimus, Typha domingensis* and *Orchis laxiflora*. In the drier parts there are *Melilotus messanensis, Lotus tenuis, Dittrichia graveolens, Ranunculus trilobus, Juncus acutus, J. bufonius, Daucus carota, Plantago coronopus, P. crassifolia, Polypogon monspeliensis, P. maritimus, Spergularia media, Trifolium squamosum* and *Atriplex* species.

Other habitats

Many other habitats will be recognised, not least the urban areas pottered round after the evening meal and in breaks between longer excursions. I hope there will not be too many specimens to sort, and perhaps by making field identification easier this book will make collection hardly necessary.

The serious student of botany will find specimens of the flora already in herbaria somewhere, and for those whose interest in plants is more aesthetic than botanical a good photo beats a herbarium specimen every time. For the competitive plant hunter ('I found 70 species, how many did you find?') a careful list is as good as anything, and the sport becomes as innocuous as cricket if it involves minimal collection. The list will bring back happy memories for years.

Wild plants everywhere have many factors stacked against their survival. These include trampling, urban development, use of weedkillers and climate change. In the wilder parts of Mallorca very heavy grazing by goats is taking its toll. Collecting is making its impact too. Careful collection of common plants may seem harmless, but I suspect this is because our own little collection makes no obvious difference *at the time that we make it*. Incrementally the effect may be enormous -some favoured spots are visited by dozens of botanists. Far worse the criminal theft of whole colonies of wild orchids, usually destined to perish, that has occurred recently in some areas here.

Many of the rarer plants in this book were painted from close-up photographs taken in the field. I did collect some specimens too. I regret in particular *Helianthemum origanifolium* subsp. *serrae*. In 1984 I collected a small specimen from what was then a substantial patch. I didn't know what it was at the time, nor that its *only known station in the world* was on waste ground adjacent to a crowded tourist resort. It is now probably extinct. Many others may have taken their small specimens from the same patch, or it may just have been trampled to death.

Fostering an interest in plants encourages people to care for them, and to this extent a little judicious collecting may be defensible. But the notion that the only purpose of the natural world is to supply the needs of mankind is losing ground. If we leave plants where we find them they may incidentally delight people yet to come. More important, they will continue to multiply and evolve to enrich the diversity of species in his lovely but beleaguered planet.

BIBLIOGRAPHY

GENERAL

Alomar, G., Rita, J., & Rosselló, J.A.(1986): *Notas Florísticas de las Islas Baleares* (III). Boll. Soc. Hist. Nat. Balears 30: 145-154. Palma.

Barceló y Combis, D.F. (1879-1881): *Flora de las Islas Baleares.* Palma.

Bonafè, F. (1977-1980): *Flora de Mallorca* (4 vols). Editorial Moll. Palma.

Bonner, A. (1982): *Plants of the Balearic Islands.* Editorial Moll. Palma.

Duvigneaud, J. (1979): *Catalogue Provisoire de la Flore des Baléares.* Second Edition. Liège. (Supplement to Fascicule no 17 of Société pour L'Échange des Plantes Vasculaires de L'Europe Occidentale et du Bassin Méditerranéen).

Greuter, W., Burdet, H.M., & Long, G. (1985-1989): *Med-Checklist.* Secrétariat Med-Checklist, Conservatoire et Jardin Botanique de la Ville de Genève.

Hansen, A. (1985): *Additions and Corrections to J. Duvigneaud: Catalogue Provisoire de la Flore des Baléares 2nd Edition.* (Unpublished circulated list).

Hutchinson, J. (1959): *The Families of Flowering Plants.* Oxford.

Knoche, H. (1921-1923): *Flora Balearica.* Montpellier.

Llorens, Ll. et al. (1991): (List of plants occurring in the Balearic Islands in course of publication).

Martin, W.K. (1965): *The Concise British Flora in Colour.* London.

Rita, J., Bibiloni, G., & Llorens, Ll. (1985): *Notas Florísticas de las Islas Baleares* (I). Boll. Soc. Hist. Nat. Balears 29: 129-133. Palma.

Smythies, B.E. (1984-1986): *Flora of Spain and the Balearic Islands.* Englera 3 (1-3). Berlin.

Tutin, T.G., Heywood, V.H., Burges, N.A., Valentine, D.H., Walters, S.M., & Webb, D.A. (1964-1980): *Flora Europaea* 1st Edition. Cambridge.

FOR PARTICULAR PLANTS OR OTHER ISLANDS

Euphorbia myrsinites: Colom, G. (1957): *Biogeografía de las Baleares.* Palma.

Filago petro-ianii: Dittrich, M. and Rita, J. in Kit Tan (Ed.) (1989): *Plant Taxonomy, Phytogeography and Related Subjects.* The Davis and Hedge Festschrift. Edinburgh University Press.

IBIZA: Kuhbier, H. (1978): Veröff. Überseemuseum Bremen 5: 6-37.

Juncus: Cope, T.A., & Stace, C.A. (1980): Watsonia 12: 113-128 (Differences between *Juncus bufonius* and *Juncus hybridus*).

Limonium: Erben, M. (1980 -1989): *Bemerkungen zur Taxonomie der Gattung Limonium.* Mitt. Bot. Staatssamml. München 16: 547-563, 17: 485-510, 22: 203-220, 27: 381-406, and 28: 313-417.

MINORCA: Cardona, A. & Rita, J. (1982): *Aportació al Coneixement de la Flora Balear.* Fol. Bot. Misc., 3: 35-42. Barcelona.

Tamarix: Baum, B.R. (1978): *The Genus Tamarix.* Jerusalem.

Thymus herba-barona: Mayol, M., Rosselló, J.A. (1990): Anales Jardín Botánico de Madrid 47 (2): 516

Torilis: Jury S.L. (1987): *A New Species of the Genus Torilis Adanson.* Bot. J. Linn. Soc. 95: 293-299.

GLOSSARY
(Numbers in brackets refer to drawings)

Acaulescent: without a stem (or with a very short one).

Achene: a dry one-seeded fruit (25c).

Acuminate: tapering to a point (1).

Alternate: (usually of leaves) strictly on one then the other side of the stem in two rows: here (as often) used to mean not in opposite pairs (2).

Amplexicaul: (of a stalkless leaf or bract): clasping the stem (3).

Anastomosing: (of veins), connected by cross-branches.

Annual plant: one which goes through its entire life-cycle in one year (often recognised by the absence of non-flowering shoots at time of flowering).

Anther: the male pollen-bearing organ of a flower (4a).

Apiculate: (usually of leaves), with a minute blunt point at the tip (5).

Appressed: pressed against (eg of hairs on a stem), as opposed to spreading.

Arista: a bristly pointed appendage, long or short (adjective **aristate**) (6).

Ascending: sloping or curving upwards.

Auricle: an ear-like projection (usually at the base of an amplexicaul leaf) (3a).

Awn: a stiff bristly pointed appendage (same as arista, but used in different contexts, especially in description of flowers of grasses) (27e and f).

Axil: the angle between a leaf or bract and the stem from which it arises (adjective **axillary**, of a stem or other part arising in the axilla). (7 shows axillary flower).

Basal: at the base or lower end (basal leaves at the base of the stem, cauline on the stem).

Berry: a fleshy fruit with one or more seeds in the pulp (seeds not enclosed in a stony endocarp, as in plum).

Biennial plant: a plant which germinates in the first year (usually producing a rosette of leaves), then flowers, fruits and dies in the second year.

Bifid: split into two parts.

Bipinnate: with the pinnae pinnate (8).

Boss: a swelling or protuberance, e.g. at the throat of the corolla-tube in Scrophulariaceae such as *Antirrhinum* (8a).

Bract: a scale or small leaf-like structure on a stem (9b, 17a, 46d). In a spike or raceme there may be a gradual transition up the stem from leaves to bracts.

Bracteole: a bract on a peduncle or pedicel, not on the main stem (17b, 20a, 46b).

Bristle: a stiff hair.

Bulbil: a small bulb produced vegetatively, often above ground e.g. in the inflorescence of *Allium* species.

Calyx: green or dull-coloured outer perianth-whorl of sepals, usually the outer of two whorls (10a, 28f), the inner being the corolla. Sometimes the only whorl where this is dull-coloured.

Capitate: gathered into a head (of an inflorescence with many flowers).

Capsule: dry, usually thin-walled fruit formed from two or more fused carpels, usually splitting when ripe (11b, 13b).

Carpel: a single unit of the gynoecium (12a) (there often only is one).

Carpophore: axis of flower between calyx attachment and base of ovary e.g. in *Silene* (13c).

Ciliate: with regularly arranged stiff projecting hairs.

Cladode: a modified branch which appears leaf-like, but is in fact a stem (e.g. in *Asparagus* and *Ruscus*).

Claw: the narrowed inner part of a petal.

Cleistogamous: fertilised without opening.

Compound: made up of more than one part as, e.g. a leaf made up of leaflets.

Connate: fused together.

Connivent: gradually convergent; approaching at the extremety: of the anthers, etc.

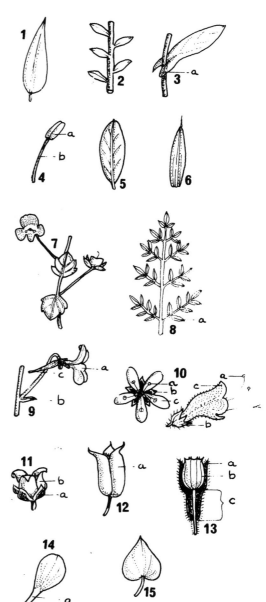

Cordate: heart-shaped with the notch downwards (15).

Corolla: a brightly-coloured perianth-whorl, composed of free or united petals (10c).

Corona: a crown-like structure. A whorl of free or united appendages attached to the inner part of petals as in Asclepiadaceae and some Caryophyllaceae, or the connate bracteoles of the florets in *Scabiosa* (16a).

Corymb: a raceme in which the pedicels get progressively shorter towards the tip of the inflorescence, which is more or less flat-topped like an umbel (17).

Crenate: wavy-edged.

Cuneate: wedge-shaped (base of leaf 18).

Cyathium (pl. cyathia): a cup-shaped structure in *Euphorbia* containing small groups of flowers with 4 or 5 glands at the top (19).

Cyme: a branched inflorescence in which the new growing points are continuously produced by division of the terminal parts so that the newer parts are at the periphery (20).

Decidious: falling off (a decidious tree is one in which all the leaves fall in autumn).

Decumbent: lying on the ground with growing tips turned upward.

Decurrent: running down, e.g. of edges of a sessile leaf running down stem to form a wing (21).

Deflexed: turned downwards.

Dehiscent: breaking open when ripe (of fruit, see 11).

Dentate: toothed (22); strictly different from serrate (q.v.), but often used interchangeably.

Denticulate: with little teeth.

Dichasial cyme: a cyme which divides repeatedly into two more or less equal branches, often with a flower at the point of each division (20).

Dichotomous: dividing into two equal branches (dichasial cyme is repeatedly dichotomous).

Drupe: a fleshy fruit containing one or more seeds, each surrounded by a stony endocarp (e.g. a plum).

Eglandular: without glands.

Emarginate: with a shallow notch at the apex (16a).

Endemic: a species native to a particular (given) area.

Entire: not toothed, notched or cut in any way (23).

Epicalyx: a calyx-like structure outside the calyx (24a).

Exserted: sticking out, not enclosed (e.g. of stamens exserted from a tubular corolla) (10, drawing on right).

Fastigiate: in bundles arising more or less from the same point.

Fertile: capable of producing viable seed or pollen.

Filament: the stalk of an anther (4b).

Floret: a small flower, usually part of a compound inflorescence (25a).

Gland: a small vesicle containing fluid, often oily or sticky and sweetly or unpleasantly scented.

Glandular hair: a gland with a stalk (or hair with a gland at the tip!) (26a).

Glume: a tough more or less scarious bract (e.g. the bracts at the base of the spikelet in grasses) (27a and b).

Gynoecium: the female reproductive parts of a flower, including the carpel or carpels each with stigma and style.

Hastate: spear-shaped.

Head: an inflorescence of many closely set florets (e.g. in Compositae).

Hedgehog-plant: a plant like a hedgehog, smallish, rounded and densely prickly. (They don't walk, however!).

Herb: a plant without woody parts.

Hermaphrodite: with male and female parts.

Hispid: with rough bristles.

Imbricate: overlapping like tiles on a roof (30).

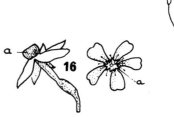
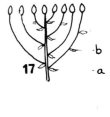
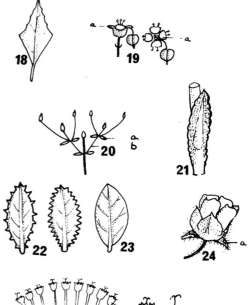
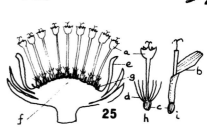

Indehiscent: not breaking open (of a capsule).

Indusium: membranous piece of tissue covering the sporangium in ferns (31a).

Inferior ovary: an ovary with the perianth inserted at the outer end. (Compare 28, which has superior ovary).

Inflorescence: the flowering part of a plant, with branches, flowers and often bracts.

Internode: the interval between nodes.

Involucre: calyx-like structure surrounding a head of flowers.

Involucral bracts: sepal-like bracts forming an involucre (25e).

Keel: the sharp edge where two surfaces meet, like the keel of a boat, as in a keeled grass-leaf (33a). Sometimes includes the surfaces too, as in most Leguminosae, where the keel is the boat-like structure formed by fusion of the two lower petals (33b, 55c).

Labellum: the lower division or lip of an orchidaceous corolla.

Lamina: the soft blade of a leaf (excluding the stalk and central vein).

Lanceolate: lance-shaped (34).

Latex: juice, often milky, especially of *Euphorbia* and some Compositae.

Leaflet: leaf-like segment of a compound leaf (8a, 41a).

Lemma: the outer bract of a single floret in a grass-spike (27c).

Ligule: a tongue-like process e.g. the membranous or hairy process at the junction of a blade of a grass leaf with the sheath, or the elongated fused perianth-segments of a floret in Compositae (25b) (the florets having ligules described as **ligulate** (25i)).

Linear: long and narrow, with more or less parallel sides (35).

Lobed: (of a leaf) deeply indented with the lamina continuous (if the lamina is divided to the mid-vein or rhachis the leaf is compound) (36).

Mucro: a short point (adjective **mucronate**).

Nectar pit: the nectar-secreting depression at the base of 'petals' in *Ranunculus* ('petals' here are strictly 'honey-leaves') (37a).

Node: a thickening in the stem where a leaf or leaves arise (38a).

Nut or **nutlet:** one seeded indehiscent fruit with hard outer covering, not breaking open spontaneously.

Ob-: a prefix meaning upside-down, as in oblanceolate, obcordate.

Obtuse: blunt or rounded.

Ochrea: a membranous sheath or partial sheath formed from fused stipules, as in *Polygonum* (39), plural **ochreae**.

Opposite: in pairs on opposite sides of the stem (40).

Ovary: the part of the gynoecium containing the ovules, consisting in one or more carpels (28c, 32c, 42c).

Ovate: egg-shaped.

Ovule: the female gamete before fertilisation (after which it becomes the seed).

Palmate: with more than 3 leaves arising from the same point (like fingers on the palm of a hand) (41).

Panicle: a branched inflorescence.

Papilla: a small fleshy projection (plural **papillae**, adj. **papillose**).

Pappus: the hairs or scales representing the calyx in the florets of Compositae (25d).

Paripinnate: pinnate with an even number of leaflets, without a terminal leaflet (43b).

Pea-flower: a flower with the general form of the flower of a garden pea, as in most of the family of Leguminosae (55).

Pectinate: comb-like.

Pedicel: the stalk of a single flower in an inflorescence (17b, 46a).

Peduncle: the stalk of an inflorescence or partial inflorescence (20b).

Perennial: a plant that continues to flower and set seed seasonally for more than one year (usually recognised by the presence of non-flowering shoots at flowering time, though this occurs in some annuals too).

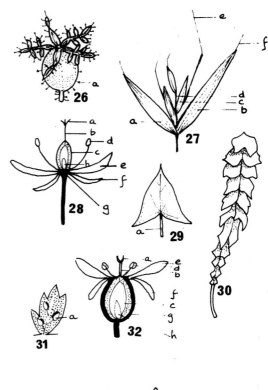

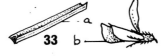

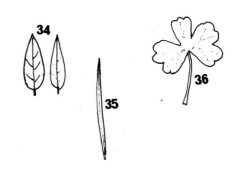

Perianth: the calyx or corolla. Both may be present, in which case there are said to be two perianth whorls.

Pericarp: wall pf ripened ovary.

Perigynous zone: the part of the receptacle of a flower between the base of the ovary and the insertion of the perianth, sometimes distinct, sometimes very small or absent (42i, compare 28 and 32).

Persistent: not caducous.

Petal: a segment of the corolla (10a).

Petaloid: like a petal (brightly coloured).

Petiole: the stalk of a leaf (29a).

Pinna: the leaflet of a pinnate leaf.

Pinnate: (of a compound leaf) with separate leaflets arranged like the parts of a feather, in two rows on either side of the central rhachis (43).

Pinnatifid: as pinnate, but not divided as far as the midrib, so that there are no separate leaflets and the leaf is simple, not compound (44).

Pinnatisect: as pinnatifid, but with some of the divisions to the midrib of the leaf.

Pinnule: the 'pinna' of a pinna in a bipinnate leaf (8a).

Procumbent: lying loosely along the surface of the ground.

Prostrate: lying closely appressed to the ground.

Puberulent: softly covered with short downy hairs.

Pubescent: as puberulent.

Raceme: strictly an unbranched inflorescence in which the pedicellate flowers are arranged along a central axis (45a) (sometimes also used of a part of a branched inflorescence).

Ray: one of the pedicels of an umbellate inflorescence or peduncles of a biumbellate inflorescence (46c).

Ray-leaf: the leaf at the base of a ray in Euphorbiaceae (compare the bract in Umbelliferae).

Raylet: the pedicel of a biumbellate umbellifer.

Receptacle: the upper part of a stem from which the parts of a simple flower arise; also the part to which the separate florets are attached in the heads of Compositae and some other families (25f).

Receptacular scales: small scales on the receptacle between the florets in some Compositae (25g).

Reticulate: forming a fine network.

Rhachis: the central axis (e.g. of a compound leaf, or of a spike or spikelet in grasses (27d).

Rhizome: an underground root-like perennial stem (adj. rhizomatous).

Ruderal: growing around some rubbish (including road-chippings, ruins of buildings and waste places in towns).

Rugose: wrinkled or with ridges.

Sagittate: arrow-shaped (47).

Scarious: stiff and scale-like, not green.

Secund: all pointing towards one side, usually of a spike or a raceme (48).

Sepal: dull-coloured perianth segment, segment of the calyx (10b).

Sepaloid: like a sepal (as opposed to petaloid).

Septum: wall dividing a compartment (e.g. between the two parts of a silicula or siliqua).

Serrate: saw-toothed (49).

Serrulate: finely saw-toothed.

Sessile: unstalked.

Shrub: a perennial with several branched woody stems from at or near ground-level.

Silicula: bivalved pod less than 3 x as long as wide, with an internal septum dividing it into two compartments (50).

Siliqua: as silicula, but more than 3 x as long as wide (51).

Simple: not compound (e.g. of a leaf not divided into leaflets).

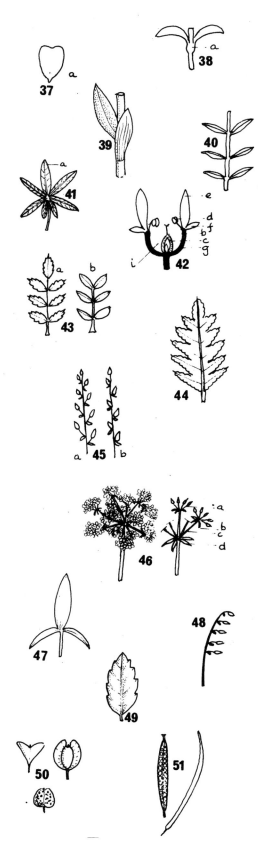

Sorus: a group of Sporangia.

Spadix: the thickened axis of a spike, as in Araceae (52a).

Spathe: a surrounding sheath, of the spadix in Araceae (52b), or the flower buds in, e.g. *Allium* (53a).

Spathulate: spoon-shaped (54).

Spike: an unbranched inflorescence with sessile flowers arranged along an elongated axis (45b).

Spikelet: a group of florets arranged along an axis, especially in Gramineae (27).

Sporangium: spore-producing bodies of Pteridophyta (e.g. fruiting bodies on the underside of the blade of a fern).

Spore: a small asexual, usually unicellular, reproductive body.

Spur: sac-like projection (9c).

Stamen: the male reproductive part of a flower, the anther with or without a filament (4).

Standard: the upper petal of the flower in Leguminosae (55a).

Stellate: star-shaped (or, of hairs, with rays arising from a single point).

Stem: the main axis of a plant, bearing leaves and inflorescence.

Stigma: the part of the gynoecium which collects the pollen (28a, 32a, 42a).

Stipule: a bract at the base of a leaf, sometimes partly fused with the petiole (56b).

Stolon: a creeping stem (normally above ground) from a plant which is otherwise upright: hence stoloniferous, bearing stolons.

Sub-: prefix meaning almost (as suborbicular = almost round).

Sulcate: grooved.

Superior ovary: an ovary lying above the point of attachment of the perianth (28c).

Tendril: specialised part of plant (usually derived from a leaflet) adapted for clinging on to surrounding plants (56a).

Terete: smooth, without projections (of a stem, smoothly rounded).

Ternate: (of a compund leaf) with three parts meeting at a point (57).

Tomentose: densely covered in cottony hairs.

Tricuspidate: with three points (e.g. of stamens in some *Allium* species, which have three points with an anther on the central point) (58).

Trifoliate: (of a compound leaf) used here to mean with three leaflets. (Trifoliolate is more correct but rarely used). This includes ternate leaves (57) and pinnately trifoliate (59).

Truncated: cut straight across, not (or hardly) pointed or shaped at end (60, base of leaf).

Tuberculate: with tubercles.

Tubercle: small swelling (often very small, as on surface of seeds).

Tubular floret: in Compositae is one without a ligule, usually with 5 short equal teeth (25h). Ligulate florets, though tubular at the base, are not called tubular florets. In other families the base of the calyx or corolla segments are commonly fused to form a tube.

Umbel: umbrella-like inflorescence with a whorl of 'spokes' arising from top of stem. The 'spokes' may be pedicels, but are more often peduncles supporting further umbels, when the inflorescence is said to be biumbellate (46).

Undulate: wavy.

Valve: the separate flaps by which a fruit opens.

Vesicle: a small vessel containing fluid.

Wing: either a thin extension of an organ, or the lateral petals, as in Leguminosae (55b).

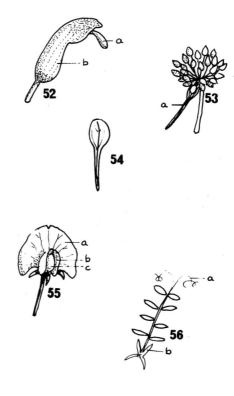

INDEX TO PLATES

With a few minor exceptions genera are in the same order as in the Flora Europaea. Brackets in the heading indicate plants probably occurring in Mallorca but not illustrated.

Plate 45: UMBELLIFERAE (3): *KUNDMANNIA, CONIUM, (MAGYDARIS), BUPLEURUM, APIUM, PETROSELINUM, RIDOLFIA, AMMI*

Plate 46: UMBELLIFERAE (4): *LIGUSTICUM, (CAPNOPHYLLUM), FERULA, PASTINACA, TORDYLIUM, LASERPITIUM, THAPSIA, TORILIS, (TURGENIA), (ORLAYA), DAUCUS, PSEUDORLAYA*

Plate 47: PYROLACEAE: *MONOTROPA*

ERICACEAE: *ERICA, ARBUTUS*

PRIMULACEAE: *PRIMULA, CYCLAMEN, ASTEROLINON, (GLAUX), ANAGALLIS, SAMOLUS, CORIS*

Plate 48: PLUMBAGINACEAE: *LIMONIUM*

Plate 49: OLEACEAE: *(JASMINUM), FRAXINUS, OLEA, PHILLYREA*

GENTIANACEAE: *BLACKSTONIA, CENTAURIUM*

Plate 50: APOCYNACEAE: *NERIUM, VINCA*

ASCLEPIADACEAE: *GOMPHOCARPUS, CYNANCHUM, VINCETOXICUM*

RUBIACEAE (1): *SHERARDIA, CRUCIANELLA, ASPERULA*

Plate 51: RUBIACEAE (2): *GALIUM, VALANTIA, RUBIA*

Plate 52: CONVOLVULACEAE: *CUSCUTA, CRESSA, CALYSTEGIA, CONVOLVULUS, IPOMOEA*

BORAGINACEAE (1): *HELIOTROPIUM*

Plate 53: BORAGINACEAE (2): *LITHOSPERMUM, NEATOSTEMA, BUGLOSSOIDES, ALKANNA, ECHIUM, NONEA, (SYMPHYTUM), ANCHUSA, BORAGO, (MYOSOTIS), (LAPPULA), CYNOGLOSSUM*

Plate 54: VERBENACEAE: *VITEX, VERBENA, LIPPIA*

CALLITRICHACEAE: *CALLITRICHE*

LABIATAE (1): *TEUCRIUM*

Plate 55: LABIATAE (2): *AJUGA, SCUTELLARIA, PRASIUM, MARRUBIUM, SIDERITIS, PHLOMIS, LAMIUM, MOLUCCELLA, BALLOTA*

Plate 56: LABIATAE (3): *STACHYS, (NEPETA), PRUNELLA, (MELISSA), (ACINOS), CALAMINTHA, (SATUREJA), MICROMERIA, (ORIGANUM), THYMUS, MENTHA, ROSMARINUS, LAVANDULA, SALVIA*

Plate 57: SOLANACEAE: *LYCIUM, HYOSCYAMUS, WITHANIA, SOLANUM, LYCOPERSICON, (MANDRAGORA), (DATURA), NICOTIANA*

Plate 58: SCROPHULARIACEAE (1): *VERBASCUM, SCROPHULARIA, ANTIRRHINUM, MISOPATES, CHAENORRHINUM*

Plate 59: SCROPHULARIACEAE (2): *LINARIA, CYMBALARIA, KICKXIA*

Plate 60: SCROPHULARIACEAE (3): *DIGITALIS, ERINUS, VERONICA, SIBTHORPIA, PARENTUCELLIA, BELLARDIA*

Plate 61: GLOBULARIACEAE: *GLOBULARIA*

(ACANTHACEAE: *ACANTHUS*)

OROBANCHACEAE: *OROBANCHE*

Plate 62: PLANTAGINACEAE: *PLANTAGO*

CAPRIFOLIACEAE: *SAMBUCUS, VIBURNUM, LONICERA*

Plate 63: VALERIANACEAE: *VALERIANELLA, FEDIA, CENTRANTHUS*

DIPSACACEAE: *CEPHALARIA, DIPSACUS, SCABIOSA, (KNAUTIA)*

CAMPANULACEAE: *CAMPANULA, LEGOUSIA, TRACHELIUM, LAURENTIA*

Plate 1

SELAGINELLACEAE: *SELAGINELLA*
ISOETACEAE: *ISOETES*
EQUISETACEAE: *EQUISETUM*
OPHIOGLOSSACEAE: *OPHIOGLOSSUM*
SINOPTERIDACEAE: *CHEILANTHES*
ADIANTACEAE: *ADIANTUM*

SELAGINELLACEAE
SELAGINELLA

1. *Selaginella denticulata* L. (Link). Toothed Clubmoss. Creeping perennial. Leaves in 4 ranks, often with fine teeth. Inner two ranks often smaller, but in mature plants all 4 ranks are similar and regularly overlapping. Common in shady places in the mountains. (Ma, Mi, I) FE I 4

ISOETACEAE
ISOETES

2. *Isoetes hystrix* Bory. Quillwort. Sporangia embedded in base of linear leaves. Rare (probably only one site, where flooded in winter).

I. durieui Bory, similar but with larger megaspores was recorded earlier. More recently both species have been found at the same site. (Ma, Mi) FE I 6

EQUISETACEAE
EQUISETUM

3. *Equisetum ramosissimum* Desf. Stems greyish-green, all alike. Branching irregular and variable. Teeth of sheaths with a long thread-like apex. Common in damp places, including higher parts of shore. (Ma, Mi, I) FE I 6

4. *Equisetum arvense* L. Common Horsetail. Fertile and sterile stems distinct. Sterile stems green with 6-19 grooves. Fertile stems brownish with 4-6 sheaths, each with 6-12 teeth. Rather rare. **NS** Seen by Duvigneaud. (From British specimen). (Ma) FE I 8

5. *Equisetum telmateia* Ehrh. Great Horsetail. Fertile and sterile stems distinct. Sterile stems broad and whitish with at least 20 shallow grooves. Fertile stems brownish with numerous sheaths, each with 20-40 teeth. Rather rare. **NS.** Seen by Duvigneaud. (From British specimen x about 1/2: small part of sterile stem shown with branches shortened). (Ma, Mi) FE I 8

OPHIOGLOSSACEAE
OPHIOGLOSSUM

6. *Ophioglossum lusitanicum* L. Portuguese Adder's Tongue. Tiny plant, with entire bract-like lamina enclosing fertile stalked spike of sporangia. Damp places, including higher parts of saltmarsh. **NS** (This from Dr H.J.M.Bowen's recent Ma specimen). (Ma, Mi, I) FE I 8

SINOPTERIDACEAE
CHEILANTHES

7. *Cheilanthes fragrans* (L. fil.) Swartz. Small coumarin-scented fern. Sori covered by deflexed lamina, which has scarious fringed margin. Occasional on mountain rocks. (x 2, detail further enlarged). (Ma, I) FE I 10

8. *Cheilanthes catanensis* (Cosent) H.P.Fuchs. Like 7, but leaves with dense hair-like scales on both sides. **NS** Rare. Not seen by Duvigneaud. (Ma, Mi, I) FE I 10

ADIANTACEAE
ADIANTUM

9. *Adiantum capillus-veneris* L. Maidenhair Fern. Rhizomatous fern with 2-3-pinnate leaves. Segments of leaf fan-shaped. Sori covered by deflexed outer margin. Common in damp places. (Ma, Mi, I) FE I 10

In Minorca:
Isoetes velata A.Braun FE I 6
Isoetes durieui Bory FE I 6

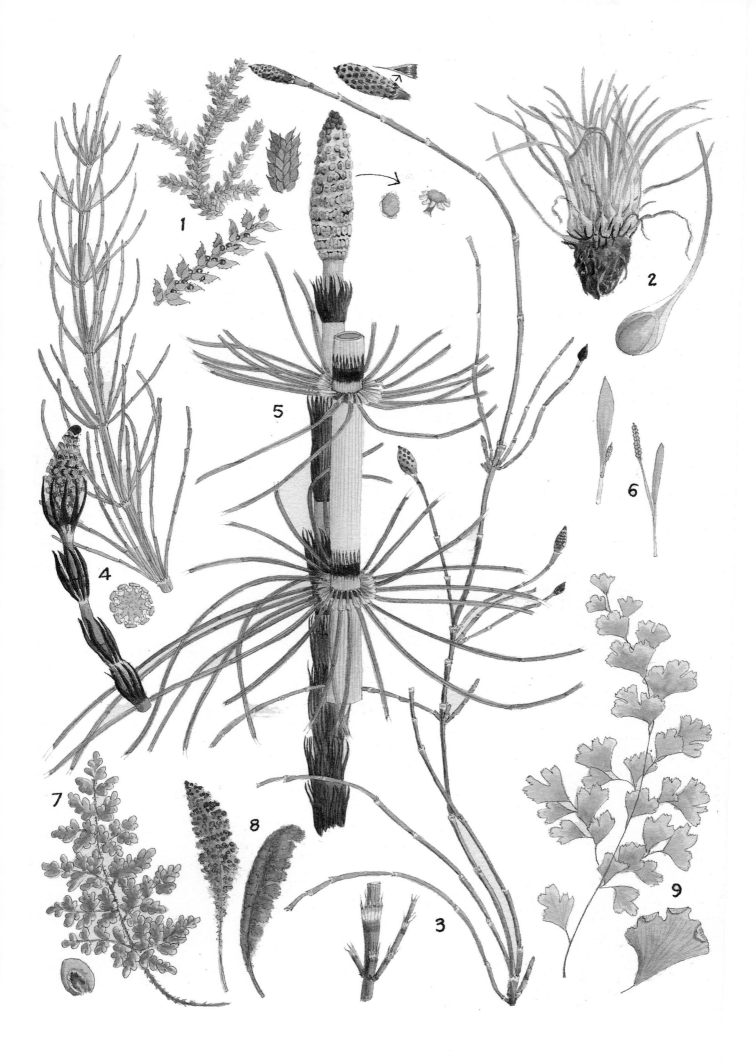

Plate 2

PTERIDACEAE: *PTERIS*
GYMNOGRAMMACEAE: *ANOGRAMMA*
HYPOLEPIDACEAE: *PTERIDIUM*
ASPLENIACEAE: *ASPLENIUM, CETERACH, PHYLLITIS*
ATHYRIACEAE: *ATHYRIUM, CYSTOPTERIS*
ASPIDIACEAE: *POLYSTICHUM, DRYOPTERIS*
POLYPODIACEAE: *POLYPODIUM*
MARSILEACEAE: *MARSILEA*

PTERIDACEAE
PTERIS
1. *Pteris vittata* L. Rhizomatous fern. Leaves pinnatisect, with 10 or more pairs of simple pinnae, slightly cordate at base. **NS.** (From Cretan specimen x about 1/2, detail of longest pinna). Not seen by Duvigneaud. Llorens lists. (Ma) FE I 11

GYMNOGRAMMACEAE
ANOGRAMMA
2. *Anogramma leptophylla* (L.) Link. Rhizomatous fern. Fertile leaves typically longer than sterile and with narrower pinnules. (In this specimen there were many sori on both kinds of leaf). Local in damp shady walls and rock crevices. (Ma, Mi, I) FE I 11

HYPOLEPIDACEAE
PTERIDIUM
3. *Pteridium aquilinum* (L.) Kuhn. Bracken. Rhizomatous fern. Height here usually less than 1m. Stems held vertically. Lamina 3-pinnate (much reduced in illustration). (Ma, Mi, I) FE I 12

ASPLENIACEAE
ASPLENIUM
Rhizomatous perennials. Leaves in apical tufts. Petiole dark, at least at base. Sori elliptical to linear, with indusium same shape.
4. *Asplenium marinum* L. Sea Spleenwort. Leaves 1-pinnate. Rhachis with green wing. **NS.** Seen by Knoche but not Duvigneaud. (From small British specimen). (Ma, Mi) FE I 15
5. *Asplenium petrarchae* (Guérin) DC. Leaves 1-pinnate. Petiole and rhachis densely covered in glandular hairs. Occasional in mountains. (Ma, Mi, I) FE I 15
6. *Asplenium trichomanes* L. Common Spleenwort. Leaves 1-pinnate, segments entire or toothed. Common in crevices of damp rocks and walls. (Ma, Mi, I) FE I 15
7. *Asplenium adiantum-nigrum* Black Spleenwort. Leaves 2-pinnate, basal pinnae the longest. Indusium white. Occasional I think. Seen by Knoche, omitted by Llorens. This illustration was from a Mallorcan specimen. Duvigneaud lists for (Ma, Mi) Not BI in FE I 16.
8. *Asplenium onopteris* L. Resembles 7, but darker and more shining, with long 'tails' at apex and apices of longer pinnae. (Small specimen). Fairly common in the mountains. (Ma, Mi, I) FE I 16
9. *Asplenium ruta-muraria* L. Wall Rue. Petiole green except at very base. Leaves very variable, with veins arranged fan-wise. Occasional in rock fissures. (Ma, Mi, I) FE I 16

CETERACH
10. *Ceterach officinarum* DC. Rusty-back. Unmistakable small 1-pinnate fern with overlapping rusty scales beneath leaves. Common on walls and rocks. (Ma, Mi, I) FE I 17

PHYLLITIS
11. *Phyllitis scolopendrium* (L.) Newman. Hart's Tongue Fern. Lamina entire, cordate at base. **NS.** Rare. (Seen by Duvigneaud) (From British specimen). (Ma, Mi, I) FE I 17
12. *Phyllitis sagittata* (DC.) Guinea & Heywood. Resembles 11, but with triangular auricles at base. Very variable, often misshapen. (Small specimen x 1, reduced specimen with double lamina). Occasional in damp, shady rock-crevices. (Ma, Mi, I) FE I 17

ATHYRIACEAE
ATHYRIUM
13. *Athyrium filix-femina* (L.) Roth. Lady Fern. Tall fern, commonly 1m, with rhizome and lower part of petiole covered in pale brown lanceolate scales. Leaves 2-pinnate, thin, green and lanceolate. Longest pinnae towards base of leaf. Sori oblong. Indusia flap-like, the lower hooked, upper nearly straight. **NS.** (From Spanish mainland specimen). Listed by Hansen and Llorens. Duvigneaud omits. (Ma) BI excluded in FE I 18

CYSTOPTERIS
14. *Cystopteris fragilis* (L.) Bernh. Brittle Bladder-fern. Delicate rhizomatous fern, up to 45cm, usually less. Leaves tufted, 2-3-pinnate, pinnae becoming increasingly distant below. Indusium white, pointed ovate. **NS.** (From British specimen). Knoche quotes Hermann (1912) and Bianor (1910-1912). Listed but not seen by Duvigneaud. Llorens lists. (Ma) FE I 18

ASPIDIACEAE
POLYSTICHUM
15. *Polystichum aculeatum* (L.) Roth. Hard Shield-fern. Stout rhizomatous fern, up to 90cm. Petioles with spreading red-brown scales. Lamina lanceolate, pinnate with deeply lobed pinnae, or 2-pinnate. Pinnules serrate with terminal bristle, narrowing down to attachment on rhachis of pinna, but not stalked or very shortly stalked. Sides of the pinnae forming an acute angle at the base. Indusium round, centrally attached among sori, which are in one row on either side of central vein. **NS.** Listed but not seen by Duvigneaud. Llorens lists. (Specimen from Spanish mainland x 1/2, detail x 4). (Ma) Not BI in FE I 20
16. *Polystichum setiferum* (Forskål) Woynar. Soft Shield-fern. Resembles 15, and most obvious difference is its softer feel to the touch. Scales of petioles yellowish, usually decurrent. Leaves always 2-pinnate, paler green, often paler still below. Distal side of each pinna with large lobe at the base, which is distinctly stalked and rounded. Distal sori in two rows as in 15, but further sori along central vein of basal lobe often alter this pattern below. **NS.** Listed but not seen by Duvigneaud. Llorens lists. (From small British specimen x 1/2, detail x 4). (Ma) BI in FE I 20.
(These two species sometimes hybridise).

DRYOPTERIS
17. *Dryopteris villarii* (Bellard) Woynar subsp. *pallida* (Bory) Heywood. Pale Buckler-fern. Rhizomatous fern, leaves tufted. Petiole with a few small reddish-brown scales. Lamina up to 40cm, usually less, with glandular hairs, triangular, bipinnate. Sori round, in two rows on each fertile pinnule, indusium kidney-shaped. Occurs here as local endemic variant, which has been described as *D. pallida* subsp. *balearica* (Litard) Maire. Basal pair of pinnae much longer than next pair above. Occasional in mountains (Ma, endemic variant or subsp.) FE I 21

POLYPODIACEAE
POLYPODIUM
18. *Polypodium australe* Fée. Southern Polypody. Very variable in size and colour. Pinnae toothed, basal pair projecting forwards. Sori elliptical, indusium absent. Very common, walls and rocks. (Small specimen x 1). (Ma, Mi, I) FE I 23

MARSILIACEAE
MARSILEA
19. *Marsilea strigosa* Willd. Rhizomatous semi-aquatic fern. Leaves with 4 leaflets, coiled in bud. Spores are produced in hairy brown 3-5mm sporocarps in axils of leaves. **NS.** Seen by Duvigneaud. Very rare, in periodically flooded places. (After Bonafe's black and white photo, coloured from FE description and garden specimen of another species). (Ma, Mi) Not BI in FE I 24

The following are also recorded from Mallorca:
Asplenium fontanum (L.) Bernh. (K quotes Bianor. Not seen by Duvigneaud. Llorens lists). (Ma) FE I 15
Asplenium billotii F.W.Schultz. Duvigneaud lists, Llorens omits. (?Ma, ?Mi) Not BI in FE I 16
Asplenium majoricum Litard. (Ma endemic) FE I 15
There are also many hybrids, especially in the Sóller area, and other species not described in FE. None of them are common, and are probably the province of the specialist.

In Minorca only:
Asplenium obovatum Viv. FE I 16
Asplenium balearicum Shivas (1969) Not in FE
Pilularia minuta Durieu FE I 24

Plate 3

PINACEAE: *PINUS*
CUPRESSACEAE: *CUPRESSUS, JUNIPERUS*
TAXACEAE: *TAXUS*
EPHEDRACEAE: *EPHEDRA*

Illustrations of trees and shrubs are much reduced. Details x 1 except where stated otherwise.

PINACEAE
PINUS
1. *Pinus halepensis* Miller. Aleppo Pine. Up to 20m, usually less. Trunk often crooked, branching low. Leaves in pairs. Unexpanded cone longer than wide. Very common, coast and hills. (Ma, Mi, I) FE I 35
2. *Pinus halepensis* var. *ceciliae* A. & Ll. Llorens. Probably a fastigiate form of 1. **NS.** (After Bonafè's black and white photo and description). (Ma, Mi, I endemic variety) Not in FE
3. *Pinus pinea* L. Stone or Umbrella Pine. Regular, upright tree, branching from upper part trunk. Unexpanded cone almost globular. Occasional. (Introduced Ma, Mi; native in Ibiza). FE I 35

CUPRESSACEAE
CUPRESSUS
4. *Cupressus sempervirens* L. Cypress. Leaves scale-like in the mature plant. Introduced here in both the fastigiate and the bushy form. (Male cone x 2). Llorens treats as a cultivated plant. FE I 37

JUNIPERUS
5. *Juniperus oxycedrus* L. Prickly Juniper. Shrub or small tree. Leaves patent, prickly acuminate when young, with two pale longitudinal bands above. Subsp. *oxycedrus* with ripe cone 8-10mm, shining, occurs in dry hilly places, and subsp. *macrocarpa* (Sibth. & Sm.) Ball with rather larger pruinose cone, is common on maritime sands. (Details only: habit of subsp. *macrocarpa* resembles that of 6, habit of subsp. *oxycedrus* is more erect, sometimes even a small tree. Both common in suitable habitats. (Ma, Mi, I) FE I 39
6. *Juniperus phoenicea* L. Phoenician Juniper. Similar to 5, but adult leaves scale-like and overlapping, not prickly. Mainly coastal. (Detail of scale-like leaves x 3). (Ma, Mi, I) FE I 39

TAXACEAE
TAXUS
7. *Taxus baccata* L. Yew. Small tree with reddish-brown scaling bark. Leaves linear, flattened, spirally arranged, but spreading on two opposite sides of twig. Seed partly surrounded by red fleshy aril. Occasional as small trees (these near peak of Massanella), or small shrubs in crevices high in mountains. (Teix, one of the higher mountains in Mallorca, is named after this species, the local name). (Ma) FE I 39

EPHEDRACEAE
EPHEDRA
8. *Ephedra fragilis* Desf. Joint Pine. Straggling shrub, with male and female flowers on separate plants, often growing through and more or less supported by other shrubs. Leaves reduced to minute scales. Flowers with yellow perianth segments on short shoots. Fruit formed by one or two seeds surrounded by 2 pairs of red fleshy bracts. May. (Ma, Mi, I) FE I 40

Plate 4

FAGACEAE: *QUERCUS*
(SALICACEAE: *SALIX*)
ULMACEAE: *ULMUS, CELTIS*
MORACEAE: *FICUS*
URTICACEAE: *URTICA, PARIETARIA, SOLEIROLIA*
(JUGLANDACEAE: *JUGLANS*)

FAGACEAE
QUERCUS

1. *Quercus coccifera* L. Kermes Oak. Usually a shrub here. Mature leaves prickly-toothed, shining with prominent veins on upper surface, pale green and smooth beneath. Fruit characteristic. Local in bushy places. (Ma, I) FE I 62

2. *Quercus ilex* L. Holm Oak. Substantial evergreen tree. Leaves leathery, grey-felted beneath, stipules thick and hairy. Acorns very bitter. Apr.-May. Dominant over much of the hillier part of Mallorca. This specimen is rather atypical. Mature leaves are often rather like those of *Q. coccifera*, but with veins more clearly visible on the dorsal surface. (Ma, Mi) FE I 63

Quercus rotundifolia Lam., with sweet acorns and membranous stipules, is very similar, occasionally seen, though probably introduced. Possibly native in Minorca. Not illustrated.

3. *Quercus faginea* Lam. Lusitanian Oak. Semi-evergreen tree, leaves with rounded teeth, shining above, more or less tomentose beneath. Known in one site in Mallorca, uncertain whether native or introduced. (Leaf only illustrated, from Mallorcan specimen). (?Ma) FE I 64

ULMACEAE
ULMUS

4. *Ulmus minor* Miller. Smooth-leaved Elm. Bush or small tree. Leaves simple, biserrate with 7-12 pairs of lateral veins. Bark fissured. Anthers purplish-red. Fruit dry, winged. Mar.-Apr. Common. (Illustrations show young twig and mature leaf slightly reduced). (Ma, Mi, I) FE I 65

CELTIS

5. *Celtis australis* L. Nettle-tree. Tree with long-pointed simply serrate leaves. Fruit a fleshy berry, eventually blackish. Widely planted for ornament and shade, seeding itself freely. Locally common. There is a fine full-grown specimen at Lluch on the N. side of the monastery. (Single leaf and fruit only). (Ma, I) Not BI in FE I 65

MORACEAE
FICUS

6. *Ficus carica* L. Fig. Spreading shrub or small tree with large aromatic palmately lobed leaves. Commonly cutivated. Small plants often naturalised in rocky places. Native in parts of S. Europe. (Ma, I) FE I 67

URTICACEAE
URTICA
(Illustrations all slightly reduced)

7. *Urtica atrovirens* Req. Perennial stinging-nettle with male and female flowers in the same raceme. The Mallorcan plant has been separated from the type as subsp. *bianorii* (Knoche) Font Quer & Garcias (not described in FE). It has very distinctive leaves, deeply serrate, with 9-13 stinging hairs on the surface arising from large conical bases (lamina indented from the back). The racemes are shorter than the adjacent petiole. May-June. Very local in the mountains. (Ma) FE I 68

8. *Urtica urens* L. Annual Stinging-nettle. Male and female flowers in the same raceme, which rarely exceeds 2cm. Petiole about 2/3 lamina. May-Oct. Common in inhabited or cultivated areas. (Ma, Mi, I) FE I 68

9. *Urtica dubia* Forskål. Like 8, but lower racemes female, shorter than the petiole, upper male and exceeding petiole, more than 2cm long, with flowers along one side of inflated axis. There are 2 stipules at each node (other species here all have 4). Common, often with 8. (Male racemes and leaf only). (Ma, Mi, I) FE I 68

10. *Urtica pilulifera* L. Roman Nettle. Annual stinging-nettle. Female flowers with inflated perianths in globular clusters. Male in erect branched uninflated clusters. May-June. Fairly common in waste places. (Ma, Mi, I) FE I 68

Note: *Urtica dioica* L. is absent from these islands, although found almost throughout Europe.

PARIETARIA

11. *Parietaria diffusa* Mart. & Koch. Pellitory-of-the-Wall. Perennial. Bracts shorter than fruiting perianth, connate at base. May-Sept. Common on walls and rocks. (Two very different specimens x 2/3. Detail of fruiting perianth and bracts enlarged). (Ma, Mi, I) FE I 69

12. *Parietaria lusitanica* L. Slender annual. Bracts equalling or exceeding fruiting perianth. May. Locally common. (Ma, Mi) FE I 69

SOLEIROLIA

13. *Soleirolia soleirolii* (Req.) Dandy. Helxine, Mother-of-thousands. This common introduced weed of greenhouses and sheltered spots in the gardens of Western Europe, is a rather rare native perennial in Mallorca. Like very slender small *Parietaria*, but creeping and rooting at the nodes. Apr.-May. (Main illustration from Mallorcan specimen, details from garden specimen). Native only in islands of the Western Mediterranean. (Ma) FE I 69

Other species recorded from Mallorca:
Salix (Willow) and *Populus* (Poplar) species are widely planted.
Juglans regia L. Walnut. Probably only associated with present or previous habitation. There is a fine specimen in a fairly remote spot on the seaward side of the Puig Roig. FE I 56
Quercus fruticosa Brot. Llorens lists *Q. humilis* Lam., which FE includes here, for Mallorca. Not BI in FE I 64

In other islands:
Quercus pubescens Willd. Not BI in FE I 64
Parietaria mauritanica Durieu. Formentera. Not BI in FE I 69

Plate 5

SANTALACEAE: *OSYRIS, THESIUM*
ARISTOLOCHIACEAE: *ARISTOLOCHIA*
RAFFLESIACEAE: *CYTINUS*
(BALANOPHORACEAE: *CYNOMORIUM*)

SANTALACEAE
OSYRIS

1. *Osyris alba* L. Small parasitic shrub with slender branches. Described in FE as having male and female flowers on separate plants, but here plants seem to have either solitary hermaphrodite flowers (slightly enlarged in illustration) or short racemes of male flowers. Fruit red, globose. May-June. Locally common. (Ma, Mi) FE I 70

THESIUM

2. *Thesium divaricatum* Jan. Leafy parasitic perennial up to 25cm, with much-branched stems. Leaves linear, not fleshy. Inflorescence pyramidal. Nut longitudinally veined. **NS.** Possibly extinct. Duvigneaud lists. Llorens queries. (Specimen from Spanish mainland). (?Ma) FE I 72

3. *Thesium humile* Vahl Fleshy parasitic annual. Nut reticulately veined. May. Occasional in sandy fields. (Ma, Mi) FE I 72

ARISTOLOCHIACEAE
ARISTOLOCHIA

4. (*Aristolochia clematitis* L. Birthwort. (From garden specimen). FE I 74 (Probably recorded here in error).

5. *Aristolochia longa* L. This taxon is now divided. The plant here is *A. paucinervis* Pomel. Flowers solitary, about 5cm. Fruit pear-shaped. Apr.-May. Rather uncommon. (Ma, Mi, I) see FE I 74

6. *Aristolochia bianorii* Sennen & Pau. Creeping perennial. Flowers usually about 2.5cm, the tube whitish, with a red-brown limb with darker stripes at maturity. May-July. Rather local in rocky places. (Main illustration x 2, details x 1). (Ma, Mi endemic) FE I 74

RAFFLESIACEAE
CYTINUS

7. *Cytinus hypocistis* (L.) L. Perennial without chlorophyll, parasitic on roots of white-flowered *Cistus* species. Perianth bright yellow, subtended by bracts and scale-like leaves which are orange or scarlet. May-June. Occasional. (Ma, Mi, I) FE I 75

8. *Cytinus ruber* (Fourr.) Komarov. Resembles 7, but flowers pinkish or cream, leaves and bracts wine-red. Parasitic on pink-flowered *Cistus* species. May-June. Rather uncommon. (Ma, I) FE I 75

Also recorded for Balearic Islands:
Asarum europaeum L. Llorens omits. Very dubious. BI in FE I 73
Osyris quadripartita Salzm. Ibiza. FE I 70
Cynomorium coccineum L. Ibiza. Not BI in FE I 75

Plate 6

POLYGONACEAE: *POLYGONUM, BILDERDYKIA, RUMEX, EMEX*

POLYGONUM

1. *Polygonum maritimum* L. Woody, more or less procumbent perennial. Leaves blue-green, narrowly elliptical with revolute margins. Apr.-May. Common on sea shores and sandy places near the sea. (Ma, Mi, I) FE I 77
2. *Polygonum aviculare* L. Knotgrass. Annual. Stems erect or procumbent. Ochreae silvery-hyaline, much shorter than internodes. Leaves lanceolate to ovate, the short petioles included in ochreae. Flowers in clusters in axils of leaves. Apr.-May. Very common. (Ma, Mi, I) FE I 78
3. *Polygonum salicifolium* Brouss. Perennial with rooting stems. Ochreae with long cilia. Flowers pink, in long, slender leafless spikes. Rather rare in or beside fresh water. (Ma, Mi) FE I 79

Other species of *Polygonum* are listed by Llorens for Balearic Islands:

1. Ochreae silvery, becoming ragged or torn: inflorescence axillary, few-flowered
2. Perennial, woody at base
3. Ochreae in inflorescence longer than internodes, those in middle part of stem less than half length internodes
4. Ochreae with 8-12 conspicuous branched veins. *P. maritimum* L. (Ma, Mi, I)
4. Ochreae with fewer, feint veins. *P. romanum* Jacq. (Listed as endemic subsp. *balearicum* Rafaelli & Villar) (Ma)
3. Ochreae much shorter than internodes. *P. equisetiforme* Sibth. & Sm. (Ma) Not BI in FE 77
2. Annual or short-lived perennial, not woody at base
5. Leaves more or less uniform in size. *P. arenastrum* Boreau (Ma, Mi, I)
5. Leaves on main stem much larger than those on branches
6. Leaves 1-4mm wide, linear or linear-lanceolate: nut slightly exserted from perianth. *P. rurivagum* Jordan
6. Leaves 5-15mm wide, lanceolate to ovate: nut included in perianth. *P. aviculare* L. (Ma, Mi, I)
1. Ochreae brownish, entire or ciliate, not lacerate, flowers in lax or dense leafless spikes
7. Flowering spikes long and lax, each flower clearly visible. *P. salicifolium* Brouss. (Ma, Mi)
7. Flowering spikes dense, some flowers more or less concealed by others
8. Peduncles with scattered glands: perianth usually white. *P. lapathifolium* L. (Ma, Mi, I)
8. Peduncles eglandular: perianth pink. *P. persicaria* L. (Ma, Mi)

BILDERDYKIA

4. *Bilderdykia convolvulus* (L.) Dumort. Black Bindweed. Twining or prostrate annual. Leaves more or less triangular, cordate at base. Not common here. (Ma, Mi) FE I 81

RUMEX

Rumex species 5-9 are tall perennial herbs with branched inflorescences. Perianth in two whorls of 3. Inner whorl enlarges to become valves enclosing fruit, often developing marginal teeth and/or dorsal tubercles which are important for identification. All species may turn red in fruit: this is not significant for identification. All flower in Apr.-May, and, except 5, occur as ruderals. (Main illustration x 1 or slightly reduced. Details of valves enlarged).

5. *Rumex intermedius* DC. Perennial. **Leaves sagittate with narrow lobes.** Widespread in rocky places. (Ma, Mi, I) FE I 85
6. *Rumex crispus* L. Curled dock. Margins of leaves undulate. Pedicels jointed below the middle, longer than valves, which are more or less **entire, with narrow inconspicuous tubercles.** Very common. (Ma, MI, I) FE I 87
7. *Rumex conglomeratus* Murray. Sharp Dock. Pedicels jointed near the middle, about equalling valves. **Valves entire, all with large egg-shaped tubercles.** Common. (Ma, Mi, I) FE I 87
8. *Rumex pulcher* L. Fiddle-Dock. Panicle usually more open and spreading than in 6 and 7. Pedicels thick, jointed near the middle, not exceeding valves. **Valves with several teeth each side.** Common. (Ma, Mi, I) FE I 87
9. *Rumex obtusifolius* L. Broad-leaved Dock. Pedicels slender, jointed near the base. **Valves toothed, only one with an enlarged tubercle.** (From British specimen, although seen in Mallorca subsequently). (Ma, I) FE I 87
10. *Rumex bucephalophorus* L. (Name means 'Bearing a Bull's head'. To me it looks as if it bears numerous small whiskered mice attached by their tails). **Small unbranched annual.** Common in sandy places near the sea. (Ma, Mi, I) FE I 88

EMEX

11. *Emex spinosa* (L.) Campd. Annual. Male flowers in terminal pedunculate clusters, female in sessile axillary clusters. Fruit in the enlarged and indurated outer perianth segments, with spreading spiny tips. Mar.-May. Common in waste places. (Ma, Mi, I) FE I 89

Plate 7

CHENOPODIACEAE (1): *CHENOPODIUM, ATRIPLEX*
(for **BETA** see Plate 8)

CHENOPODIUM

Mostly annual herbs. Leaves flattened, often mealy. Perianth segments 2-5 in one whorl, persistent and surrounding fruit.

1. *Chenopodium ambrosioides* L. Mexican tea. Hairy aromatic annual, with numerous sessile glands. Leaves entire, toothed or irregularly divided. Inflorescence of small sessile clusters. Native of tropical America, formerly cultivated as a vermifuge. **NS.** (From garden specimen). (Ma, Mi, I) FE I 93

2. *Chenopodium bonus-henricus* L. Good King Henry. Perennial. Leaves triangular or spear-shaped, entire except for basal lobes. **NS.** (From British specimen). Probably casual only. (Ma) FE I 93

3. *Chenopodium glaucum* L. Oak-leaved Goosefoot. Annual. Leaves variable in shape, green above and densely bluish mealy beneath. Apr.-May. Occasional. (Ma) BI excluded in FE I 93

4. *Chenopodium vulvaria* L. Stinking Goosefoot. Foul-smelling greyish annual, more or less mealy, especially on underside of leaves. Leaf-shape variable, often rhombic, with tooth on either side opposite widest part. May-Sept. Fairly Common. (Ma, Mi0 FE I 94

5. *Chenopodium murale* L. Nettle-leaved Goosefoot. Very robust, much-branched annual with shiny, coarsely toothed dark green leaves, often turning yellow or red. Seeds black with acute keel round margin and closely adherent testa. Mar.-Sept. Common in waste places. (Ma, Mi, I) FE I 94

6. *Chenopodium opulifolium* Schrader. Grey Goosefoot. Annual. Leaves broader than long, densely grey-mealy at least below. **NS.** (From Italian specimen). (Ma, Mi, I) FE I 94

7. *Chenopodium album* L. Fat Hen. Green to greyish mealy annual. Leaves longer than wide, more-or-less diamond-shaped, variably toothed. Seeds with blunt margins. Common. (Ma, Mi, I) FE I 94

8. *Chenopodium suecicum* J. Murr. Like 7, but leaves thin and rather bright green. Cymes lax. Testa with deep radial furrows. (Probably casual: single plant found by F. Rumsey in Gorg Blau, May 1990: illustrated from his specimen). Not BI in FE I 95

ATRIPLEX

Annual herbs or perennial shrubs. Leaves flattened and often mealy. Male flowers with 5 perianth segments, female usually with none, but with two bracteoles which enlarge and enclose fruit.

9. *Atriplex halimus* L. Shrubby Orache. Small to medium shrub, with leathery silver-green leaves. Aug.-Sept. Local near sea, also planted as hedging. (Ma, Mi, I) FE I 95

10. *Atriplex rosea* L. Procumbent whitish annual. Cymes axillary. Bracteoles up to 12mm, diamond-shaped and toothed, becoming hard in lower half. (Ma, Mi, I) FE I 96

11. *Atriplex patula* L. Common Orache. Mealy annual. Upper leaves lanceolate, lower more or less diamond shaped. Apr.-Sept. Common near the sea. (Ma, Mi, I) FE I 96

12. *Atriplex hastata* L. Spear-leaved Orache. Green-leaved annual with spear-shaped lower leaves. Inflorescence often red. Common, usually near coast. (Ma, Mi, I) FE I 97

Also recorded from Mallorca:

Chenopodium ficifolium Smith. Fig-leaved Goosefoot. Recorded by Garcias (1905-1958) and listed by Duvigneaud but not Llorens. FE I 96

Atriplex tornabenei Tineo. Listed by Duvigneaud and Llorens (Ma, Mi, I) See FE I 96 under *A. tatarica* L. (BI not included).

Plate 8

CHENOPODIACEAE (2): *BETA, HALIMIONE, BASSIA, ARTHROCNEMUM SALICORNIA, SUAEDA, SALSOLA*

BETA

1. *Beta vulgaris* L. subsp. *maritima* (L.) Arcangeli. Sea Beet. Perennial, or occasionally annual. Usually procumbent. Basal leaves usually rhombic. Short (1 or 2-flowered) cymes arranged in spike-like inflorescence, dense but often interrupted near base. Bracts small or absent at apex of inflorescence. Receptacle bowl-shaped with incurved segments up to 3mm in fruit. Fruits connate by swollen bases. Saline habitats. Common. (Single stem leaf, basal part of fruiting spike x 2). (Ma, Mi, I) FE I 91

2. *Beta macrocarpa* Guss. Resembles 1, but annual, with inflorescence lax and clearly bracteate to apex. Segments of fruiting perianth up to 5mm, erect, often incurved at apex. **NS.** Seen by Duvigneaud. Llorens queries except for Ibiza. (x 2, specimen from Spanish mainland). (?Ma, ?Mi, I) Not BI in FE I 92

HALIMIONE

3. *Halimione portulacoides* (L.) Aellen. Sea Purslane. Decumbent small shrub, with upright silvery-mealy stems. Leaves opposite below. Flowers and fruit as *Atriplex* (Plate 7), but paired bracteoles in fruit connate almost to apex. Common in saltmarshes. (Ma, Mi, I) FE I 97

BASSIA

4. *Bassia hyssopifolia* (Pallas) Volk. Erect hairy annual up to 1m, with numerous strict branches. Perianth segments 5, enlarging and developing a spine in fruit. Saline soils. (From garden specimen, but seen wild in Mallorca: seen by Duvigneaud). (Ma, introduced) Not BI in FE.I 98

ARTHROCNEMUM

Shrubby perennials, leaves scale-like, the basal part fused to form a segment. Fertile segments have two three-flowered cymes immersed in a pair of bracts formed from the node above.

5. *Arthrocnemum perenne* (Miller) Moss. Shrubby Glasswort. Has creeping underground stems and green erect branches, becoming red or brownish, up to 1m. Flowers of each segment fall to leave a tripartite hollow in the segment. Testa of seed greenish brown, covered with curved or hooked hairs. Rather rare in saltmarshes. (Illustration from fragment of specimen from Spanish mainland x 4, with seed x 10). Probably **NS.** (Ma, Mi) FE I 101

6. *Arthrocnemum fruticosum* (L.) Moq. As 5, but blue-green and without underground creeping stems. Testa covered in short conical hairs. (Non-flowering shoot x 1, seed from specimen from Spanish mainland x 10. This one had a few curved hairs at one end, though most seeds were tuberculate). Fairly common in saltmarshes. (Ma, Mi, I) FE I 101

7. *Arthrocnemum glaucum* (Delile) Ung.-Sternb. Erect bluish shrub, becoming yellow-green or reddish. Segments generally broader than long. Flowers of each segment protruding, free, falling to leave undivided hollow. Testa black with very small tubercles. Common in saltmarshes. (Flowering branch x 1, small sterile branch x 1, seed x 10). (Ma, Mi, I) FE I 101

SALICORNIA

8. *Salicornia ramosissima* J.Woods. Glasswort. Like *Arthrocnemum*, but annual. Up to 20cm, sometimes becoming prostrate. Dark green, becoming yellow-green or purplish. Upper edge of fertile segments with conspicuous scarious margin. (Whole plant x 1/3, left detail x 6, right shows top of plant x 2). Fairly common in saltmarshes. (Ma, Mi, I) Not BI in FE I 101

SUAEDA

9. *Suaeda vera* J.F.Gmelin. Shrubby Seablite. Small green shrub, usually less than 1m. Leaves cylindrical, often blue-green. Fruiting perianth green. Common in saltmarshes. (Ma, Mi, I) FE I 103

10. *Suaeda maritima* (L.) Dumort. Annual Seablite. As 9, but annual up to 50cm, often much less. Common in saltmarshes. (Ma, Mi, I) FE I 103

SALSOLA

11. *Salsola soda* L. Erect annual, about 15cm here. Lower leaves opposite, upper alternate with short mucro. (x 1, details x 3). Rare in saltmarshes. Not seen by Duvigneaud. Listed by Llorens. (From fresh Mallorcan specimen). (Ma, Mi) FE I 105

12. *Salsola kali* L. Saltwort. Erect or spreading annual. Bracteoles with long spiny apex. Common in sandy saline places. (Ma, Mi, I) FE I 105

13. *Salsola vermiculata* L. Hairy shrub, about 1m. Leaves semicylindrical to thread-like. Local in dry soils. (x 1. Details show shoot with small axillary branches, and single leaf enlarged). FE I 106

Also recorded from Mallorca:

Beta patellaris Moq. Procumbent annual. Perianth segments 1-1.5mm in fruit, incurved or erect. Rare. Seen by Duvigneaud. Llorens lists. (Ma) Not BI in FE I 92

Kochia scoparia (L.) Schrader. (Ornamental Asian species sometimes escaping from cultivation). Seen by Duvigneaud. Not BI in FE I 98

Suaeda splendens (Pourret) Gren. & Godron. Annual. Leaves acuminate or mucronate. Fruiting perianth much inflated. Rare. Seen by Duvigneaud. Llorens lists. (Ma) FE I 104

In Ibiza:

Salsola verticillata Schousboe (*Salsola oppositifolia* Desf. In Llorens' list). Not BI in FE I 106

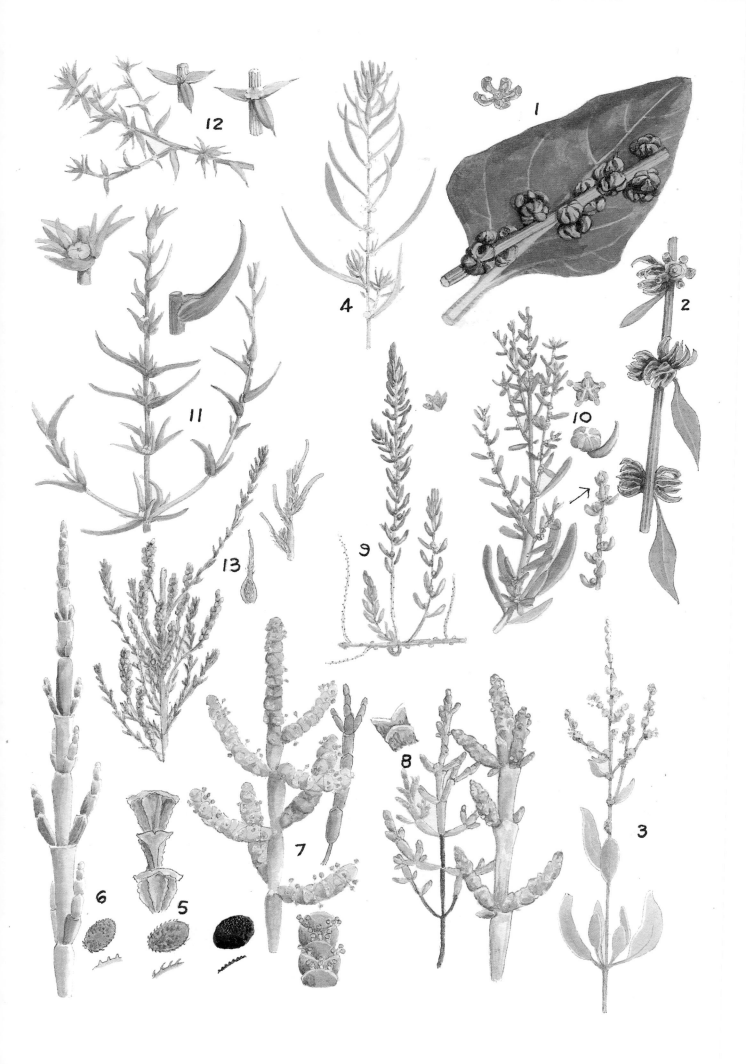

Plate 9

AMARANTHACEAE: *AMARANTHUS*
(NYCTAGINACEAE: *MIRABILIS)*
PHYTOLACCACEAE: *PHYTOLACCA*
AIZOACEAE: *AIZOON, CARPOBROTUS, LAMPRANTHUS,*
   MESEMBRYANTHEMUM
(TETRAGONIACEAE: *TETRAGONIA)*
PORTULACACEAE: *PORTULACA*

AMARANTHACEAE
AMARANTHUS

Weedy introduced plants of waste places and urban roadsides. All annuals except 3 and 6. Inflorescence bracteate, bracteoles 2-5. Perianth of one whorl, dry and scarious, 4-5-merous, segments free or connate at base. Fruit with membranous (rarely fleshy) wall, breaking open in various ways, sometimes not breaking open. Most are natives of America, flowering June-September. The taxonomy is difficult: as my specimens were identified from FE 1st Edition, the names used here follow this, although many have now been regrouped.

1. *Amaranthus hybridus* L. Only detail of single flowers, with long mucronate bracts x 2 perianth. Otherwise resembles *A. cruentus* (2). (Ma, Me, I) Not BI in FE I 109
2. *Amaranthus cruentus* L. Inflorescence dense, terminal, with short branches at base. Bracteoles about 1 1/2 x acute perianth segments. Common. As is the very similar *A. hybridus* (detail 1a, with bracteoles 2 x perianth segments, recurved when dry). Both (Ma, Mi, I) Not BI in FE I 109
3. *Amaranthus muricatus* (Moq.) Gillies. Decumbent perennial. Leaves linear to narrow ovate-lanceolate. Inflorescence a branched panicle with groups of flowers widely spaced. Fruit not breaking open, warty. Fairly common. (x 1, detail enlarged). (Ma, Mi, I) Not BI in FE I 109
4. *Amaranthus blitoides* S.Watson. Erect or decumbent. Leaves with a distinct membranous margin, often white-blotched. Capsule breaking open transversely. Occasional. (slightly reduced, details x 1). (Ma, I) Not BI in FE I 110
5. *Amaranthus albus* L. Usually erect. Leaves slightly notched, mucronate. Inflorescence of short axillary clusters. Bracteoles curved, with spiny tip. Capsule breaking open transversely. Common. (Slightly reduced, detail x 4). (Ma, Mi, I) FE I 110
6. *Amaranthus deflexus* L. Procumbent perennial, densely puberulent on upper part of flowering stem (less so in fruit). Inflorescence dense, terminal, spike-like, often interrupted and/or leafy at base. Occasional. (x 1, detail x 2). (Ma, Mi, I) FE I 110
7. *Amaranthus lividus* L. Leaves often emarginate. Inflorescence terminal, more or less branched, the branches long and spicate. Fruit ridged, breaking open irregularly or not at all. Occasional. (x1, detail x 3). (Ma) Not BI in FE 1 110

PHYTOLACCACEAE
PHYTOLACCA

8. *Phytolacca americana* L. Pokeweed. Tall fleshy perennial. Flowers green or pink. Formerly cultivated for the red dye obtained from the fruit. June-Aug. Locally common near houses. Introduced from N. America. (Ma, Mi, I) FE I 112

AIZOACEAE
AIZOON

9. *Aizoon hispanicum* L. Fleshy papillose annual with greenish-white sepaloid perianth and 10 stamens. Very rare. (One station, where plants are very small). **NS.** (From Greek specimen). Seen by Duvigneaud. Llorens lists. (Ma, I) FE I 112

CARPOBROTUS

10. *Carpobrotus acinaciformis* (L.) L. Bolus. Very fleshy procumbent perennial. Leaves blue-green, widest at or above the middle. Flowers purple, stamens purple. Apr.-Aug. Native of S. Africa, naturalized, especially on higher parts sandy beaches. (x 1/3). (Ma, I) Not BI in FE I 112
11. *Carpobrotus edulis* (L.) N.E.Br. Hottentot Fig. As 10, but leaves not blue-green and not broadening about the middle. Flowers yellow or purple, stamens yellow. Native of S. Africa, very widely naturalized, especially on higher parts sandy beaches. (x 1/3). (Ma, I) Not BI in FE I 112

LAMPRANTHUS

12. *Lampranthus glaucus* (L.) N.E.Br. Small blue-green fleshy perennial. Flowers orange, with raised ring surrounding 5 prominent stigmas. Apr.-May. Introduced from S. Africa. (x 1). Not BI in FE I 113
13. *Lampranthus roseus* (Willd.) Schwantes. Similar to 11, but not blue-green. Flowers pink. Introduced from S. Africa. Not described in FE.

MESEMBRYANTHEMUM

14. *Mesembryanthemum nodiflorum* L. Gasoul. Small fleshy annual. Flowers white. Apr.-July. Local on sea-shore. (Ma, Mi, I) FE I 113
15. *Mesembryanthemum crystallinum* L. Ice plant. Fleshy annual, often about 40cm. Whole plant covered in translucent watery papillae. May-June. Common on waste sites near the sea in the South. (Ma, Mi, I) FE I 113

PORTULACACEAE
PORTULACA

16. *Portulaca oleracea* L. Purslane. Fleshy procumbent annual. Flowers with 5 yellow petals. May-Oct. Occasional, especially near the sea, including shingle beaches. (x 3/ 4, including single leaf from base of plant. Detail of flower x 2). (Ma, Mi, I) FE I 114

Others recorded for Mallorca (all introduced plants: in addition many Aizoaceae from S. Africa are cultivated for ornament and more or less established on tips):
Amaranthus retroflexus L. Pigweed. Very like 1, but perianth segments more or less spathulate, obtuse or truncate. (Ma, Mi, I) FE I 109
Amaranthus graecizans L. Resembles 4, but bracteoles not spinescent. (Ma, Mi, I) FE I 110
Mirabilis jalapa L. Perennial herb with opposite leaves. Perianth tubular with 5-lobed limb, yellow or red. Garden escape. Native of tropical America. (Ma, I) FE I 111
Tetragonia tetragonioides (Pallas) O. Kuntze. New Zealand Spinach. Bonafè records as naturalized. (Ma) Not BI in FE 114

In other islands:
Amaranthus caudatus L. Ibiza. FE I 109
Phytolacca dioica L. Ibiza. Not BI in FE I 112
Carpobrotus chilensis (Molina) N.E.Br. Minorca and Ibiza. Not BI in FE I 113

Plate 10

CARYOPHYLLACEAE (1): *ARENARIA, MOEHRINGIA, MINUARTIA STELLARIA, CERASTIUM*

Unless otherwise stated: herbs with opposite leaves, without stipules on this Plate. Flowers regular, 4 or 5 -merous. Petals white. Fruit a capsule opening with teeth equalling the number of styles or twice as many.

ARENARIA

Here: flowers 5-merous, white. Petals entire. Styles 3.

1. *Arenaria grandiflora* L. Very variable. Leaves linear-lanceolate, 5-10mm or perhaps more. Stems usually with 1-3 flowers on longish pedicels. **Flowers large** (2cm or more). May. Occasional in mountains. (Ma) FE I 119

2. *Arenaria balearica* L. **Mat-forming** perennial with thread-like stems. Leaves 2-4mm, ovate to spathulate with more or less pointed tips. **Flowers** about 1cm, **solitary** on stalks usually less than 3cm. Apr.-May. Fairly common in shady damp places in mountain area. (Ma) FE I 119

3. *Arenaria serpyllifolia* L. Thyme-leaved Sandwort. Much-branched annual, roughly hairy, with ovate leaves up to 8mm, but usually much smaller, the lower petiolate, the upper sessile. Sepals up to 4.5mm, ovate or ovate-lanceolate. Petals shorter. **Capsule slightly exceeding sepals**, less than twice as long as wide, and distinctly swollen at base. Mar.-Apr. Common. Llorens lists for (Ma), Duvigneaud for (Mi) too. FE I 121

4. *Arenaria leptoclados* (Reichenb.) Guss. Very like 3, but plant more delicate, often prostrate. **Capsule** length more than 2 x width, **equalling or shorter than sepals** and not swollen at base. Common. (Ma, Mi, I) FE I 121

MOEHRINGIA

5. *Moehringia pentandra* Gay. Ascending annual. Sepals 2-4mm with a wide scarious margin. **Petals absent or rudimentary**. Pedicels elongated and deflexed in fruit, slightly swollen above. (Easily overlooked as 'Chickweed', no 8). Apr.-May. Shady places in mountains. (Ma, Mi) FE I 124

MINUARTIA

6. *Minuartia hybrida* (Vill.) Schischkin. Fine-leaved Sandwort. Annual, usually glandular-hairy. Stems much-branched, erect, rather rigid, with long internodes. Leaves narrow lanceolate. Sepals 2-4mm, petals rather shorter. **Capsule teeth obtuse**, everted when ripe. Apr.-May. Occasional, usually in mountains. (Ma, Mi, I) FE I 127

7. *Minuartia geniculata* (Poiret) Thell. Glandular hairy perennial, easily taken for Spergularia species (Plate1) since flowers are **pink**. But **without stipules**. Apr.-May. Common in dry places. (Ma) FE I 132

STELLARIA

Weak straggling annuals (here). Petals deeply bifid (to at least halfway). Styles 3, capsule with 6 teeth.

8. *Stellaria media* (L.) Vill. Chickweed. **Stems with hairs all round.** Lower leaves ovate, acute, with long petioles. Upper more or less sessile. **Petals shorter or slightly longer than sepals.** Seeds dark reddish-brown. Common. (Ma, Mi) FE I 134

9. *Stellaria pallida* (Dumort) Piré. Lesser Chickweed. Like 8, only usually more slender. **Stems with 1 line of hairs down each internode**, rarely hairless. Leaves usually all petiolate, **petals absent or minute**. Seeds pale yellowish-brown with rounded or conical tubercles. Common. (Ma, Mi, I) FE I 134

10. *Stellaria ?media* subsp. Like 8, but more robust. This, from specimens and photos around the Monastery at Lluch, resembles *S. neglecta* Weihe in the robust habit, with broad stems, and pedicels reflexed in fruit, also in the reddish-brown seeds with conical tubercles. It keys out in the FE key as *S. media*, and has other features

described for this species (petals shorter than sepals, stamens 5). This might prove to be a new endemic subspecies, but doesn't exactly conform to *S. neglecta*, which D records having seen, although Llorens omits. *S. neglecta* Weihe, of course, may exist apart from this plant that looks so like it. For *S. neglecta* Llorens lists ?Ma. Not BI in FE I 134

CERASTIUM

Annual herbs here. Petals usually bifid or notched, but not deeply bifid as in *Stellaria*. Styles usually 5.

11. *Cerastium brachypetalum* Pers. subsp. *roeseri* (Boiss. & Heldrich.) Nyman. Stem with long eglandular and **glandular** hairs. **Pedicels longer than sepals, deflexed below larger buds and fruit, erect in flower.** Calyx with eglandular hairs protruding beyond apex. Petals longer or shorter than sepals. **Capsule curved, slightly exceeding sepals.** Mar.-May. Common in mountain areas. (Ma) FE I 143

12. *Cerastium glomeratum* Thuill. Another **glandular** annual. Flowers in compacts clusters, **pedicels shorter than sepals, not deflexed in bud or in fruit.** Calyx with eglandular hairs protruding beyond apex. **Capsule** curved, **up to twice length of sepals.** (Ma, Mi, I) FE I 144

13. *Cerastium* cf. *semidecandrum* L. Specimens used here keyed out as *C. pumilum* Curtis in FE, but resembled specimens of *C. semidecandrum* var. *sennenii* in herbarium of the Universitat de les Illes Balears. Pedicels equalling or slightly exceeding sepals, **bracts with short scarious tips** (typically *C. semidecandrum* has bracts often almost entirely scarious, always so in upper 1/3. Stem and sepals with dense glandular and eglandular hairs, **not protruding beyond apex of sepals.** Petals equalling or exceeding sepals, bifid up to about 1/4. Mar.-Apr. Occasional. (Details from above down: flower x 4, capsule x 3, upper bract x 6, stem leaf x 3). *C. semidecandrum*: Llorens lists 2 subsp. and 3 vars. of subsp. *semidecandrum* here: the plants used in illustrations 13 and 14 were not reliably identified. (Ma, Mi) FE I 144

14. *Cerastium diffusum* Pers. subsp. ?*diffusum*. Annual. Upper bract completely herbaceous or with just discernible scarious tip. Pedicels longer than sepals. Sepals with narrow scarious margin. Petals shorter than sepals, about 1/5 bifid. Apr.-May. Occasional. Llorens lists subsp. *diffusum* (Ma), and subsp. *gussonei* (Tod. Ex Lojac) P.D.Sell & Whitehead. (Ma, I) Not BI in FE I 145

Also recorded from Mallorca:

Minuartia mediterranea (Link) K.Maly. Resembles 6, but pedicels not longer than sepals, and cymes crowded. Llorens lists (Ma, Mi) FE I 127

Cerastium fontanum Baumg. Mouse-ear Chickweed. Perennial. Dubious here. Llorens omits.

Cerastium pumilum Curtis. **Bracts only marginally scarious.** Petals equalling or slightly longer than sepals. Pedicel longer than very slightly curved capsule. Llorens lists (Ma) FE I 145

Cerastium siculum Guss. **Bracts entirely herbaceous.** Flowers clustered with **pedicels shorter than sepals.** Duvigneaud saw in Mallorca. Llorens lists (Ma, Mi) FE I 145

Key (after FE) to the 4 species of *Cerastium* in which eglandular hairs do not protrude beyond apex of sepals: (the 4 difficult ones!). In spite of the key they seem very difficult to distinguish.

1. Bracts entirely herbaceous
2. Pedicels shorter than sepals: flowers clustered. *C. siculum*
2. Pedicels equalling or exceeding sepals. *C. diffusum*
1. Bracts scarious at least at tip
3. Bracts scarious in upper 1\3 or more, often almost entirely scarious. *C. semidecandrum*
3. Bracts scarious for 1/4 length or less
4. Petals equalling or slightly longer than sepals. *C. pumilum*
4. Petals shorter than sepals. *C. diffusum*

Plate 11

CARYOPHYLLACEAE (2): *SAGINA, (CORRIGIOLA), PARO-NYCHIA, HERNIARIA POLYCARPON, SPERGULARIA, AGROSTEMMA, SAPONARIA, (VACCARIA), PETRORHA-GIA, (DIANTHUS)*

SAGINA

1. *Sagina apetala* Ard. Annual Pearlwort. Small tufted annual. **Leaves linear, long-mucronate to aristate.** Flowers 4-merous. Petals minute or absent. **Ripe capsule equalling or exceeding sepals.** Apr.-May. Streets and other dry places. Occasional. (Ma, Mi, I) FE I 147
2. *Sagina maritima* G.Don. Sea Pearlwort. Rather like 1, but often denser, with a great many stems. **Leaves linear-lanceolate, slightly fleshy, with very short mucro.** Ripe capsule **equalling sepals or shorter.** Apr.-May. Common, usually near the sea. (Ma, Mi, I) FE I 148

PARONYCHIA

3. *Paronychia argentea* Lam. Procumbent perennial. **Flowers small in axillary clusters** with conspicuous large silvery bracts. Mar.-May. Fairly common in dry places. (Ma, Mi, I) FE I 150
4. *Paronychia capitata* (L.) Lam. More or less erect tufted perennial. Stems much-branched. **Flowers in conspicuous terminal clusters,** concealed by silvery bracts. Mar.-May. Rather local. (Ma, Mi, I) FE I 150

HERNIARIA

5. *Herniaria hirsuta* L. (including *H. cinerea* DC.). Rupture Wort. Hairy prostrate annual. Small flowers without petals in dense leaf-opposed clusters. Apr.-June. Common in dry places. (Ma, Mi, I) FE I 152

POLYCARPON

Small herbs. Leaves opposite, sometimes appearing whorled. Flowers small in clusters with white scarious bracts. Sepals and petals 5, petals very small.

6. *Polycarpon tetraphyllum* (L.) L. All-seed. Usually annual. Stems much-branched. Leaves mostly in whorls of 4. **Flowers usually numerous, in lax inflorescence, with many conspicuous branches.** Apr.-June. Common. (Ma, Mi, I) FE I 153
7. *Polycarpon alsinifolium* (Biv.) DC. Often perennial, more robust than 6. Some leaves in whorls of 4. **Flowers very numerous in dense inflorescence, largely concealing branches.** (Ma, Mi, I) FE I 153
8. *Polycarpon polycarpoides* (Biv.) Zodda. Perennial with woody stock. Leaves ovate, fleshy, in pairs. **Flowers few, in lax inflorescence.** Stipules small, greyish. Apr.-June. NS. Uncommon, on coastal rocks. (From Minorcan specimen, slightly enlarged). Seen by Duvigneaud. (Ma, Mi) FE I 153

SPERGULARIA

Herbs. Leaves linear, with pale papery stipules. Perianth 5-merous. Fruit a capsule, opening with 3 valves. Beware of misidentifying *Minuartia geniculata* (Poiret) Thell. Plate 9: very like *Spergularia*, but without stipules.

9. *Spergularia media* (L.) C.Presl. Greater Sea Spurrey. **Robust perennial,** hairless throughout or glandular-hairy above. Leaves linear, mucronate. **Petals uniformly white or pink. Capsule 7-9mm.** Seeds usually winged. Coastal, common. (Ma, Mi, I) FE I 155
10. *Spergularia marina* (L.) Griseb. Sea Spurrey. Usually annual, often glandular above. **Petals pink, white towards base,** not exceeding sepals. **Capsule 4-6mm,** usually exceeding sepals. **Some seeds usually winged.** Coastal, less common than 9. (Ma, Mi, I) FE I 155
11. *Spergularia rubra* (L.) J.&C.Presl. Sand Spurrey. Upper bracts about equalling leaves. Petals uniformly pink. Capsule 4-5mm. Seeds never winged. Often inland, in sandy places. (Ma, Mi, I) FE I 155

AGROSTEMMA

12. *Agrostemma githago* L. Corn Cockle. Annual, with long appressed hairs. Petals deep pinkish-purple, exceeded by long calyx-teeth. NS. Not seen by Duvigneaud. Probably introduced from Eastern Mediterranean. Llorens lists. (Ma) FE I 157

SAPONARIA

13. *Saponaria officinalis* L. Soapwort. Perennial up to 90cm. June-Sept. **NS.** (From Garden specimen). Llorens treats as garden escape. FE I 185

PETRORHAGIA

14. *Petrorhagia nanteuilii* (Burnat) P.W.Ball & Heywood. Annual. Flowering stems usually about 30cm, with terminal cluster of pink-like flowers enclosed by broad scarious brownish bracts. This species differs from others that might be found in this area with the tuberculate seeds and leaf-sheaths less than twice as long as wide. Local in sandy soils. (Ma, Mi) FE I 188

Other species recorded for Mallorca:
Spergularia diandra (Guss.) Boiss. (Ma, Mi, I) FE I 155
Spergularia bocconei (Scheele) Ascherson & Graebner. (Ma, I) FE 156
Spergularia heldreichii Fouc. (Ma) FE 156
    These 3 *Spergularia* species are all reliably recorded. They differ from the species illustrated in having capsules 3.5mm or less, and can be distinguished by the following key:
1. Inflorescence ebracteate above: petals narrowly elliptical, equalling sepals. *S. diandra*
Inflorescence bracteate throughout: petals ovate, sometimes shorter than sepals
2. Seeds grey-brown, tuberculate. *S. bocconei*
2. Seeds black, smooth or slightly ridged. *S. heldreichii*
Spergularia nicaeensis Sarato. Resembles *S. rubra* (above), but the upper bracts are shorter than the leaves, and the plant is rather robust. Llorens lists with a query. (?Ma) FE I 155
Vaccaria pyramidata Medicus. A blue-green herb with an inflated calyx with 5 green wings, and long-clawed pink flowers. Llorens lists (Ma, Mi) Not BI in FE I 186
Dianthus rupicola Biv. A *Dianthus* species has been recorded from time to time. Knoche records that Rodríguez was unable to identify a *Dianthus* species found by another collector, and a similar specimen was collected later. Bonafè lists *D. rupicola* with a good photo, and Duvigneaud and Llorens both list this species. Another botanist reports seeing inaccessible (and so unidentifiable) *Dianthus* species on the cliffs below the lighthouse at Formentor. (Ma) FE 1 201

In other islands:
Paronychia echinulata Chater. Minorca. FE I 150
Loeflingia hispanica L. Ibiza. Not BI in FE I 153
Spergularia fimbriata Boiss. Ibiza. Not BI in FE I 155

Plate 12

CARYOPHYLLACEAE (3): *SILENE*

SILENE species are herbs (rarely shrubs) with regular 5-merous flowers with clawed petals. The calyx is tubular with conspicuous longitudinal veins and 5 short teeth, often inflated in fruit. The fruit is a capsule opening by a variable number of teeth, twice as many as the number of styles. All flower April-June unless otherwise stated. (Small illustrations of calyx in flower and (where different) in fruit are x 1, main illustration x 2/3 to 1).

1. *Silene mollissima* (L.) Pers. Softly hairy robust woody perennial. Flowers white. Calyx glandular. Local in N. (Illustration from Mallorcan specimen). Llorens lists (Ma, Mi). Ibiza only according to FE I 163

2. *Silene vulgaris* (Moench) Garcke. Bladder Campion. A very variable perennial with characteristic inflated calyx. Flowers white usually, occasionally pinkish. Jan.-Oct. Common. (Ma, Mi, I) FE I 168

3. *Silene pseudotocion* Desf. Viscid, softly hairy annual with large (about 1cm) entire pink petals. Confined to one locality, but abundant there. An African species, this is probably its only Europaean station, though there is one unconfirmed record from the Spanish mainland. (Ma) FE I 175

4. *Silene rubella* L. Softly hairy annual. Leaves undulate. Calyx not enlarging significantly in fruit. Field weed, often among Broad Beans or Lucerne. (Ma, Mi, I) FE I 175

5. *Silene sedoides* Poiret. Small, much-branched viscid annual. Rather rare. (Ma, Mi) FE I 176

6. *Silene nicaeensis* All. Viscid annual with pink or whitish flowers. NS. (From herbarium and garden specimens) Knoche quotes Garcia (1905). Llorens queries. (?Ma) BI in FE 178

7. *Silene colorata* Poiret. Softly hairy annual. Flowers solitary, terminal on stems usually around 10cm. Very local on sandy ground and shore in SE. Llorens lists (Ma) Not BI in FE I 180

8. *Silene nocturna* L. Annual. Flowers very small, whitish, sometimes included in calyx. Veins of calyx conspicuously anastomosing. Fairly common. (Ma, Mi, I) FE I 179

9. *Silene gallica* L. Small-flowered Catchfly. Annual, sticky above. Petals usually entire and pink here, may be white or notched. Widespread, especially near sea. (Ma, Mi, I) FE I 179

10. *Silene bellidifolia* Juss. Softly hairy annual, with elegant secund racemose cymes of numerous pink flowers, with deeply bifid, inrolled petals. Locally common. (Ma, Mi) FE I 179

11. *Silene cerastioides* L. Rather like 9, but with deeply emarginate petals which are often white. Knoche and Duvigneaud both list this species. Llorens omits. Seems common around Bay of Pollensa. (Ma, Mi, I) FE I 179

12. *Silene disticha* Willd. Hispid annual with subcapitate inflorescence. Petal almost included in calyx. Rare. NS. (from Corsican specimen). Knoche quotes Marès & Vigineix (1880). Llorens lists. (Ma, Mi, I) FE I 180

13. *Silene secundiflora* Otth. Annual. Leaves almost hairless. Calyx hairy, much enlarged in fruit, with conspicuously anastomosing veins. Seeds narrowly grooved between two dorsal undulate wings. Locally common near sea and in mountain areas. (Ma, Mi, I) FE I 180

14. *Silene apetala* Willd. (including *S. decipiens* Barc.). Hairy annual. Calyx 7-10mm, petals small or absent. Seeds dark brown, deeply grooved between undulate wings (13 the only other species here with winged seeds). Feb.-Mar. Rare (or overlooked because early and inconspicuous). **NS**. (Specimen from Spanish mainland). (Ma, I) FE I 180

Other species recorded from Mallorca:

Silene muscipula L. Knoche records. Duvigneaud omits. Llorens queries. ?BI in FE I 176

Silene almolae Gay. Llorens lists (Ma). Stems up to 20cm, unbranched. Calyx 15-18mm with short, triangular, acute teeth and veins distinctly anastomosing. Petals very pale pink. Seeds reniform, up to 1.4mm with 2 rows of tubercles on the back. Llorens lists for (Ma) BI not included in FE I 178

Silene sclerocarpa Léon Dufour. Llorens lists for (Ma, Mi, ?I). Not in FE (even the index), could this be related to or included in no 11 above?

In Ibiza:

Silene hifacensis Rouy. FE I 163

Silene cambessedesii Boiss. & Reuter. (? Same as or close to *Silene littorea* Brot. FE I 178, BI in FE)

Silene tridentata Desf. FE I 180

Plate 13

(NYMPHAEACEAE: *NYMPHAEA)*
CERATOPHYLLACEAE: *CERATOPHYLLUM*
RANUNCULACEAE (1): *HELLEBORUS, NIGELLA, DELPHINIUM, ANEMONE, CLEMATIS, ADONIS, MYOSURUS*

CERATOPHYLLACEAE
CERATOPHYLLUM
1. *Ceratophyllum demersum* L. Submerged aquatic perennial. Leaves in dense whorls, forked once or twice. Flowers tiny, axillary, unisexual. Nut with terminal spine. Common in fresh water. (Ma, Mi) Not BI in FE I 206

RANUNCULACEAE (1)
These are herbs or, sometimes in the case of *Clematis*, woody climbers. The flowers are mainly regular, hermaphrodite with a superior ovary. There are numerous sepals, and the gynoecium consists of one or many carpels, usually spirally arranged. The perianth includes sepals and petals, petals here including honey-leaves, which are petal-like structures bearing nectaries.

HELLEBORUS
2. *Helleborus foetidus* L. Stinking Hellebore. Robust branched perennial. Leaves divided into 7-9 narrow segments. Feb.-May. Local in mountains. (Small part inflorescence, slightly reduced). (Ma) FE I 210
3. *Helleborus lividus* Aiton, subsp. *lividus*. Leaves trifoliate, ovate. Flowers pinkish. Feb.-Apr. Local in shady places in the mountains. (x 1/2). (Ma, endemic subsp.) FE I 207

NIGELLA
4. *Nigella damascena* L. Love-in-a mist. Annual. Flowers blue, with central black united follicles, and much divided leaves with linear segments. Upper leaves form an involucre round the flower. Apr.-May. Common in cultivated ground. (Ma, Mi, I) FE I 210

DELPHINIUM
5. *Delphinium staphisagria* L. Licebane. Hairy biennial. Leaves palmately lobed. Flowers deep blue, with a very short spur from the upper petal. May-June. Occasional, stony places in mountains. (Plant here x 1/5, details x 1, including large seed). (Ma, Mi, I) FE I 216
6. *Delphinium pictum* Willd. Similar to 5, but flowers white (dark blue on drying), with a 6-8mm spur from the upper petal, bilobed at tip. (Details of flower x 1: above them a middle stem-leaf with more or less linear shining segments). May-June. Occasional in stony places. (Ma) FE I 216

ANEMONE
7. *Anemone coronaria* L. Corolla red or blue. Flowering stem with a whorl of partly united leaves. Feb.-Mar. (From garden specimen, seen once in Mallorca). Not common and probably introduced. (Ma, Mi) FE I 219

CLEMATIS
8. *Clematis flammula* L. Maiden's Bower. Leaves irregularly bipinnate. Flower clusters creamish-white. Petals hairless on upper surface. May-Oct. Fairly common on fences and in rocky places. (Ma, Mi, I) FE I 221
9. *Clematis vitalba* L. Old Man's Beard. Leaves irregularly pinnate. Flowers greenish-white, petals tomentose on both surfaces. June-Aug. **NS.** Seen by Duvigneaud. Llorens lists. (From British specimen). (Ma) Not BI in FE I 221
10. *Clematis cirrhosa* L. (var. *balearica* (L.C.M.Richard) Willk.: not described in FE). Leaves 3-lobed. Flowers solitary, pendent, white, often tinged with green or pink, with red spots inside. (Ma, Mi, I) FE I 221

ADONIS
11. *Adonis annua* L. Pheasant's Eye. Small annual with 5-8 red petals. Achenes forming an elongated head in fruit, each achene with a straight inner margin. Mar.-June. Fairly common in cultivated ground. (Ma, Mi) FE I 222
12. *Adonis microcarpa* DC. Like 11, but corolla usually yellow. Inner margin of achene with a projection near beak. **NS.** Seen by Duvigneaud. Llorens lists. (Detail from Greek specimen). (Ma, Mi, I) FE I 223

MYOSURUS
13. *Myosurus minimus* L. Mouse tail. Small annual. Flowers solitary. Petals pale greenish-yellow, small. Achenes numerous, receptacle greatly elongated in fruit. **NS.** Seen by Duvigneaud. (From British specimen). Llorens lists. (Ma) (FE I 238)

Other species recorded for Mallorca:
Nymphaea alba L. White Water-Lily. Probably extinct here as a wild plant (Bonafè). Llorens lists. (Ma) FE I 204
Ceratophyllum submersum L. Resembles 1, but leaves forked 3 or 4 times. Nut without basal spine. (Seen by several botanists recently). Llorens lists. (Ma) Not BI in FE I 206
Consolida ambigua (L.) P.W.Ball & Heywood. Larkspur. Occasional escape from cultivation. (Ma, Mi) FE I 217
Adonis aestivalis L. Llorens lists. (Ma) Not BI in FE I 223

In other islands:
Nigella gallica Jordan. Minorca. Not BI in FE I 209
Delphinium halteratum Sibth. & Sm. Ibiza. Not BI in FE I 215
Consolida regalis S.F.Gray. Ibiza. BI excluded in FE I 217

Plate 14

RANUNCULACEAE (2): *RANUNCULUS* (part 1)

RANUNCULUS

1. *Ranunculus repens* L. Creeping Buttercup. Stoloniferous perennial, rooting at nodes. Basal leaves with 3 leaflets, the central one stalked. Achenes compressed, bordered, with a curved beak. Apr.-June. **NS.** Seen by Duvigneaud. (From British specimen). Llorens lists. (Ma, ?Mi, ?I) FE I 227

2. *Ranunculus macrophyllus* Desf. Robust hairy perennial. Basal leaves 12cm or more across, deeply cordate, with 3-5 segments. Stem leaves much smaller, uppermost trifid with entire segments or simple. Achenes compressed, bordered, minutely pitted or hairy. Mar.-June. Common in damp places. (Ma, Mi, I) FE I 229

3. *Ranunculus bulbosus* L. Bulbous Buttercup. Softly hairy perennial, bulbous rooted. Upper leaves deeply cut into more or less linear segments. Sepals reflexed in mature flower. Achenes 2-4mm, beak short, hooked, with twisted tip. Mar.-June. Occasional. (Ma) FE I 229

4. *Ranunculus sardous* Crantz. Hairy Buttercup. Annual, resembling 3, but without bulbous base. Leaves in middle part of stem sessile, much lobed, opposite pairs often overlapping to form a sort of 'ruff' round stem. Achenes about 3mm, with blunt tubercles forming a ring inside border: centre of face smooth. Mar.-June. Widespread. (Ma, ?Mi, ?I) FE I 230

5. *Ranunculus trilobus* Desf. Annual, almost hairless. Lowest leaves simple, others 3-lobed. Achenes 2mm with a short beak, the face covered with low tubercles. Mar.-May. Common in marshy places. (Ma, Mi, I) FE I 230

6. *Ranunculus muricatus* L. Annual, almost hairless. Leaves shallowly lobed. Petals small, little longer than sepals. Achenes 7-8mm, with spiny face and a smooth margin. Mar.-May. (Ma, Mi, I) FE I 230

7. *Ranunculus arvensis* L. Corn Buttercup. Annual. Flowers 4-12mm. Sepals spreading. Achenes 6-8mm, few, with long curved spines from the border and shorter ones from ridges on the face. Mar.-June. Widespread in cultivated areas. (Ma, Mi) FE I 230

8. *Ranunculus ?parviflorus* L. Softly hairy spreading more or less decumbent annual. Flowers 3-6mm. Sepals deflexed. Pedicels recurved in fruit, and **slightly thickened.** Achenes 3mm with long beak, face covered in tubercles, some of which are pointed or slightly hooked. (This does not fit description in FE I 230 exactly (recurved pedicel not mentioned: beak of achene short in FE description): Hansen records this species as 'most likely = *R. chius* here'). Apr.-June. Common throughout mountains and uncultivated areas. (Ma, Mi, I) FE I 230

9. *Ranunculus chius* DC. Resembles 8, but with **much thickened** recurved pedicels in fruit. Beak at least 1/2 length achene. **NS.** (From Greek specimen). Llorens lists. (?Ma, I) FE I 230

10. *Ranunculus monspeliacus* L. Now deleted from the Balearic Flora, having been recorded as doubtful for years! FE I 231

Plate 15

RANUNCULACEAE (3): *RANUNCULUS* (continued)
PAEONIACEAE: *PAEONIA*
LAURACEAE: *LAURUS*

RANUNCULACEAE (3)
RANUNCULUS (continued)

1. *Ranunculus paludosus* Poiret. Fan-leaved Buttercup. Stoloniferous perennial. Flowers large, up to 3cm. Receptacle much elongated in fruit. Achene punctate, keeled on back, tapering gradually to long straight beak with small hook at tip. Mar.-Apr. Very local. (Ma, I) FE I 231

2. *Ranunculus sceleratus* L. Celery-leaved Buttercup. Hairless annual. Basal leaves large, broader than long, 3-lobed. Flowers small (5-10mm), numerous. Sepals deflexed. Receptacle much elongated in fruit. Apr.-May. Occasional in wet places. (Ma, Mi) FE I 233

3. *Ranunculus ficaria* L. Lesser Celandine. (A robust subsp. *ficariiformis* Rouy & Fouc. here). Hairless perennial with shining long-petiolate leaves. Petals about 10. Mar.-Apr. Fairly common near streams. (Ma, Mi) FE I 233

4. *Ranunculus weyleri* Marès. Small (up to 20cm) tufted perennial. Leaves up to 2cm, deeply trilobed. Flowers solitary, small. **NS.** Very rare. (Specimen from Cambridge University Botanic Garden, achene x 3). (Ma endemic) FE I 235

5. *Ranunculus ophioglossifolius* Vill. Snakes-tongue Crowfoot. Annual, up to 40cm, usually less. Leaves undivided. Flowers numerous, 5-9mm diameter. Apr.-May. Local in wet places. (Ma, Mi) FE I 235

There seems to be some doubt about which white aquatic species occur here. They are often difficult to identify.

6. *Ranunculus peltatus* Schrank. Annual or perennial with laminate or capillary leaves or both. Petals usually more than 10mm, contiguous. Pedicel in fruit usually more than 50cm, exceeding subtending leaf. (Ma, Mi) FE I 237

7. *Ranunculus trichophyllus* Chaix. Laminate leaves absent. Petals 5mm or less. Pedicels in fruit less than 40cm. Apr.-May. Local in or by fresh water. Listed by Llorens. (Ma) BI excluded in FE I 237

PAEONIACEAE
PAEONIA

8. *Paeonia cambessedesii* (Willk.) Willk. Basal leaves hairless, more or less bluish green with purplish veins. Flower large and pink. Very local in the mountains. (Ma, Mi endemic) FE I 244

LAURACEAE
LAURUS

9. *Laurus nobilis* L. Sweet Bay. Evergreen shrub. Leaves entire. Flowers small, subsessile, cream with numerous stamens. **NS.** Very local, except in cultivation. Seen by Duvigneaud. (Ma, Mi) FE I 246

Other species recorded for Mallorca:

Ranunculus bullatus L. Leaves all simple, basal, crenate. Knoche's only site now very trampled. Llorens lists. (Ma). BI in FE I 234

Ranunculus baudotii Godron. Duvigneaud and Llorens query this species. BI in FE I 237

Ranunculus pseudofluitans (Syme) Newbould, seems to correspond with *Ranunculus penicillatus* (Dumort) Bab., which Llorens lists (Ma, Mi, I) Not BI in FE I 237

Plate 16

PAPAVERACEAE (1): *PAPAVER, ROEMERIA, GLAUCI-UM, CHELIDONIUM, HYPECOUM*

PAPAVER

Annuals here, with latex. Flowers with 2 sepals and 4 entire petals, crumpled in bud. Stigmas sessile (the rays on the disc). Stamens numerous.

1. *Papaver somniferum* L. subsp. *setigerum* (DC.) Corb. Opium Poppy. Bluish-green annual. Mar.-June. Common. (Ma, Mi, I) FE I 247
2. *Papaver rhoeas* L. Field Poppy. Hairs spreading on upper part of stem. Petals sometimes with dark area at base. **Filaments blackish-purple, anthers bluish. Capsule not or hardly elongated.** Mar.-June. Common. (Ma, Mi, I) FE I 248
3. *Papaver dubium* L. Long-headed Poppy. Very much like 2, but petals usually a more orange red. Hairs appressed at top of stem. **Filaments blackish-purple, anthers bluish. Capsule** at least **twice as long as wide.** Mar.-June. Common, but less so than 2. (Ma, Mi) FE I 248
4. *Papaver pinnatifidum* Moris. Much like 2 and 3, but **filaments violet, anthers yellow. Capsule** elongated, **ribbed.** Less common, but fairly widespread. (Ma, Mi, I) FE I 248
5. *Papaver argemone* L. Like a small Field Poppy, but **capsule elongated and bristly. NS,** and not seen by Duvigneaud. (From British specimen). Llorens lists (Ma, I) FE I 248
6. *Papaver hybridum* L. Often has a bluish tinge to colour of petals, but very variable (two illustrations). Filaments purple, anthers white or very pale yellow. **Capsule globular, ribbed and bristly.** Fairly common. (Ma, Mi, I) FE I 249

ROEMERIA

7. *Roemeria hybrida* (L.) DC. Like a small **lavender-violet** poppy. **Capsule narrow, much elongated, 5-10cm. NS.** (From garden specimen). Seen by Duvigneaud. Llorens lists. (Ma, I) FE I 251

GLAUCIUM

8. *Glaucium flavum* Crantz. Yellow Horned Poppy. Much-branched bluish-green biennial or perennial. **Yellow petals** up to 3cm, and **much elongated capsule** (15-30cm). Apr.-Sept. Common near the sea. (Ma, Mi, I) FE I 251
9. *Glaucium corniculatum* (L.) J.H.Rudolph. Bristly annual. **Petals red**, but easily distinguished from *Papaver* species by the long hairy **capsule (up to 20cm). NS.** (From garden specimen). Seen by Duvigneaud. (Ma) FE I 251

CHELIDONIUM

10. *Chelidonium majus* L. Greater Celandine. Branched perennial. Flowers much like those of 8, but much smaller (petals up to 1cm). Capsule elongated with constrictions between seeds. **NS.** (From British specimen). Llorens treats as garden escape. FE I 251

HYPECOUM

11. *Hypecoum imberbe* Sibth. & Sm. Hairless annual, with 2 outer petals much larger than the two inner. Lateral lobes of outer petals as large as or larger than the middle one. Not common. (Ma, Mi) FE I 252

Also occurring or possibly occurring in Mallorca:

Eschscholzia californica Cham. Naturalised in BI according to FE I 251

Hypecoum procumbens L. Differs from 11 in that lateral lobes of outer petals are much smaller than middle one (and in other respects). Knoche quotes Barceló. Duvigneaud lists but did not see. Very rare (Prof. Llorens). (Ma, I) FE I 252

In Minorca only:
Hypecoum pendulum L. Not BI in FE I 252

Plate 17

PAPAVERACEAE (2): *FUMARIA*
CAPPARIDACEAE: *CAPPARIS*
CRUCIFERAE (1): *SISYMBRIUM, (DESCURAINIA), (ARABIDOPSIS)*

PAPAVERACEAE (FUMARIACEAE)
FUMARIA

Weak-stemmed annuals. Leaves 2-4-pinnatisect. Inflorescence racemose, each pedicel subtended by a small bract. Calyx of 2 small sepals. Corolla irregular with 4 petals, the upper with a sac-like spur at the base and wings at the tip. The two inner (lateral) petals are dark-tipped, and the lower petal is narrow, often spathulate.

1. *Fumaria agraria* Lag. Mature leaves with broad flat segments. **Corolla 12-14mm. Wings of upper petal pink or white.** Feb.-Mar. Rare. **NS.** (From Portuguese specimen). Not seen by Duvigneaud. Llorens lists. (Ma, Mi, I) FE I 256
2. *Fumaria capreolata* L. Leaves with broad flat segments. **Corolla** whitish, often becoming pinkish-red, **10-14mm, wings of upper petal blackish-purple.** Pedicels recurved in lower part inflorescence. Apr.-May. (Ma, Mi, I) FE I 256
3. *Fumaria bastardii* Boreau. This specimen was thought to be *F. bicolor* Sommier (hence two illustrations) see:
4. *Fumaria bastardii* Boreau. Raceme usually longer than the peduncle (but this varies). Sepals 2-3mm. Corolla 9-12mm, pink. **Upper petal** narrow and laterally compressed, **usually with pink wings** (though they may be dark). Lateral petals with dark tips. Fruit ovoid, rugose when ripe. Fairly common. (Ma, Mi) FE I 257
5. *Fumaria densiflora* DC. **Corolla 5-7mm.** Racemes dense with 20-25 flowers, **peduncle very much shorter than raceme, if any. Bracts usually exceed fruiting pedicel. NS.** Seen by Duvigneaud. (Detail only x 2, from British specimen). (Ma, I) FE I 257
6. *Fumaria officinalis* L. Leaf segments narrow, flat or channelled. Raceme longer than peduncle. **Corolla 7-9mm, purplish pink.** Wings of upper petal and apex of inner ones black. **Apex of fruit truncate or slightly emarginate.** 2 subspecies here, both common: subsp. *wirtgenii* (Koch) Arcangeli, has 10-20 flowers and sepals less than 2mm, subsp. *officinalis* has more than 20 flowers and sepals 2.5-3.5mm. (Ma, Mi) FE I 257
7. *Fumaria parviflora* Lam. **Leaves pale bluish-green, segments very narrow, channelled.** Racemes very dense, more or less sessile. Corolla **5-6mm,** usually white, but sometimes turning pink. Wings of upper petal white. Very common. Apr.-May. (Ma, Mi, I) FE I 258

CAPPARIDACEAE
CAPPARIS

8. *Capparis spinosa* L. Caper. Shrub with hairless orbicular leaves and spiny stipules. Flowers 4 petalled, the two upper petals rather smaller than the two lower. Stamens long-exserted, very numerous. June-Oct. Common in cultivation (especially in the South), rarer in wild places. (Ma, I) FE I 259

CRUCIFERAE

Herbs (here) annual to perennial. Flowers usually in a terminal raceme, mostly ebracteate except sometimes below. Flowers with 4 clawed petals alternating with sepals, which are free in 2 pairs. Stamens usually 6. Pod a capsule, called a siliqua when at least 3 x as long as wide, a silicula if shorter than this.

SISYMBRIUM

Annuals here, 12 sometimes biennial. Fruit a siliqua.
9. *Sisymbrium irio* L. London Rocket. Annual. Variably hairy. Lower leaves pinnatifid, the terminal lobe much larger than the lateral lobes, stem leaves lobed or entire, spear-shaped at base. Inflorescence without bracts. Petals 2.5-3.5mm, yellow. **Pedicels in fruit up to 20mm,** much thinner than **torulose siliqua,** which is 25-65mm long, held **erect.** Mar.-June. Common in waste places. (x 1/2). (Ma, Mi, I) FE I 264
10. *Sisymbrium orientale* L. Eastern Rocket. Similar to 9, but stem and **leaves grey-hairy.** Petals pale yellow, 8-10mm. **Siliquae held less erect,** often spreading, **not torulose.** Apr.-June. Occasional. (x 1/5). (Ma, I) FE I 265
11. *Sisymbrium erysimoides* Desf. Like 9, but petals smaller (1-2.5mm). Siliquae **not torulose, spreading in a line with very short fruiting pedicel** (up to5mm, usually shorter). Common. (x 1/2). (Ma, I) FE I 266
12. *Sisymbrium officinale* (L.) Scop. Hedge Mustard. Differs from the others here in the **short (10-20mm) conical siliquae, appressed to stem.** Mar.-Sept. Common. (Main illustration x 1/3, detail of siliqua x 2). (Ma, Mi, I) FE I 266

Also recorded from Mallorca:
Fumaria vaillantii Loisel. Llorens lists with query. BI in FE I 258
Sisymbrium polyceratium L. **Inflorescence bracteate to apex.** Fruiting pedicels 1mm or less, **siliquae 10-25mm, recurved, torulose,** with a **thin style.** Seen by Duvigneaud. Llorens lists. (Ma, Mi) Not BI in FE I 265
Sisymbrium runcinatum Lag. Like *S. polyceratium*, but **pod not torulose** and **style in fruit almost as thick as siliqua.** Duvigneaud quotes FE. Llorens lists. (Ma) BI in FE I 266
Descurainia sophia (L.) Webb. Knoche quotes Barceló (1867-1877). Listed but not seen by Duvigneaud. Llorens lists. (Ma) BI not excluded in FE I 266
Arabidopsis thaliana (L.) Heynh. Knoche quotes Bianor (1910-1914). Listed but not seen by Duvigneaud. Llorens lists. (Ma, MI) BI not excluded in FE I 266

Possible species in other islands:
Fumaria bella P.D.Sell seems to be *F. barnolae* Sennen & Pau listed by Llorens for Ibiza. *F. bella* Not BI in FE I 256
Fumaria gaillardotii Boiss. Llorens lists for Ibiza. Not BI in FE I 256
Fumaria flabellata Gaspar. Llorens lists for Minorca. BI in FE I 256
Fumaria muralis Sonder. Llorens lists for Ibiza. Not BI in FE I 256
Platycapnos spicata (L.) Bernh. Llorens lists for Ibiza. Not BI in FE 258
Capparis ovata Desf. BI in FE I 259
Erysimum grandiflorum BI in FE I 271

Plate 18

CRUCIFERAE (2*): (MALCOLMIA), MARESIA, CHEI-RANTHUS, MATTHIOLA, NASTURTIUM, CAR-DAMINE, ARABIS, LOBULARIA, CLYPEOLA*

MARESIA

1. *Maresia nana* (DC.) Batt. Tiny branched annual, more or less densely covered in stellate hairs (often greyish). May be confused with *Malcolmia ramosissima* (Desf.) Thell., but distinguished by presence of style (absent in *M. ramosissima*) and translucent septum of siliqua (opaque in *M. ramosissima*). May. Sandy places near sea. Occasional. (Ma, I) FE I 278 (Illustration x 2, details x 4)

CHEIRANTHUS

2. *Cheiranthus cheiri* L. Wallflower. Perennial. Feb.-Apr. **NS.** From garden specimen. Introduced species (native Aegean region). (Ma, Mi, I) FE I 279

MATTHIOLA

3. *Matthiola incana* (L.) R.Br. Stock. Flowers white, violet or pink. Apr.-May. Introduced. **NS.** (Ma, Mi, I) FE I 280

4. *Matthiola sinuata* (L.) R.Br. Sea Stock. Usually biennial, up to 60cm. Densely white tomentose. Apr.-June. Fairly common on sand-dunes. (Ma, Mi, I) FE I 280

5. *Matthiola tricuspidata* (L.) R.Br. Annual up to 40cm. Siliqua with 2 horns. **NS.** (From Greek specimen). Rare. (Ma, Mi) FE I 280

NASTURTIUM

6. *Nasturtium officinale* R.Br. Watercress. Flowers throughout the year. Common in running water. (Ma, Mi) FE I 284

CARDAMINE

7. *Cardamine hirsuta* L. Hairy Bittercress. Annual, up to 30cm, usually much less. Feb.-June. Common. (Ma, Mi, I) FE I 289

ARABIS

8. *Arabis hirsuta* (L.) Scop. Short-lived perennial. Stem leaves sessile, often half-clasping. Petals 4-5mm. Siliqua 15-35mm. (From Welsh specimen with sagittate stem-leaves: found subsequently in Mallorca high in mountains with stem leaves not sagitate and less pointed, but otherwise similar). (Ma) FE I 292

9. *Arabis collina* Ten. Perennial. Stem-leaves ovate below to lanceolate above, sessile, not clasping. Petals 8-10mm. Siliqua 60-90mm. Apr.-May. Uncommon in mountains. (Ma, Mi) FE I 292

10. *Arabis verna* (L.) R.Br. Annual. Flowers deep violet. Common in damp places in mountain area. (Ma) FE I 293

LOBULARIA

11. *Lobularia maritima* (L.) Desv. Sweet Alison. Common in sandy places by the sea and as a weed of sandy fields. (Ma, Mi, I) FE I 307

CLYPEOLA

12. *Clypeola jonthlaspi* L. Greyish-hairy annual. Silicula more or less orbicular with a distinct wing. Local, mainly in mountains. (Ma, I) FE I 307

Other plants recorded from Mallorca:

Malcolmia africana (L.) R.Br. Annual. Siliqua patent, 25-65mm, more or less 4-angled, densely hispid. Llorens includes this species. Not BI in FE I 277

Matthiola parviflora (Schousboe) R. Br. Annual up to 20cm. Petals 6-10mm, purple or brownish-purple. Llorens lists for Mallorca and Ibiza. BI in FE I 280

Arabis sagittata (Bertol.) DC. Resembles 8. Included by Bonafè. Llorens omits. Not BI in FE I 291

Arabis muralis Bertol. Very like 9, and has been treated as a subsp. Duvigneaud has it in his list, Llorens omits. ?BI in FE I 292

In other Balearic Islands:

Malcolmia ramosissima (Desf.) Thell. (See *Maresia nana* above). (Mi, I) FE I 277

Malcolmia maritima (L.) R.Br. Night-scented Stock. (Mi) FE I 277

Matthiola fruticulosa (L.) Maire. (I) FE I 280

Plate 19

CRUCIFERAE (3): *EROPHILA, (CAMELINA), NESLIA, CAPSELLA, HYMENOLOBUS, HORNUNGIA, THLASPI, (IBERIS), BISCUTELLA, LEPIDIUM, CARDARIA, CORONOPUS*

Main illustrations approximately x 1, unless otherwise stated.

EROPHILA
1. *Erophila verna* (L.) Chevall. Whitlow Grass. Small annual with basal leaf-rosette. Stems not usually exceeding 6cm, with terminal racemose inflorescence, elongating in fruit. Petals deeply bifid, white. Feb.-Apr. Common. (Ma) FE I 312

NESLIA
2. *Neslia paniculata* (L.) Desv. Ball Mustard. Annual. Stem leaves sagittate, sessile, with acute auricles. Flowers small, bright yellow. Fruit globose or sometimes compressed, 1.5-3mm diameter. Mar.-May. Occasional casual. (Ma, I) FE I 315

CAPSELLA
3. *Capsella bursa-pastoris* (L.) Medicus. Shepherd's Purse. Annual. Basal leaves in a rosette, varying from entire to pinnatifid. Stem leaves sagittate-amplexicaul. Petals 2-3mm, white, longer than the sepals. Fruit a more or less triangular silicula, with septum at right angles to the flat face. Sides of siliqua straight or slightly convex. Most of year. Common. (Ma, Mi, I) FE I 316
4. *Capsella rubella* Reuter. Pink Shepherd's Purse. Very like 3, but flowers scarcely exceeding sepals, sometimes reddish. Siliqua with concave lateral margins. Common. (Details x 4). (Ma, Mi) FE I 316

HYMENOLOBUS
5. *Hymenolobus procumbens* (L.) Nutt. Small annual with scattered simple hairs, resembling 1, but with branched stems and entire petals. Fruit an elliptical to ovate siliqua, with septum at right angles to the widest diameter. Mar.-Apr. Common. (Ma, Mi, I) FE I 317

HORNUNGIA
6. *Hornungia petraea* (L.) Reichenb. Rock Hutchinsia. Small annual. Leaves all pinnate, the lower forming a rosette. Flowers minute, petals 1mm or less. Fruit similar to that of 5. Apr.-May. Common in rocky places, cracks of walls etc, often very small. (Both illustrations x 1). (Ma, I) FE I 317

THLASPI
7. *Thlaspi arvense* L. Penny Cress. Annual. **Fruit almost circular** (including wings), 10-15mm, with a **deep narrow notch at the apex**. Flowers small, white. Apr.-Sept. **NS.** (From British specimen). Duvigneaud lists, but not as seen. Llorens lists. (Ma) FE I 319

8. *Thlaspi perfoliatum* L. Resembles 7, but **fruit heart-shaped**, with **wide notch at the apex. NS.** Seen by Duvigneaud. (Specimen from Spanish mainland). (Ma) FE I 319

BISCUTELLA
9. *Biscutella auriculata* L. Annual. Stem leaves sessile, amplexicaul, with blunt apex and rounded basal lobes. Petals pale yellow with long claw, up to 15mm. Outer sepals strongly saccate at base. Silicula like two adjacent shields, strongly flattened. **NS.** Listed but not seen by Duvigneaud. Llorens lists. (Ma, I) FE I 329

LEPIDIUM
10. *Lepidium graminifolium* L. Perennial 1m or more, inflorescence much branched. Upper leaves linear or narrow spathulate, inflorescence racemose. Sepals 0.5mm with narrow white margin, petals equalling sepals or slightly longer. Fruit 2.5-4mm, pointed ovate. Apr.-Sept. Fairly common in waste places and drier parts of saltmarshes. (Ma, Mi) FE I 333

CARDARIA
11. *Cardaria draba* (L.) Desv. Hairless or sparsely hairy perennial. Stem leaves sagittate, amplexicaul. Flowers in a dense panicle. Fruit heart-shaped, inflated. Mar.-June. Common wayside weed. (Illustration x 1/2, fruit x 2). (Ma, Mi, I) FE I 333

CORONOPUS
12. *Coronopus squamatus* (Forskål) Ascherson. Swine-cress. Annual or biennial, often prostrate. Flowers very small. **Fruit** kidney-shaped, **apiculate**, with deep irregular ridges. Widespread in trampled places. (Ma) Not BI in FE
13. *Coronopus didymus* (L.) Sm. Lesser Swine-cress. Like 12, but smaller. **Fruit notched**, not apiculate, with shallow pits and ridges. Mar.-May. Occasional. (Ma, Mi, I) FE I 333

Also possibly occurring in Mallorca:
Camelina microcarpa Andrz. ex DC. Annual or biennial with densely hairy stem and leaves. Petals pale yellow. Fruiting racemes elongate and rigid with numerous siliculae, 5-7mm. Valves hard and woody. Llorens lists. (Ma). FE I 315

In other islands, or listed BI in FE:
Biscutella laevigata L. Ibiza. FE I 328
Biscutella frutescens Cosson. BI in FE I 327
Lepidium spinosum Ard. Minorca. FE I 331
Lepidium ruderale L. Minorca. FE I 332

Plate 20

CRUCIFERAE (4): *(CONRINGIA), MORICANDIA, DI-PLOTAXIS, BRASSICA, SINAPIS, ERUCA, HIRSCH-FELDIA*

MORICANDIA
1. *Moricandia arvensis* (L.) DC. Violet Cabbage. Hairless, blue-green perennial, often much branched. Mar.-May. Occasional casual. (Ma, I) FE I 334

DIPLOTAXIS
Fruit a long linear siliqua with a short beak. Valves compressed with a prominent median vein. Seeds in 2 rows in each loculus.
2. *Diplotaxis ibicensis* (Pau) Gomez-Campo 1981. Shrubby perennial. Stems leafy, much branched at base. Leaves pinnatifid. Flowers pale yellow. Rare, on a sandy shore. (Ma, I) Not described in FE
3. *Diplotaxis erucoides* (L.) DC. Annual. Petals white with purple or pink claw. Feb.-Mar. Common field weed. (Ma, Mi, I) FE I 335
4. *Diplotaxis viminea* (L.) DC. Slender annual. Leaves confined to a basal rosette. Petals 3-4mm. Outer 2 stamens sterile. Rare or overlooked. **NS.** (Illustration from Mallorcan specimen collected by Bianor). Mar.-Apr. (Ma, ?Mi, I) FE I 335
5. *Diplotaxis muralis* (L.) DC. Annual Wall-rocket. Stinkweed. Annual, biennial or perennial. Leaves usually confined to a basal rosette. Petals bright sulphur yellow, 4.5mm or more. Stamens all fertile. Mar.-Sept. Fairly common. (Ma, Mi) FE I 335

BRASSICA
Fruit a siliqua, the valves convex with a prominent median vein.
6. *Brassica balearica* Pers. Hairless small shrub. Leaves nearly all basal. Rock crevices in mountains, rather local. (Ma endemic) FE I 336

SINAPIS
Leaves pinnatifid or pinnatisect. Sepals patent. Fruit a siliqua with a long beak, valves 3-7-veined. Seeds in one row in each loculus.

7. *Sinapis arvensis* L. Charlock. Bristly annual weed. Siliqua patent, 25-45mm long, beak 10-15mm, not or hardly compressed. Common. (x 1/2, immature pod, and mature pod front and side view x 1). (Ma, Mi, I) FE I 339
8. *Sinapis alba* L. White Mustard. Resembles 7, but siliqua 10-30mm, with beak strongly compressed and often as long as the body or longer. (x 1/2, details x 1). (Ma, I) FE I 339

ERUCA
Resembles *Sinapis*, but sepals erect and valves of the siliqua 1-veined. Seeds in 2 rows in each loculus.
9. *Eruca vesicaria* (L.) Cav. Garden Rocket. Petals 15-20mm, white or yellow with violet veins. Common. (Ma, Mi, I) FE I 340

HIRSCHFELDIA
10. *Hirschfeldia incana* (L.) Lagrèze-Fossat. Hoary Mustard. Like *Sinapis*, but sepals almost erect. Siliqua with short beak swollen at base, valves of siliqua 3-veined when young, obscurely veined when mature. Widespread. (From Turkish specimen, not differing materially from Ma specimens seen later). (Ma, Mi, I) FE I 342

Also recorded from Mallorca:
Conringia orientalis (L.) Dumort. Hare's Ear Cabbage. Hairless, blue-green annual. Stem leaves simple. Cordate-amplexicaul. Flowers inconspicuous, yellowish-green. Siliqua 6-14cm, 4-angled. (Ma, Mi introduced from Central and East Europe). FE I 334
Brassica tournefortii Gouan. Annual up to 50cm. Stem leaves few, sessile. Petals pale yellow with violet base, becoming whitish. Llorens lists for Ma. Not BI in FE I 338

Recorded from other islands:
Diplotaxis tenuifolia (L.) DC. Minorca. FE I 335
Brassica rapa L. Minorca. FE I 337
Brassica barrelieri (L.) Janka. ?Ibiza ?BI in FE I 338
Erucastrum gallicum (Willd.) O.E.Schulz. Ibiza. Not BI in FE I 340

Plate 21

CRUCIFERAE (5): *CARRICHTERA, SUCCOWIA, CAK-ILE, RAPISTRUM, RAPHANUS*
RESEDACEAE: *RESEDA*

CRUCIFERAE
CARRICHTERA

1. *Carrichtera annua* (L.) DC. Bristly annual. Leaves 2-3 pinnatisect, with blunt linear segments. Inflorescence a raceme with very short pedicels. Flowers pale yellow, calyx often red. Fruit with a more or less globose prickly lower segment, and a tongue-like flattened upper segment. Mar.-May. Fairly common. (Ma, Mi, I) FE I 342

SUCCOWIA

2. *Succowia balearica* (L.) Medicus. More or less scabrid annual. Leaves pinnatisect. Flowers bright yellow. Fruit with a lower round segment covered in spines, the upper segment long and conical. Apr.-May. Rather uncommon. (From garden specimen: seen subsequently in Mallorca, where not significantly different, except rather lanky and straggling). (Ma, Mi, I: not endemic in spite of name) FE I 342

CAKILE

3. *Cakile maritima* Scop. Sea Rocket. Succulent hairless blue-green annual. Petals clawed, violet. Fruit characteristic (see detail, x 2). Mar.-Sept. Sea shores, common. (Ma, Mi, I) FE I 343

RAPISTRUM

4. *Rapistrum rugosum* (L.) All. Bastard Cabbage. Annual, hispid below, often hairless above. Basal leaves pinnate, stem leaves simple. Numerous stems arising from basal rosette. Inflorescence with long, slender spreading branches, many held horizontally. Silicula globose, abruptly contracted into a short beak. Apr.-June. Common wayside weed. (x 1/10, details x 1). (Ma, Mi, I) FE I 344

RAPHANUS

5. *Raphanus raphanistrum* L. Wild Radish. Hispid annual. Petals white, pale yellow or violet, usually with dark violet veins. Siliqua with a negligible lower segment, and a broad upper segment, torulose at least above, with a long beak. The siliqua breaks up transversely, not longitudinally as in most other siliquate species. Mar.-Sept. Common weed of roadsides and cutivated places, also coastal. (Ma, Mi, I) FE I 346

RESEDACEAE
RESEDA

6. *Reseda luteola* L. Weld. Biennial, up to 1.5m, stiffly erect, usually unbranched until the main stem has nearly finished flowering. **Leaves entire. Petals pale yellow. Sepals 4. Carpels 3.** May-Oct. Waste ground, roadsides. (Ma, Mi, I) FE I 347

7. *Reseda alba* L. White Mignonette. Leaves pinnatifid. **Petals white. Sepals 5. Carpels 4.** Feb.-Apr. Common. Waste ground. (Ma, Mi, I) FE I 347

8. *Reseda phyteuma* L. Annual or biennial. Leaves usually entire, spathulate (sometimes with 1 or 2 lobes at the base). **Petals white. Sepals 6. Carpels 3. NS.** Listed but not seen by Duvigneaud. Llorens lists. (From garden specimen). (Ma, Mi, I) FE I 348

9. *Reseda lutea* L. Wild Mignonette. Leaves mostly pinnatifid. **Petals pale yellow. Sepals 6. Carpels 3.** May-Sept. Common in waste places. (Ma, Mi, I) FE I 348

Other species recorded:
Reseda media Lag. BI in FE I 348
Reseda odorata L. Garden Mignonette. Casual in BI according to FE I 348

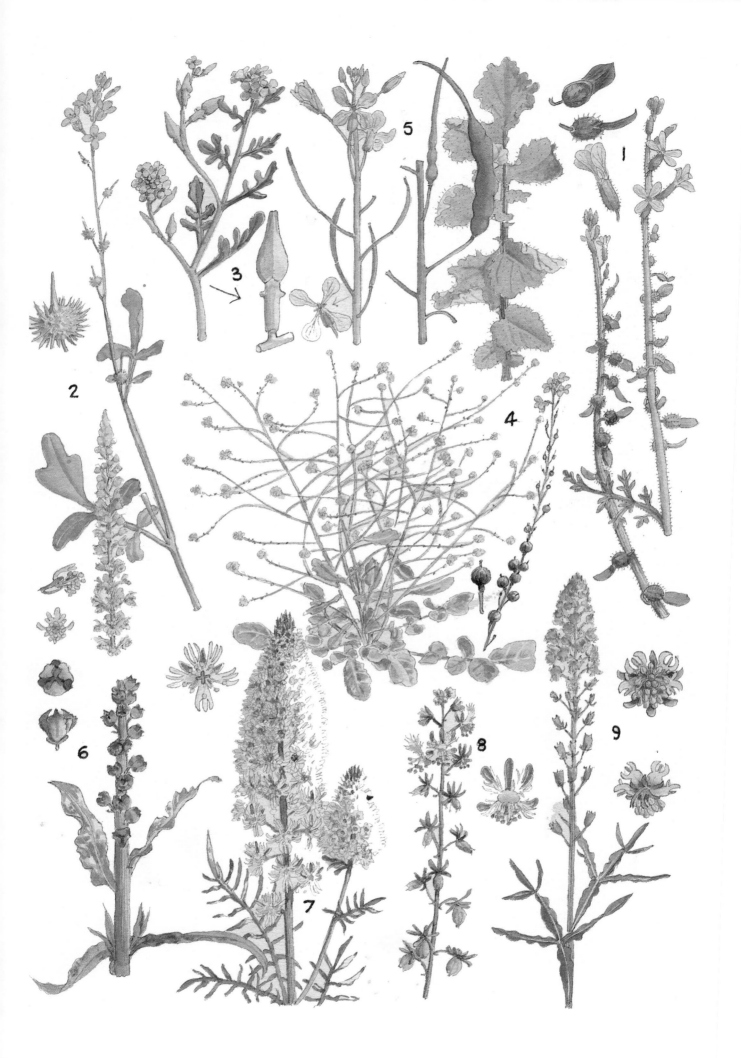

Plate 22

CRASSULACEAE: *CRASSULA, UMBILICUS, AEONI-UM, SEDUM*
SAXIFRAGACEAE: *SAXIFRAGA*

CRASSULACEAE
CRASSULA

1. *Crassula tillaea* Lester-Garland. Minute, moss-like, hairless annual. Flowers sessile in axils of opposite connate leaves. Occasional. (Ma, Mi, I) FE I 351
2. *Crassula vaillantii* (Willd.) Roth. Annual, 2-6cm. Flowers pedicellate in leaf-axils. **NS.** (Seen by Duvigneaud). Locally common. (Ma, Mi) FE I 351

UMBILICUS

3. *Umbilicus rupestris* (Salisb.) Dandy. Wall Pennywort. Raceme dense, occupying more than half stem. Stem leaves relatively few. Pedicels 3-9mm, flowers pendent. Apr.-June. Common on walls and rocks. (Ma, Mi) FE I 352
4. *Umbilicus horizontalis* (Guss.) DC. Perennial, raceme occupying less than half stem, often with short branches. Flowers narrow, subsessile. Stem leaves very numerous. Apr.-June. Common on walls and rocks. (Ma, Mi, I) FE I 352
5. Intermediate forms are common. This one resembles 3 in the long raceme and fewer stem leaves, but pedicels are rather short and the narrow flowers are held horizontally as in 4. (The leaves, however, are more typical of *U. horizontalis* than in the illustration of this species – which may perhaps be a hybrid too).

AEONIUM

6. *Aeonium arboreum* (L.) Webb & Berth. Rather woody perennial, about 1m. Dec.-Apr. Common in waste places (x about 1/2). (Native of Morocco, introduced Ma, I) FE I 356

SEDUM

7. *Sedum sediforme* (Jacq.) Pau. Robust perennial, often bluish-green. Stems commonly about 25cm. Inflorescence branched, with recurved branches. Petals 5-8, greenish or pale yellow. Common on walls and rocks. (Ma, Mi, I) FE I 358
8. *Sedum dasyphyllum* L. Creeping perennial, glandular hairy at least in the inflorescence. Leaves ovoid, flattened on upper surface, greyish, often pink-tinged. Petals 5 or 6, pinkish-white. May-Aug. Common on walls and rocks. (Ma, Mi, I) FE I 361
9. *Sedum stellatum* L. Small hairless annual. Leaves green, flat, more or less triangular. Petals 5, narrow, pink. Fruit stellate when ripe. Local in dry places. (All x 1 except details of flower, fruit and leaf). (Ma) FE I 362
10. *Sedum rubens* L. Glandular-hairy annual. Leaves linear, semi-circular in section. Flowers with 5 petals, usually white with a red mid-vein. Follicles spreading when ripe to form a red star. Locally common, especially in mountain area. (Ma, Mi, I) FE I 363

SAXIFRAGACEAE
SAXIFRAGA

11. *Saxifraga tridactylites* L. Annual, usually glandular-hairy, with reddish stems, often completely red-tinged. Stem leaves wedge-shaped, 3-lobed. Flowers about 5mm, white, with 5 petals. Mar.-Apr. Common, especially on walls. (Ma, Mi, I) FE I 370

Also in Mallorca:
Sedum caespitosum (Cav.) DC. Resembles 10, but Hairless with broadly ovoid leaves. Seen by Duvigneaud. (Ma, Mi) Not BI in FE I 363

In Ibiza only
Sedum album L. FE I 360
Saxifraga corsica (Duby) Gren. & Godron. FE I 376

Plate 23

PLATANACEAE: *PLATANUS*
ROSACEAE (1): *RUBUS, ROSA*

PLATANACEAE
PLATANUS

(The 2 species illustrated are listed by Duvigneaud as introduced here. Llorens et al. (1991) give *P. hispanica* Miller, *P. occidentalis* L. and *P. orientalis* L. The Med-Checklist gives only *P. orientalis,* possibly because only this species is truly naturalised in this area. All species are large trees with scaling bark).

1. *Platanus orientalis* L. Oriental Plane. Leaves lobed to more than half way: fruiting heads 3-6. (From Cretan specimen, reduced). (Ma) FE I 384

2. *Platanus hybrida* L. Hybrid Plane. Leaves lobed to less than half way: fruiting heads usually 2. (From British specimen, reduced). FE I 384

ROSACEAE
RUBUS

3. *Rubus ulmifolius* Schott. Blackberry, Bramble. Densely tangled shrub with arching branches rooting at apex. Leaves white-tomentose beneath. Fruit with numerous druplets. Apr.-May. Common. (Ma, Mi, I) FE II 15

4. *Rubus caesius* L. Dewberry. Low straggling bush, with prostrate rooting stems. Fruit with 2-20 druplets, often with a bluish waxy coating. Mar.-Apr. **NS.** Seen by Duvigneaud. (From British specimen). (Ma, Mi, I) FE II 25

ROSA

5. *Rosa sempervirens* L. Leaves shining, leathery. Inflorescence 3-7-flowered. Flowers pure white. Styles connate into a column at least as long as the stamens. Apr.-June. Commonest rose in lowland parts of Mallorca, hedgerows and bushy places. (Ma, Mi, I) FE II 27

6. *Rosa arvensis* Hudson. Inflorescence usually 1-3-flowered. Flowers white, with connate styles like 5. (All the others here have free styles). Flowers white. **NS.** (From British specimen). Seen by Duvigneaud. (Ma, Mi) FE II 27

7. *Rosa canina* L. Dog Rose. Leaflets without glands or with few glands confined to margins and main veins beneath. Flowers pink or white. Styles free. Not common (fruit from British specimen). Llorens lists for (Ma, Mi) FE II 29

Other species of *Rosa:*

Knoche's *Rosa* species nos 554 and 555 seem to include any species, and it seems impossible to distinguish them or determine which he actually saw. Several species are given for BI in FE which are not listed by Bonafè or Duvigneaud. In some places (eg. Around the Embalse de Cúber) there seem to be ?hybrids which can easily be keyed out to *Rubiginosa* agg., but differ in some respects from species described in FE. Many of the white flowered plants in this area are close to *R. agrestis*, but have glandular sepals, while the pink flowered ones with glandular pedicels seem nearer *R. rubiginosa* or *R. micrantha* (though leaves are wedge-shaped at base). One of my specimens matched description of *R. rubiginosa* in all respects, but fruit was not seen.

8. *R. ?rubiginosa* L. Apple-scented bush. Leaflets rounded at base. Pedicels densely glandular-hairy. Petals deep pink. Styles hairy. (Main illustration from Mallorcan specimen, fruit from garden specimen). Duvigneaud quotes FE. Llorens lists with query. (?Ma) BI in FE II 31

9. *Rosa* sp. cf. *R. agrestis* Savi. Apple-scented bush. Leaves usually narrow, wedge-shaped at base. Pedicels hairless or with sparse stalked glands. Petals white. (Plant here, otherwise fitting FE description, has glandular sepals). Apr.-June. Common in mountain areas. Duvigneaud saw *R. Agrestis*, Llorens lists for (Ma, I) FE II 31

10. *Rosa* sp. cf. *R. micrantha* Borrer. Resembles 9, but pedicels have stalked glands and sepals are glandular. Flowers pink (according to Bonafè; in FE to be presumed white as in *R. agrestis*). In this specimen leaflets were mostly wedge-shaped at base: FE describes leaflets of *R. micrantha* as 'usually rounded at base'. Duvigneaud apparently did not find it: Bonafè lists records from several places. (This from a Mallorcan specimen: but is it this species? Llorens lists for (Ma) BI in FE II 32

Also recorded from Mallorca:

Rubus candicans Weihe. Duvigneaud quotes FE. Llorens omits. (?Ma) BI in FE II 16

Rosa pouzinii Tratt. Resembles 7, but has pedicels and sometimes the base of the fruit, covered in stalked glands. Seen by Duvigneaud. Llorens lists. (Ma) FE II 29

Rosa corymbifera Borkh. Resembles 7, but leaves hairy at least on veins below, sometimes all over both surfaces. Pedicels hairless. Duvigneaud quotes FE. Llorens lists with a query. (?Ma) BI in FE II 30

Plate 24

ROSACEAE (2): *AGRIMONIA, SANGUISORBA, POTEN-TILLA, APHANES, SORBUS, AMELANCHIER, CRATAEGUS, PRUNUS*

AGRIMONIA

1. *Agrimonia eupatoria* L. Agrimony. Perennial. Leaves pinnate with smaller leaflets between the pairs of larger ones. Flowers in spike-like raceme. Fruit with hooked bristles. Occasional. (Ma, Mi) FE II 32

SANGUISORBA

2. *Sanguisorba minor* Scop. Salad Burnet. Flowers small in dense terminal heads. Petals absent, sepals 4, green. Stamens numerous. May-Sept. Common. (Ma, Mi, I) FE II 33

POTENTILLA

3. *Potentilla reptans* L. Creeping Cinquefoil. Creeping perennial, with digitate leaves. Flowers solitary, axillary, with 5 yellow petals. May-Sept. Common. (Ma, Mi, I) FE II 45

4. *Potentilla caulescens* L. Shrubby cinquefoil. Hairy perennial. Leaves digitate. Flowers white in lax cymes. Apr.-May. **NS**. Local in the mountains. Seen by Duvigneaud. (From Austrian specimen). (Ma) FE II 45

APHANES

5. *Aphanes ?arvensis* L. Parsley Piert. Hairy procumbent slender annual. Leaves all petiolate. In this specimen sepals erect in fruit 1.9mm. (This fits *A. microcarpa* (Boiss. & Reuter) Rothm. better) Mallorcan specimen, from high in mountains, but could have been misidentified (and the little bit I took didn't survive long enough for somebody else to have a look!) Duvigneaud lists this species as seen. Llorens omits. BI not excluded in FE II 64

6. *Aphanes floribunda* (Murb.) Rothm. Erect robust annual with long white hairs. Upper leaves sessile. Fruit more than 2.75mm, with slightly spreading sepals. Occasional. (Ma) FE II 64

SORBUS

7. *Sorbus domestica* L. Small white-flowered tree. Fruit globose to pyriform. May-June. (Seen apparently wild here; illustration from garden specimen). Introduced for edible fruit. (Ma, Mi) FE II 68

8. *Sorbus aria* (L.) Crantz. Whitebeam. Small tree with ovate leaves (badly shown here), densely white-tomentose on the under surface. Inflorescence corymbose, flowers white, 5-petalled. (From British specimen, but seen in Mallorca as a small shrub high in the mountains). (Ma) FE II 68

AMELANCHIER

9. *Amelanchier ovalis* Medicus. Snowy Mespilus. Shrub up to 3m, with ovate leaves. Petals narrow, 10-13mm. Fruit purple-black. Apr.-May. **NS**. Rare in mountains. Not seen by Duvigneaud, but listed by Duvigneaud and Llorens. (Ma) FE II 71

CRATAEGUS

10. *Crataegus monogyna* Jacq. Hawthorn. Shrub or small tree. Flowers usually in dense corymbs. Fruit red with a large stone occupying most of it (brighter than in N. Europe: subsp. *brevispina* (Kuntze) Franco here). Apr.-May. Widespread in hilly places. (Ma, Mi) FE II 75

PRUNUS

11. *Prunus spinosa* L. Sloe, Blackthorn. Spiny shrub. White flowers appear before the leaves. Mar.-Apr. Common. (Ma, Mi) FE II 78

12. *Prunus dulcis* (Miller) D.A.Webb. Almond. Small tree with pink or white blossom. Feb.-Mar. Formerly the main crop here, and planted literally in millions. Occasional naturalised, then rather spiny. (Ma) FE II 78

Also recorded for Mallorca:
Aphanes cornucopioides Lag. Resembles 6, but all leaves sessile. Llorens lists. Not BI in FE II 64

Plate 25

LEGUMINOSAE (1): *CERATONIA, ANAGYRIS, CALICO-TOME, GENISTA, SPARTIUM, ARGYROLOBIUM, ASTRAGALUS, PSORALEA*

CERATONIA

1. *Ceratonia siliqua* L. Carob. Substantial tree. Leaves leathery, paripinnate. Flowers in catkins, without petals and with 5–7 free stamens. **Ripe fruit a hard black pod 10-20 x about 2cm.** Not native here, but often appears wild. (Ma, Mi, I) FE II 83 (This species belongs to Caesalpinoideae, a division of Leguminosae more widely represented in the tropics. All the others here are Lotoideae, which generally have characteristic 'Pea' flowers (see Glossary), with petals, and 10 stamens, either all united basally into a tube, or with 9 united and one free. (*Anagyris*, however, has free stamens).

ANAGYRIS

2. *Anagyris foetida* L. Bean Trefoil. Tall shrub or small tree. Leaves trifoliate. Corolla dirty-yellowish, the **standard much shorter than wings and keel.** Stamens 10, free. Fruit a **pod** nearly as large as that of 1, but **brown and constricted between seeds.** Feb.-Mar. Local. (Ma, Mi, I) FE II 85

CALICOTOME

3. *Calicotome spinosa* (L.) Link. Robust prickly shrub. Leaves trifoliate. Flowers yellow, gorse-like. **Calyx tubular with 5 short teeth.** Apical part of calyx is pushed off as flower expands and can be seen as **brown cap on tips of buds just before they open.** Mar.-May. Common, especially in Northern part of mountain range. (Ma, Mi, I) FE II 86

GENISTA

Spiny or unarmed shrubs. Flowers yellow in axillary heads or clusters. Calyx bilabiate, **upper lip deeply bifid, lower 3-toothed.**

4. *Genista cinerea* (Vill.) DC. subsp. *leptoclada* (Willk.) Bolòs & Molinier. Small **spineless** shrub with many thin grey-green branches with dense appressed hairs. Flowers usually in pairs. Mar.-Apr. Mainly in central part of mountain range. (Ma endemic) FE II 96

5. *Genista lucida* Camb. Erect shrub with short more or less **straight axillary spines. Leaves simple.** Flowers in terminal racemes. Common in hilly area South of Arta peninsula, and in South West, rarer elsewhere. Feb.-Mar. (Ma endemic) FE II 99

6. *Genista balearica* Porta & Rigo. Resembles 5, but **very dense and robust,** with **spines** thicker and more or less **curved.** Leaves very few. Two small patches only, one on a beach and one in the mountains. (Ma endemic) Not in FE

SPARTIUM

7. *Spartium junceum* L. Spanish Broom. Large shrub or small tree. Leaves few, on young shoots only. Flowers showy in lax terminal racemes, **Calyx spathe-like, split above.** Corolla yellow, 20-25mm. Widely planted, sometimes naturalised. (Native in Minorca) FE II 101

ARGYROLOBIUM

8. *Argyrolobium zanonii* (Turra) P.W.Ball. **Procumbent small woody perennial. Pods and undersides of trifoliate leaves** silky-hairy. Calyx with upper lip deeply bifid, lower 3-toothed. Flowers yellow. Pod slightly torulose. Apr.-May. Stony places. Occasional. (Ma, I) FE II 106

ASTRAGALUS

Annual or perennial herbs or small shrubs. **Leaves pinnate, terminating in a leaflet or a spine** (here).

9. *Astragalus boeticus* L. **Robust erect leafy annual.** Leaves up to 20cm, with 10-15 pairs of leaflets. Peduncles half as long as leaves, bearing a dense many-flowered terminal raceme of creamish yellow flowers. Calyx with blackish hairs. **Pod 20-40 x 7-8mm, deeply grooved beneath.** Mar.-Apr. Fairly common. (Ma, Mi, I) FE II 111

10. *Astragalus hamosus* L. Similar to 9, but much smaller. Leaves up to 10cm, with 9-11 pairs of leaflets, hairy beneath with medifixed hairs. Raceme lax, with 2-5 white flowers. **Pod 10-20 x 5-7mm, laterally compressed and curved.** Mar. Occasional, roadsides and waste places. (Ma, Mi, I) FE II 113

11. *Astragalus balearicus* Chater. **Hedgehog-like spiny dwarf shrub** (1m or more in high places such as plateau below peak of Teix: usually only up to 15cm or so). Leaflets 3-5 pairs, terminal leaflet in most leaves replaced by a spine. Corolla white or pinkish, with darker markings. Common in hilly areas and mountains. (Illustration of plant much reduced, details x 1 and slightly enlarged). (Ma, Mi endemic) FE II 119

PSORALEA

12. *Psoralea bituminosa* L. Pitch Trefoil. Large clover-like plant. Trifoliate leaves smelling of pitch when crushed underfoot (some people get unpleasant rashes if they crush it by hand). Flowers pinkish or bluish violet in terminal heads on long rather rigid peduncles. Apr.-June. (Ma, Mi, I) FE II 127

Also recorded for Mallorca:

Astragalus stella Gouan. Annual. Stems procumbent or ascending. Leaves 2-8cm, with 9-11 pairs of leaflets. Racemes dense, on long peduncles, with 7-12 flowers. **Pod 10-15 x 3-4mm, almost straight, laterally compressed, with 2cm curved beak** and densely appressed-hairy valves. Llorens lists. (See Alomar et al. 1986). Not BI in FE II 113

Astragalus epiglottis L. Small annual. Leaves 2-4cm, with 5-10pairs of leaflets. **Hairs on leaves and stems medifixed, with one arm much longer than the other. Pod** densely hairy. 7-9mm, **triangular-ovate, flattened and broadly cordate at base.** Llorens lists. (Ma, I) Not BI in FE II 113

Recorded in other islands:
Chronanthus biflorus (Desf.) Frodin & Heywood. FE II 93: Ibiza
Teline linifolia (L.) Webb & Berth. FE II 94: Minorca (cultivated in Mallorca)
Genista hirsuta Vahl. FE II 98: Ibiza
Genista dorycnifolia Font Quer. FE II 99: Ibiza
Ulex parviflorus Pourret. FE II 102: Ibiza
Lupinus micranthus Guss. FE II 105: Minorca
Robinia pseudoacacia L. FE II 106: Naturalized in Ibiza
Astragalus sesameus L. Not BI in FE II 113: Formentera
Astragalus incanus L. ?BI in FE II 122 ?Minorca
Biserrula pelecinus L. FE II 127: Minorca

Plate 26

LEGUMINOSAE (2): *CICER, VICIA, LENS*

CICER

1. *Cicer arietinum* L. Chick Pea. Hairy annual. Leaves with 3-8 pairs of **deeply toothed leaflets.** Cultivated, possibly escaping. May-July. (Ma, introduced) Not BI in FE II 128

VICIA

Annual (unless stated) or perennial herbs, often climbing by means of tendrils.

There is no simple way of distinguishing between *Lathyrus* (Plate 27) and *Vicia*. *Vicia* never has winged stems, *Lathyrus* often does. *Lathyrus* tends to have only one pair of leaflets, with parallel veins, *Vicia* to have several pairs of leaflets with one main vein from which any lateral veins arise. In *Vicia* the style is hairy all round or on the lower side, or else hairless. In *Lathyrus* it is hairy on the upper side, or rarely hairless. This requires close observation, but is at least a constant difference.

The next 2 species here belong to Section Cracca SF.Gray, with many leaflets, and large (10mm or more) flowers in many-flowered long-pedunculate racemes.

2. *Vicia villosa* Roth. Up to 2m. Leaflets 4-12 pairs. Corolla 10-20mm. Lower 3 calyx teeth longer than tube, upper 2 much shorter. **Standard purple, wings and keel paler or white. NS.** Seen by Duvigneaud. (Ma, Mi) FE II 132
3. *Vicia benghalensis* L. Villous plant resembling 2, but with 2-12-flowered racemes of **reddish flowers: wings often with blackish-purple markings at base.** Lower 3 calyx teeth much longer than upper 2, exceeding length of tube. Occasional. (Ma, Mi) FE II 132

The next 6 species here belong to Section Ervum (L.) S.F.Gray, with more than 4 pairs of leaflets, and few small flowers in long pedunculate racemes. **It should be noticed that in nos 4-6 calyx-teeth are equal, in nos 7-10 unequal.**

4. *Vicia ervilia* (L.) Willd. Leaves without tendril, **leaflets 8-16 pairs.** Racemes 1-4-flowered. Corolla **white tinged red or purple.** Calyx teeth all equal. Pod 10-30 x 4-6mm, **torulose.** May – July. Cultivated, sometimes escaping. **NS.** (From herbarium specimen) (seen by Duvigneaud). Llorens lists. (Ma, I) Not BI in FE II 133
5. *Vicia leucantha* Biv. Leaflets 5-10 pairs. Racemes 2-10-flowered. **Corolla 6-10mm. Pale blue, white at base. Keel with blackish tip. Calyx teeth equal.** Mar.-Apr. Rare. (Illustration from street weed collected in Alcudia: possibly only casual). Llorens lists. (Ma) ?BI in FE II 133
6. *Vicia hirsuta* (L.) S.F.Gray. Hairy Tare. Leaflets 4-10 pairs. **Calyx-teeth equal,** longer than tube. Corolla 2-4mm, dingy whitish purple. **Pod small, black and hairy with 2 seeds. NS.** (From British specimen). Seen by Knoche, not by Duvigneaud. Llorens lists. (Ma, I) FE II 133
7. *Vicia tenuissima* (Bieb.) Schinz & Thell. Slender Tare. **Leaflets** 2-5 pairs, linear **(10-25 x 1-3mm). Racemes with 2-5 flowers,** longer than leaves. **Calyx-teeth unequal,** shorter than tube. **Pod hairy or not, brown with 4-6 seeds.** Corolla 6-9mm, pinkish-lilac, or pale purple, often bicoloured. Apr.-May. Common. FE II 133
8. *Vicia tetrasperma* (L.) Schreber. Rather like 7, but leaflets usually shorter, **racemes 1 or 2 flowered. Calyx-teeth unequal, all shorter than tube. Pod brown, usually hairless,** with 3-5 seeds. **NS.** (From British specimen). Seen by

Knoche but not by Duvigneaud, Llorens lists. (Ma, Mi) FE II 133
9. *Vicia pubescens* (DC.) Link. Like 8. Sparsely hairy. **Racemes up to 6-flowered, lower calyx-teeth equalling or longer than tube.** Apr.-May. Common. (Ma, Mi) FE II 133

Section Vicia. Leaflets more than 3 pairs. Flowers solitary or few-flowered, sessile or in shortly pedunculate racemes. Corolla usually more than 10mm.

10. *Vicia sativa* L. CommonVetch. A very variable plant, with several subspecies recorded here. **Flowers purple,** often with darker wings and keel, usually solitary, sometimes 2 together. **Stipules toothed, often with a dark blotch.** Apr.-May. Common. (The main illustration here is subsp. *nigra*, common in mountain areas, with linear leaflets and a narrow black pod. Other details are from other subsp. occurring here, cultivated or wild). (Ma, Mi, I) FE II 134
11. *Vicia lutea* L. Yellow Vetch. Flowers yellow, sometimes purplish-yellow, in groups of 1-3. Stipules entire or toothed. Pod yellowish-brown to black, with tuberculate based hairs. Apr.-May. Occasional. (Ma, Mi) FE II 135

Section Faba (Miller) S.F.Gray. Leaflets 1-3 pairs. Flowers large, 10mm or more, solitary or (here) in shortly pedunculate few-flowered racemes.

12. *Vicia bithynica* (L.) L. Bithynian Vetch. Leaflets 2-3 pairs, varying from almost linear to broadly elliptical. Peduncle short, but obvious. **Standard purple, wings and keel white.** Common, waysides and dry stony places. (Ma, Mi) FE II 135
13. *Vicia faba* L. Broad Bean. Peduncle very short or 0. **Corolla white with black-blotched wings.** Cultivated, sometimes as relic of cultivation. FE II 135

LENS

Like *Vicia*, but calyx-teeth equal and at least 2 x tube length. Pod strongly compressed with flat orbicular seeds.

14. *Lens culinaris* Medicus. Lentil. **Racemes about equalling the leaves. Stipules entire.** Widely cultivated. FE II 136
15. *Lens ervoides* (Brign.) Grande. So like *Vicia* sec. Ervum that easily overlooked. **Racemes longer than leaves. Stipules half spear-shaped or toothed.** Tendrils usually absent, or only on upper leaves. May-Aug. Locally common. (Ma) FE II 136

Other species recorded for Mallorca:

Vicia monantha Retz. (Section Cracca, see above) **Stipules bipartite, the lobes entire.** (*Vicia villosa* has stipules entire, not bipartite; *V. benghalensis* has entire or toothed stipules, not bipartite). Corolla pale purple, pod yellow, Hairless. Not common. Seen by Duvigneaud. Llorens lists. (Ma, I) FE II 133

Vicia peregrina L. (Section Vicia) Rather like *Vicia sativa*, but stipules entire (toothed in *V. sativa*). Listed but not seen by Duvigneaud. Llorens lists. (Ma, Mi, I) FE II 135

Vicia hybrida L. (Section Vicia) Very like *Vicia lutea* (no 11 above), but standard hairy on the back (Hairless in *V. lutea*) Knoche quotes Barceló (1867-1877). Listed but not seen by Duvigneaud. Llorens lists. (Ma, Mi) BI in FE II 135

In Minorca:

Vicia disperma DC. FE II 133

Vicia bifoliata (Mi endemic) FE II 133

Plate 27

LEGUMINOSAE (3): *LATHYRUS, PISUM*

LATHYRUS

1. *Lathyrus latifolius* L. Broad-leaved Everlasting Pea. Conspicuous perennial with 5-15 large flowers (corolla 2-3cm) on a long peduncle. Apr.-May. Common. (x about 1/2, pod x 1). (Ma) FE II 141

2. *Lathyrus saxatilis* (Vent.) Vis. Small annual. Stem unwinged, leaves without a tendril. Leaflets of lowest leaves obcordate with 3 teeth at apex. Flowers small, solitary, bluish or yellowish. Mar.-May. Roadsides, not common. (Ma, I) FE II 141

3. *Lathyrus sphaericus* Retz. Annual. Stem unwinged (FE) or commonly very narrowly winged. Flowers solitary, orange-red, peduncles aristae. Calyx teeth equalling or slightly longer than calyx tube. Pod 30-70 x 4-7mm.with 8-15 seeds. Local in rocky places. (x about 2/3). (Ma, Mi) FE II 141

4. *Lathyrus cicera* L. Red Vetchling. Annual. Flowers solitary. Calyx teeth large, equal, longer than the tube. Pod with 2 keels on dorsal suture. Mar.-May. Common. (Ma, Mi, I) FE II 142

5. *Lathyrus annuus* L. Fodder Pea. Annual. Stem winged. Racemes with 1-3 yellow flowers, often with red markings. Pod glandular when young. (Immature pod here. Mature pod straight, up to 30-80x 7-12mm). Apr.-June. Occasional in bushy places. (Ma, Mi) FE II 142

6. *Lathyrus clymenum* L. Annual. Stem winged. Lower leaves without leaflets, with rhachis broad and leaf-like. Standard notched, pinkish-red. Wings violet or lilac. Pod with channelled dorsal suture. Apr.-June. Common. (Ma, Mi) FE II 142

7. *Lathyrus articulatus* L. Very like 6. Difference in leaflet width described in FE seem not to be constant here. Wings of flower are white. Pod is torulose without a dorsal suture. Apr.-June. Common. (Ma, Mi) FE II 142

8. *Lathyrus ochrus* (L.) DC. Annual. Petiole and rhachis of leaves very broadly winged. Lower leaves with tendrils and no leaflets. Pod with two wings on dorsal suture. Common. (Ma, Mi, I) FE II 142

9. *Lathyrus aphaca* L. Yellow Vetchling. Leaves on mature plant without leaflets but with a tendril. Stipules large, arrow-shaped and leaf-like. Flowers solitary, yellow. Mar.-May. Common. (Ma, Mi, I) FE II 143

PISUM

Like *Lathyrus,* but stems terete. Stipules large and leaf-like. Wings adnate to keel.

10. *Pisum sativum* L. Pea. Two subsp., one with white flower and one as illustrated. Escape from cultivation. Mar.-May. FE II 143

Also recorded from Mallorca:
Lathyrus setifolius L. Annual, much like 3, but peduncles not aristate and pod broader, with 2-3 seeds. FE II 142
Lathyrus amphicarpos L. Dubious. Llorens omits. BI in FE II 142

Recorded from Ibiza only:
Lathyrus sativus L. Not BI in FE II 142

Plate 28

LEGUMINOSAE (4): *ONONIS, MELILOTUS*

ONONIS

Annual or perennial herbs or dwarf shrubs. Leaves simple or with 3 leaflets (very occasionally more). Flowers yellow or pink. Fruiting pedicels usually deflexed.

1. *Ononis natrix* L. Dwarf (up to 60cm) sticky shrub, densely glandular-hairy, upper leaves 3-foliate, lower sometimes pinnate. **Leaflets ovate to linear, margins not undulate.** Corolla yellow, often red-veined. Subsp. *natrix* has flowers 12-20mm and dark brown minutely tuberculate seeds: subsp. *hispanica* has flowers less than 12mm and smooth grey seeds. May-July. Both locally common. (Subsp. *hispanica* illustrated x 3/4, pod x 1). (Ma, Mi, I) FE II 144

2. *Ononis crispa* L. Resembles 1, but **leaflets round with undulate margins.** May-July. Not common. **NS.** (Specimen from Spanish mainland). Seen by Duvigneaud. (Ma, Mi) FE II 145

3. *Ononis ornithopodioides* L. Small sticky erect annual. **Leaves all with 3 leaflets. Flowers yellow. Pod torulose,** 12-20mm. Mar.-Apr. Occasional. (x 1/2, pod x 1). (Ma, I) FE II 145

4. *Ononis reclinata* L. Small erect or procumbent annual. **Leaves all with 3 leaflets. Flowers pink. Pod smooth,** 8-14mm. Mar.-Apr. Common.(Ma, Mi, I) FE II 145

5. *Ononis pubescens* L. Sticky annual. **Upper and lower leaves simple,** middle leaves with 3 leaflets. Branches of inflorescence **without arista** (compare 6). Flowers yellow. Rather uncommon. (Ma) ?BI in FE II 145

6. *Ononis viscosa* L. subsp. *breviflora* Nyman. Rather robust erect annual (up to 80cm). **Leaves all simple, or middle ones with 3 leaflets.** Branches of inflorescence with one yellow flower and a **conspicuous long arista** (commonly 25-30mm). Common. (Ma, Mi) FE II 145

7. *Ononis minutissima* L. Stiff shrublet. **Nearly hairless.** Leaves all with 3 leaflets. **Calyx erect and stellate in fruit.** Flowers yellow in dense terminal racemes. Pod 6-7mm, black. Common in dry rocky places. (Ma, Mi, I) FE II 146

8. *Ononis spinosa* L. subsp. *antiquorum* (L.) Arcangeli. Spiny Restharrow. Rather variable shrublet. Stems erect, usually **very spiny. Flowers pink.** Common. (Ma, Mi, I) FE II 147

9. *Ononis baetica* Clemente. Robust annual. **Corolla pink, equalling the calyx.** Two plants found in Puerto Alcudia, possibly originating from birdseed. (x 1/2). Not BI in FE II 148

MELILOTUS

Annuals here, with trifoliate leaves. Flowers small, yellow (here), in axillary racemes. Ripe pod usually necessary for identification.

10. *Melilotus italica* (L.) Lam. **Racemes lax,** elongating in fruit. **Corolla 6-9mm. Pod strongly reticulate-veined.** Feb.-May. Uncommon. (From Bianor's specimen: subsequently seen in Mallorca). (Ma, I) FE II 149

11. *Melilotus indica* (L.) All. **Racemes dense,** elongating in fruit. **Corolla 2-3mm. Pod strongly reticulate-veined.** Apr.-May. Common. (Ma, Mi, I) FE II 149

12. *Melilotus elegans* Salzm. Racemes lax, hardly elongating in fruit. Corolla 4-5mm. **Pod compressed with transverse, slightly S-shaped veins.** Feb.-May. Not common. (Ma, Mi, I) FE II 150

13. *Melilotus sulcata* Desf. Racemes lax, slightly elongating in fruit. **Stipules toothed. Corolla 3-4mm. Pod globose, concentrically striate.** Mar.-May. Common. (Ma, Mi, I) FE II 150

14. *Melilotus segetalis* (Brot.) Ser. Rather like 13, but **stipules entire below, toothed above. Corolla 4-8mm.** Pod very like that of 13. Apr.-May. Common. Seen by Knoche and Duvigneaud. Llorens omits. BI in FE II 150

15. *Melilotus messanensis* (L.) All. **Peduncle and raceme very short,** not exceeding subtending leaf. **Pod acute,** ovoid, concentrically striate. Mar.-May. Locally common in marshy ground near the coast. (Ma, Mi, I) FE II 150

Others recorded from Mallorca:

Ononis pusilla L. Small shrublet resembling 7, but leaves with eglandular hairs, **calyx-teeth with long glandular and eglandular hairs.** Listed but not seen by Duvigneaud. Llorens lists. Not BI in FE II 146

Ononis mitissima L. Erect or procumbent annual resembling 9. **Corolla pink, 10-12mm, exceeding the calyx.** Listed by Duvigneaud and Llorens. (Ma, Mi) FE II 147

Melilotus neapolitana Ten. Duvigneaud quotes FE. Llorens omits. BI in FE II 149

In Minorca only:

Melilotus infesta Guss.

Plate 29

LEGUMINOSAE (5): *TRIGONELLA, MEDICAGO*

TRIGONELLA

1. *Trigonella monspeliaca* L. Star-fruited Fenugreek. Annual, leaves trifoliate. Racemes almost sessile, with 4-14 flowers. Corolla 4mm, yellow. Pod linear, curved, with thick oblique veins. **NS.** Seen by Duvigneaud. (Ma, I) FE II 152

MEDICAGO

Annual herbs (except 4 and 7, which are perennials, and 3, sometimes perennial). Leaves trifoliate, stipulate. Flowers yellow (except sometimes 3) in axillary pedunculate racemes. Pods usually spirally coiled (sizes below indicate diameter). Flowering Apr.-June. Illustrations x 1, with enlarged details.

Note: Pod features are seen best on a flat circle from the middle of the coil when pulled apart. Transverse veins arise from the inner edge of the coil. The marginal veins run parallel to the outer edge, and there may be a submarginal vein parallel to this and inside it. Between the marginal and submarginal veins on the one hand, and the transverse veins on the other there is sometimes a veinless border.

2. *Medicago lupulina* L. Black Medick. Easily mistaken for *Trifolium*, with dense long-pedunculate heads of yellow flowers. **Pod kidney-shaped, black.** Common. (Ma, Mi, I) FE II 154

3. *Medicago sativa* L. subsp. *sativa*. Lucerne. Up to 80cm, erect. **Flowers blue or purplish.** Cultivated for fodder, often escaping. Pod in a loose spiral, 4-6mm diameter, with a hole through the middle. Common. (Ma, Mi, I) FE II 154

(Subsp. *falcata* (L.) Arcangeli, with yellow flowers and a straight or curved pod also seen occasionally)

4. *Medicago orbicularis* (L.) Bartal. Disc Medick. **Pod at least 1cm diameter, flattened, disc-like,** black or brown when ripe. Locally common. (Ma, Mi, I) FE II 155

5. *Medicago ciliaris* (L.) All. **Pod barrel-shaped,** hairy with glandular hairs, **12mm or more.** Spines always present, usually short and straight or with recurved apices. (Ma, I) FE II 155

6. *Medicago scutellata* (L.) Miller. Pod 1cm or more, glandular-hairy, bowl-shaped, the outer coils enclosing the inner. Spines always absent. (Ma, I) FE II 155

7. *Medicago marina* L. **White tomentose perennial. Pod** usually about 5mm **with a hole** through the middle, and short spines. Local on sea-shores. (Ma, Mi, I) FE II 156

8. *Medicago truncatula* Gaertner. **Peduncle aristate. Pod cylindrical more or less truncate** at ends, **5-8mm,** usually villous. Spiral tight, submarginal veins above and below the marginal veins are separated from the marginal vein by a distinct groove, so that the **pod seems to have 3 keels when seen from the side. Spines** always present, **curved,** arising partly from the marginal and partly from the submarginal veins. Occasional. (Ma, Mi, I) FE II 156

9. *Medicago littoralis* Rohde ex Loisel. Sparsely villous. **Pod hairless, 4-6mm, usually cylindrical and truncate with**

few turns. 3 keels, as in 8 at first, but on ripening they become confluent and one. Spines sometimes present, arising from submarginal vein only. Very common in dry sandy places. (Ma, Mi, I) FE II 156

10. *Medicago aculeata* Gaertner. **Pod 7-10mm diameter, globose to ellipsoid,** often with dense short glandular or eglandular hairs, with or without spines. **3-keeled,** as in 8. Spines if present usually conical. **NS.** Not seen by Duvigneaud. (Specimen from Spanish mainland). (Occurrence here possibly dubious) FE II 156

11. *Medicago turbinata* (L.) All. **Leaflets obovate. Pod hairless, cylindrical or conical** (distal coils smaller) 5-7mm, always spiny. Spines usually short and broad. **Transverse veins** are slender, and **end in a wide veinless border** 1/4-1/3 x radius of the spiral (see detail of 12). Occasional. (Ma, Mi) FE II 156

12. *Medicago murex* Willd. Resembles 11, but **leaflets obcordate or triangular. Margin with 3 keels. Transverse veins end in a wide veinless border.** Spines absent, or longer and less conical than in 11. Very local, but plentiful in places. (Ma, Mi) FE II 156

13. *Medicago arabica* (L.) Hudson. Spotted Medick. **Leaves commonly with a black spot. Pod 5-6mm, hairless,** in a **lax** barrel-shaped **spiral** (like a stretched spring, with light between the coils viewed from the side: all those above from no 4 have tight spirals). Margin of pod with 3 conspicuous grooves (central one is sulcate marginal vein). Usually spiny. (Ma, Mi) FE II 156

14. *Medicago polymorpha* L. Rather like 13, but without black spot. Marginal vein not sulcate, so there are 3 keels separated by two grooves. Common and variable. (Ma, Mi, I) FE II 156

15. *Medicago praecox* DC. Small hairy plant. **Stipules more or less pectinate.** Peduncles short. **Pod puberulent, 3-4mm,** spiny, with only one keel. Base of spiral usually wide and flat, with transverse veins clearly visible. Spiral lax (see 13). Feb.-Apr. Common. (Ma, Mi, I) FE II 157

16. *Medicago minima* (L.) Bartal. Small **dark-greyish woolly** plant. **Stipules more or less entire,** sometimes shallowly toothed near base. Pod globose, 3-5mm, nearly always spiny. Common, often on higher parts of beaches. (Ma, Mi, I) FE II 157

Also recorded from Mallorca:

Medicago secundiflora Durieu. Whitish-hairy annual with 3-10 secund flowers. Pod as 2. Listed by Duvigneaud and Llorens. BI in FE II 154

Medicago rigidula (L.) All. Resembles 8, but pod usually densely glandular-hairy, submarginal vein present at first, becoming confluent with marginal vein as pod ripens Listed by Duvigneaud and Llorens. BI in FE II 156

In other islands:

Medicago arborea L. Ibiza. FE II 155

M. disciformis DC. ?Formentera. Not BI in FE II 157

Plate 30

LEGUMINOSAE (6): *TRIFOLIUM*

TRIFOLIUM

Annual, biennial or perennial herbs. Leaves here always with 3 leaflets. Flowers usually in terminal or axillary pedunculate heads of numerous small flowers. (Main illustration x 1 unless stated otherwise, details enlarged).

1. *Trifolium repens* L. White Clover. **Perennial** with creeping stems. White or creamish flowers in dense long-pedunculate **globose** heads: peduncles usually erect, in axils of long-petiolate **leaves**, which **usually have white marking** as shown. Upper 2 calyx teeth usually longer than lower 3. Corolla becoming red-brown, **pedicels deflexed after flowering.** Apr.-Sept. Common in cultivated areas. (Ma, I) FE II 162

2. *Trifolium nigrescens* Viv. Very like 1, but **annual.** Heads laxer with fewer flowers, **pedicels not deflexed after flowering.** (Detail beside illustration of 1, for comparison. Main illustration bottom right. (Ma, Mi) FE II 163

3. *Trifolium glomeratum* L. **Completely hairless** annual. **Heads** globose, **8-12mm** diameter, dense, **remote, sessile** or nearly so in leaf-axils (petioles often hidden by the heads). Flowers small, sessile, corolla pinkish or white. (May-Aug.). (Ma, MI) FE II 164

4. *Trifolium suffocatum* L. Similar to 3, but **heads 5-6mm, confluent,** not remote, petioles generally longer. Mar.-Aug. **NS.** (Illustration x 2 from British specimen). Seen by Duvigneaud. (Ma, Mi) FE II 164

5. *Trifolium fragiferum* L. Strawberry Clover. More or less hairy perennial, with creeping stems. Flowers white in **hemispherical** heads (differentiating from 1 which it slightly resembles when not in fruit). In fruit heads are globose, with **calyces greatly inflated.** May-Aug. Damp places. Not common. (Ma, Mi, I) FE II 164

6. *Trifolium resupinatum* L. Hairless annual. **Flowers** pink or reddish-purple, **inverted** (with standard below keel), in small hemispherical, pedunculate axillary heads. Calyx much inflated in fruit, sparsely hairy to tomentose, in resupinate heads. The **two upper calyx-teeth are long-pointed and divergent, and stick well out of these more or less fluffy fruiting heads.** Apr.-June. Widespread in cultivated area, often an escape from cultivation. (Ma, Mi, I) FE II 165

7. *Trifolium tomentosum* L. Very like 6, but fruiting heads with shorter peduncles and not resupinate, always woolly, with the **two upper calyx teeth** much shorter and **almost concealed.** Apr.-June. (Ma, Mi, I) FE II 165

8. *Trifolium campestre* Schreber. Hop Trefoil. Annual. **Heads 20-30 flowered,** in terminal and axillary heads, peduncle equalling or exceeding subtending leaf. **Corolla yellow.** Apr.-Oct. Common. (Ma, Mi, I) FE II 166

9. *Trifolium micranthum* L. Rather small annual, **heads 3-15-flowered** (usually nearer 3). **Corolla yellow. NS.** Seen by Duvigneaud. (From British specimen). (Ma, Mi, I) FE II 166

10. *Trifolium striatum* L. Hairy annual. **Heads** sessile, axillary, **enfolded when young in dilated stipules** of subtending leaves. **Stipules** ovate. Heads in a short few-flowered spike. Corolla pink. Calyx conspicuously ribbed, with short spiny teeth in fruit. **NS.** Very rare. (From British specimen). Llorens lists (Ma, Mi) FE II 166

11. *Trifolium scabrum* L. Hairy annual. **Leaflets toothed, with lateral veins recurved and prominent at margins.** Heads numerous, sessile, often paired, more or less cylindrical. Superficially resembles 3, but 3 is hairless. Apr.-June. Common in dry places. (Ma, Mi, I) FE II 167

12. *Trifolium stellatum* L. Star Clover. Hairy annual. Heads ovoid, terminal. Peduncles mostly exceeding 3cm. Corolla pink. **Calyx teeth twice as long as tube, spreading in fruit to produce characteristic stars.** Apr.-June. Common in dry places. (Ma, Mi, I) FE II 168

13. *Trifolium lappaceum* L. Bright green annual. Heads terminal, globose or ovoid. **Corolla pink, inconspicuous, not exceeding calyx teeth. Calyx teeth longer than tube, purplish-black, very fine, hairy above.** Apr.-May. Not common. (Ma, Mi) FE II 169

14. *Trifolium cherleri* L. Rather like 13, but **heads subtended by broad, whitish, conspicuously-veined involucre.** Head abscissing below involucre in fruit. Corolla pinkish or white, inconspicuous. Apr.-May. Locally common. (Ma, Mi) FE II 169

15. *Trifolium angustifolium* L. Hairy annual. **Leaflets linear or linear-lanceolate.** Heads terminal, solitary, **elongated cone-shaped.** Corolla pink. Apr.-July. Common. (Ma, Mi) FE II 170

16. *Trifolium squamosum* L. Annual, procumbent or erect. **Stipules linear,** the free herbaceous tip longer than membranous base. **Upper pair of leaves opposite.** Heads ovoid, terminal. Corolla pink. May-June. Fairly common, especially in damp places near the sea. (Ma, Mi) FE II 171

17. *Trifolium subterraneum* L. Usually has only 2-5 flowers together. **Peduncles become recurved in fruit, and** bury the **pods** in the soil, where they become **anchored by numerous rigid sterile calyces** which appear at this time. Apr.-June. Occasional. (Main illustration from rather weak-looking British specimen, detail below from robust specimen found subsequently in Mallorca). (Ma, Mi) FE II 171

Other species recorded from Mallorca:

Trifolium ornithopodioides L. Heads usually only 2-4-flowered. Pods 6-8mm, slightly curved and exserted. Llorens lists (see Rita J. et al. 1985). (Ma, Mi) FE II 161

Trifolium bocconei Savi. Annual with densely hairy stems. Heads dense, cylindrical or conical, terminal heads often paired but unequal. Listed but not seen by Duvigneaud. Listed by Llorens. (Ma, Mi) FE II 167

Trifolium ligusticum Balbis. Annual. Stems dark green with long spreading hairs. Heads ovoid, often paired, one axillary and long-pedunculate, one terminal and short-pedunculate. Corolla 3-4mm, much shorter than calyx. Calyx 4-6mm, teeth 1-2 x length tube. Not seen by Duvigneaud. Listed by Llorens. (Ma, Mi, I) FE II 167

Trifolium diffusum Ehrh. Annual or biennial up to 40cm or more with much-branched hairy stems. Heads 15-25mm, globose to ovoid, sessile. Corolla about 12mm, reddish-purple, not or scarcely exceeding calyx. Calyx teeth thread-like, 2 x length tube. Not seen by Duvigneaud. (Ma, Mi) FE II 169

Trifolium vesiculosum Savi FE II 164

In Minorca but not Mallorca:
Trifolium spumosum L. FE II 164
Trifolium arvense L. FE II 167
Trifolium squarrosum L. Not BI in FE II 172

Plate 31

LEGUMINOSAE (7): *DORYCNIUM, LOTUS, TETRA-GONOLOBUS*
Main illustration x 1.

DORYCNIUM

Perennial herbs or shrubs. Leaves with 5 leaflets, the lowest pair stipule-like. Flowers in axillary heads. Corolla white (here), with blunt dark red or black keel.

1. *Dorycnium hirsutum* (L.) Ser. Scrambling hairy shrub. **Leaves with very short rhachis or none. Flowers 10-20mm in heads of 4-10.** Pod 6-12mm, usually red, not contorted. Apr.-June. Common in bushy places, rather variable (2 illustrations). (Ma, Mi, I) FE II 172.
2. *Dorycnium rectum* (L.) Ser. Perennial herb or shrub. **Rhachis of middle and lower leaves at least 5mm. Flowers 5-6mm in dense 20-40-flowered heads.** Pod 10-20mm, contorted when seed released. May-June. Rather local in wet places. (Ma, Mi, I) FE II 172
3. *Dorycnium pentaphyllum* Scop. Herb (usually here) or small shrub. **Leaflets narrow without a rhachis. Flowers 3-6mm in heads of 5-15.** Pod 3-5mm, ov oid to globose. Common in dry places. (Ma, Mi, I) FE II 173
4. *Dorycnium fulgurans* (Porta) Lassen. Small '**hedgehog plant**'. **Branches very spiny.** Leaves few. Flowers mostly solitary or in pairs, about 3mm. May. Very local. (Ma, Mi endemic) Not in FE under any name.

LOTUS

Annual or perennial herbs. Leaves with 5 leaflets (except 11), the lowest pair stipule-like. Flowers solitary or in bracteate heads, yellow.

5. *Lotus tenuis* Waldst. & Kit. ex Willd. Straggling perennial. **Leaflets of upper leaves more than 3 x as long as wide.** Heads usually 1-4-flowered. May-Sept. Common in wet places. (Ma, Mi, I) FE II 174
6. *Lotus corniculatus* L. Bird's Foot Trefoil, Bacon-and-Eggs. Similar to 5, but generally more compact. **Upper leaves less than 3 x as long as wide.** Heads 2-7-flowered. May-June. Common. (Ma, Mi, I) FE II 174
7. *Lotus angustissimus* L. Hairy annual. Like 5 and 6, but much slenderer. Heads 1-3-flowered. **Keel strongly angled on lower border** (see detail). Pod 1-2mm diameter. May-June. NS. Not seen by Duvigneaud. (Specimen from Spanish mainland). Llorens lists. (Ma, Mi) FE II 175

8. *Lotus edulis* L. Like 10 in most respects, but **1-2-flowered. Pod strongly inflated**, sulcate on the upper border. Flower often seems to be twisted so that wings are above and below the keel. Common. (Ma, Mi, I) FE II 175
9. *Lotus cytisoides* L. **Densely silvery-haired** perennial. Heads 2-6-flowered. **Keel of flower with short purple beak.** Ma.-May. Local on coastal sands. (Ma, Mi, I) FE II 176
10. *Lotus ornithopodioides* L. Hairy annual, often forming dense clumps. **Heads 2-5-flowered, exceeded by three broad oval leaf-like bracts.** Mar.-May. Very common. (Ma, Mi, I) FE II 176
11. *Lotus tetraphyllus* L. Small neat perennial. **Leaflets only 4. Flowers nodding, solitary**, back of standard usually red-striped. Fairly common in mountain areas. (Ma, Mi endemic) FE II 176

TETRAGONOLOBUS

Like *Lotus,* but the lowest pair of 'leaflets' are treated as stipules. There are therefore 3 leaflets. Flowers (here) crimson, solitary or paired. Pod almost square in transverse section.

12. *Tetragonolobus purpureus* Moench. Asparagus Pea. Pod with **undulating wing on all 4 angles.** Apr.-May. **NS.** Not seen by Duvigneaud. (From garden specimen). Llorens lists. (Ma, I) FE II 177
13. *Tetragonolobus requienii* (Mauri ex Sanguinetti) Sanguinetti. **Pod winged on two angles** (pod in this specimen not really angular). Apr.-May. (Main illustration from garden specimen, detail of flower with stamen-like marking, complete with shadow under the stamen, found later in Mallorca. This marking also found in the only other site where I have seen this plant, many miles from the first finding). Occasional. (Ma) FE II 177

In other islands:
Lotus preslii Ten. Minorca. FE II 175
Lotus parviflorus Desf. Minorca. FE II 175
Lotus subbiflorus Lag. Minorca. FE II 175
Lotus halophilus Boiss. & Spruner. Ibiza. FE II 176

Plate 32

LEGUMINOSAE (8): *ANTHYLLIS, ORNITHOPUS, CORONILLA, HIPPOCREPIS, SCORPIURUS, HEDYSARUM*

ANTHYLLIS

1. *Anthyllis cytisoides* L. Small shrub. Leaves and stems white-felted. Leaves simple and trifoliate, terminal leaflet much larger than the lateral. Flowers solitary or 2-3 together in the axils of leaf-like bracts. Apr.-June. Locally very common, dominant in roadside vegetation of much of SW end of C710 road, but rare in the north. (Ma, Mi) FE II 178

2. *Anthyllis vulneraria* L. Kidney-vetch. Annual to perennial. Most leaves pinnate, with the terminal leaflet larger than the others. Flowers in paired heads subtended by pinnate bracts. Flowers reddish-pink in the subspecies here. Apr.-June. Widespread in dry sunny places. (Ma, Mi, I) FE II 179

3. *Anthyllis tetraphylla* L. Bladder Vetch. Creeping hairy annual. Leaves pinnate, with the terminal leaflet larger than the others. Flowers axillary, 1-7 together. Calyx much inflated, becoming more so in fruit. May-Aug. Common. (Ma, Mi, I) FE II 181

ORNITHOPUS

4. *Ornithopus compressus* L. Hairy annual. Leaves pinnate with 7-18 pairs of leaflets. Flowers small in 3-5-flowered head. Pod up to 50mm, curved, sometimes compressed. Mar.-May. Uncommon. (Ma, Mi) FE II 181

CORONILLA

5. *Coronilla valentina* L. subsp. *glauca* (L.) Batt. Scorpion Vetch. Bluish-green hairless shrub. Leaves with 2-6 pairs of heart-shaped leaflets. (Detail shows standard wing and keel x1). Flowers in long-pedunculate heads. Occasional and often planted. (Ma, Mi) FE II 183

6. *Coronilla juncea* L. Thin shrub with rush-like stems. Leaves inconspicuous, falling soon after development, with 1-3 pairs of narrow leaflets. Flowers in heads (look at the buds to see why this was named Coronilla = Little Crown). Common in southern end of mountain range, where, like 1, it is dominant on long stretches of roadside. (Ma, Mi) FE II 183

7. *Coronilla scorpioides* (L.) Koch. Scorpion Senna. Hairless, more or less bluish annual. Leaves sessile, trifoliate, the terminal leaflet much larger than the laterals. Heads usually 2 flowered on axillary peduncles. Pods narrow, long and curved. Feb.-June. Fairly common, mainly as weed of cultivation. (Ma, Mi, I) FE II 183

HIPPOCREPIS

Annual or perennial herbs with pinnate leaves. Flowers yellow, solitary or in pedunculate axillary heads. Pod characteristic, with 'horseshoes' lined up side by side, separating at maturity.

8. *Hippocrepis balearica* Jacq. **Showy perennial.** Corolla 9-12mm, in heads of 10 or more. Petals long-clawed. Feb.-Mar. Exposed rocky places in the mountain area. (Ma, Mi, I endemic) FE II 185

9. *Hippocrepis ciliata* Willd. Slender annual. Peduncle about equalling leaves. Pod with long papillae. **Opening of 'horseshoes' on concave curve** of pod. Apr.-May. Not common. (Mallorcan specimen, plus mature pod from Spanish mainland). (Ma, Mi, I) FE II 185

10. *Hippocrepis multisiliquosa* L. As 9, but pod with very small papillae or none, **opening of 'horseshoes' on convex curve of pod. NS.** Seen by Duvigneaud. (Specimen from Spanish mainland). (Ma, Mi) FE II 185

11. *Hippocrepis unisiliquosa* L. Prostrate annual. **Flowers usually solitary,** occasionally 2-3 with very short peduncle. Pod usually without papillae. Mar.-June. Common. (Ma, Mi, I) FE II 185

SCORPIURUS

12. *Scorpiurus muricatus* L. Variable annual, some botanists divide up this species in several ways. Leaves entire. Flowers up to 6 together on long axillary peduncles. Pod irregularly coiled, spiny. Apr.-June. Common. (Ma, I) FE II 185

HEDYSARUM

13. *Hedysarum coronarium* L. French Honeysuckle. Spectacular bushy perennial up to 1m or more. Leaves pinnate. Flowers 12-15mm, bright pinkish red, in clover like head. Cultivated for fodder, but widespread in more or less wild situations. Probably not native. (Ma, Mi) FE II 186

14. *Hedysarum spinosissimum* L. Annual. Flowers pink, usually up to 4 together. Pod with 2-4 flat prickly segments. Apr.-May. Occasional in grassy places. (Ma, Mi, I) FE II 186

Other possible species for Mallorca:
Ornithopus pinnatus (Miller) Druce. Known to occur in Minorca. Llorens lists ?Ma. FE II 182
Scorpiurus vermiculatus L. Llorens lists ?Ma. Not BI in FE II 185

In Minorca only:
Anthyllis hermanniae L. FE II 178
Coronilla repanda (Poiret) Guss. FE II 183

Plate 33

GERANIACEAE: *GERANIUM, ERODIUM*

GERANIUM

All species here are annual. Flowers are usually in pairs, and 'Maypole' arrangement of ripe fruit is characteristic of *Geranium* species (see illustrations 1 and 4).

1. *Geranium rotundifolium* L. Leaves shallowly lobed, softly hairy. **Petal not or hardly notched**, limb longer than claw. **Sepals aristate.** Apr.-June. Common. (Ma, Mi, I) FE II 198

2. *Geranium molle* L. Dove's Foot Cranesbill. **Petals deeply notched**, limb longer than claw. Mar.-June. Common (often white-flowered). (Ma, Mi, I) FE II 198

3. *Geranium columbinum* L. Lower leaves deeply divided. Pedicels 2-6cm. Petals rounded, notched or apiculate, limb longer than claw. Sepals aristate. Apr.-June. Locally common. (Sometimes white-flowered). (Ma, Mi) FE II 198

4. *Geranium dissectum* L. Lower leaves deeply divided. Pedicels 0.5-1.5cm. Petals notched, limb longer than claw. Mar.-June. Common. (Ma, Mi, I) FE II 198

5. *Geranium lucidum* L. Shining Cranesbill. Lower leaves 5-lobed, shining, sparsely hairy or hairless. Claw of petal longer than limb. Mar.-June. Common. (Ma) FE II 198

6. *Geranium purpureum* Vill. Petals 6-9mm, claw longer than limb. Pollen yellow. Mar.-July. Common. (Ma, Mi, I) FE II 198

ERODIUM

Flowers usually in an umbel (no 9 has single flowers). Fruit has a long beak, which usually becomes spiral on ripening.

7. *Erodium chium* (L.) Willd. Annual, biennial or perennial. Leaves rounded to pinnatifid, with not more than 1 pair of distinct leaflets. Pit at apex of fruit without a furrow beneath (see illustration, and compare no 8, in which the fruit has a furrow). Feb.-June. Locally common. (Ma, Mi, I) FE II 200

8. *Erodium malacoides* (L.) L'Hér. Much as 7, but apical pit of fruit with deep furrow beneath it, and petals often a deeper pink. Jan.-May. Common. (Ma, Mi, I) FE II 200

9. *Erodium reichardii* (Murray) DC. Small mat-forming perennial. Flowers solitary, pale pink with darker veins. Most of year, especially May-June. Locally common. Damp rocky places in shade. (Ma, Mi endemic) FE II 201

10. *Erodium ciconium* (L.) L'Hér. (including *E. senneni* Bianor). Annual or biennial. Leaves with small leaflets alternating with larger ones. Flowers bluish. Beak of fruit 6-10cm. Apr.-May. Very local. (This specimen was found in a crowded popular resort where Knoche found his 'forme sennenii'. It wasn't a crowded popular resort in his day). (Ma) FE II 201

11. *Erodium cicutarium* (L.) L'Hér. Common Storksbill. Usually annual. Leaves pinnate, leaflets pinnatifid or more divided. Flowers varying in colour, the two upper petals often smaller than the other 3, with a dark blotch at the base. Dec.-July. Common. (Ma, Mi, I) FE II 202

12. *Erodium moschatum* (L.) L'Hér. Musk Storksbill. Annual or biennial musk-scented plant, with glandular hairs. Leaves pinnate, almost throughout their length, sometimes pinnatifid near apex. Dec.-July. Locally common. (Ma, Mi, I) FE II 203

Other species recorded from Mallorca:

Geranium robertianum L. Herb Robert. Very like no 6, but with larger flowers and orange pollen. Llorens omits. Possibly recorded in error for no 6. FE II 198

Erodium laciniatum (Cav.) Willd. Has been recorded from Is. Cabrera. FE II 200

Erodium maritimum (L.) L'Hér. Has been recorded from Dragonera. FE II 201

Erodium botrys (Cav.) Bertol. Caulescent annual. At least upper leaves pinnatifid or pinnatisect. Beak of fruit 50-110mm, with two furrows under pit at apex. Not common. (Ma, Mi) FE II 201

Plate 34

OXALIDACEAE: *OXALIS*
TROPAEOLACEAE: *TROPAEOLUM*
ZYGOPHYLLACEAE: *FAGONIA, ZYGOPHYLLUM, TRIBULUS*
LINACEAE: *LINUM, (RADIOLA)*

OXALIDACEAE

1. *Oxalis corniculata* L. Small procumbent perennial. Common, usually as a street weed. All year. (Ma, Mi, I) FE II 192
2. *Oxalis pes-caprae* L. Bermuda buttercup. Tufted perennial. A common field and roadside weed. Double flowered plants occasional, usually with reddish coloration. A South-African native, now common throughout the Mediterranean and often a serious weed. (Ma, Mi, I) FE II 193

TROPAEOLACEAE

3. *Tropaeolum majus* L. Garden Nasturtium. Trailing plant, annual to perennial. Native of S. America, well established here in stream beds. (Ma) FE II 204

ZYGOPHYLLACEAE
FAGONIA

4. *Fagonia cretica* L. Prostrate perennial with spiny stipules. Apr.-May. Not common. (Ma, I) FE II 205

ZYGOPHYLLUM

5. *Zygophyllum fabago* L. Syrian Bean-caper. Erect, rather fleshy perennial. June. Native of SE Europe. Locally established here. (Ma) FE II 205

TRIBULUS

6. *Tribulus terrestris* L. Caltrop. Procumbent hairy annual. Fruit very spiny. July-Sept. Common. (Ma, Mi, I) FE II 205

LINACEAE
LINUM

7. *Linum narbonense* L. Hairless perennial, up to 50cm. **NS**. (From garden specimen: not recently recorded). (?Ma) FE II 208
8. *Linum bienne* Miller. Pale Flax. Flowers always pale blue. (Differs from the annual cultivated Flax *Linum usitatissimum* L. in being biennial or perennial with a capsule up to 6mm: the cultivated Flax has a larger capsule up to 9mm). Mar.-May. Widespread. (Ma, I) FE II 209
9. *Linum maritimum* L. Sea Flax. Perennial, up to 80cm. June-Sept. Sandy places near coast. Very local. (Ma) FE II 210
10. *Linum trigynum* L. Annual, up to 30cm. Leaves entire. May-June. Common. (Ma, Mi, I) FE II 210
11. *Linum strictum* L. Annual up to 45cm. Leaves minutely toothed (teeth easily felt by rubbing leaf-margin with thumb). May-June. Common. (Ma, Mi, I) FE II 210

Also in Mallorca:
Oxalis ferae Llorens, Cardona & Boi. A new endemic described in 2005 (botanical Journal of Linnaean Society 2005, 148 p489).

In Minorca only:
Radiola linoides Roth. (Linaceae). An annual with tiny 4-merous white flowers. FE II 211

Plate 35

EUPHORBIACEAE (1): *CHROZOPHORA, MERCURIALIS, RICINUS, EUPHORBIA* (1)
(Scale refers to main illustration unless otherwise stated)

CHROZOPHORA

1. *Chrozophora tinctoria* (L.) A.Juss. Turn-sole. Stellate-hairy annual. Flowers in racemes, with very short stalked erect male flowers at tip and long stalked drooping female flowers at base. Fruit 3-valved. Apr.-Oct. (Slightly reduced, details x 1). Common in waste places. (Ma) FE II 211

MERCURIALIS

2. *Mercurialis annua* L. Annual Mercury. Much branched Hairless plant up to 75cm. Male and female flowers distinct, either on the same plant or (as usually here) on different plants. Male flowers in clusters on long axillary spikes, female sessile. Mar.-May. Common in waste places. (Branch from 60cm female plant x 1. Details enlarged). (Ma, Mi, I) FE II 212

RICINUS

3. *Ricinus communis* L. Castor-oil Plant. Very robust annual up to 4m. Leaves peltate, palmately divided. Flowers in panicles, the male with numerous yellow stamens, the female smaller with a perianth which quickly falls and 3 bilobed red styles. Fruit 10-20mm with long conical projections. Cultivated, now mainly for ornament, sometimes established in waste places. (x 1/5. Fruit x 1). (Ma) FE II 213

EUPHORBIA

The appearance of *Euphorbia* species varies with maturity. Repeated dichotomous branching from beneath the cyathia leads to proliferation of new shoots, so that a mature plant is much more intricately branched than a young one. Most species lose their lower stem leaves when older. The habit, for this reason, is often of less use in identification than the number of rays, shape of raylet-leaves and ornamentation of glands, capsule and seed.

4. *Euphorbia nutans* Lag. Procumbent or ascending annual up to 60cm. Capsules 1.8-2mm. Seeds 1.1mm, black, rugulose. Apr.-May. Local in disturbed ground. Native of N. America. (Terminal part of stem and small section from near base of stem showing single leaf and stipule x 1. Capsule and seed enlarged: illustration from a Mallorcan specimen). Ma. Not BI in FE II 215

5. *Euphorbia peplis* L. Procumbent fleshy, often greyish annual. Leaves entire, asymmetrical. Glands reddish-brown with small appendages. Seed smooth, greyish, egg-shaped, about 3mm. June-Sept. Sea-shores. (Slightly reduced, details enlarged). (Ma, Mi, I) FE II 216

6. *Euphorbia chamaecyse* L. Procumbent hairless or villous annual. Leaves usually 3-7 x 2.5-4.5mm, deep green, slightly asymmetric at base, usually serrulate, often notched at apex. Glands with rounded white appendages. Seed 2mm, elongated quadrangular, with 4 sharp longitudinal angles and faint transverse ridges. June-Oct. Common. (x 1, details enlarged). (Ma, Mi, I) FE II 216

7. *Euphorbia dendroides* L. Tree Spurge. Dense, dome-shaped shrub up to 200cm. Leaves lanceolate, often becoming bright red towards autumn. Glands yellow to reddish, irregularly lobed. Seeds 3mm, laterally compressed. Locally common near sea. (Part of inflorescence x 1. Shrub much reduced, smaller details enlarged). (Ma, Mi, I) FE II 216

8. *Euphorbia serrata* L. Hairless, blue-green perennial up to 50cm. Leaves sharply serrate. Ray and raylet leaves usually bright greenish-yellow. Capsule 5-6mm. Seeds 3mm, grey, smooth or shallowly punctate. Mar.-July. Common. (x 1/3, details enlarged). (Ma, Mi, I) FE II 216

9. *Euphorbia pubescens* Vahl. Hairy perennial up to 1m. Stem usually with axillary rays. Terminal rays 5 or 6. Capsule 3-4mm, tuberculate. Seeds about 2mm, almost globular, with dark tubercles and prominent comma-shaped white caruncle. Jan.-Oct. Local in marshy places. (x 1/3, details enlarged). (Ma, Mi, I) FE II 220

10. *Euphorbia pterococca* Brot. Hairless annual, rather like less robust forms of 11. Capsule winged. Glands entire, rounded. Apr.-May. Locally common. (x 1, details enlarged). (Ma, Mi) FE II 221

11. *Euphorbia helioscopia* L. Sun Spurge. Annual. The common garden weed of Britain often looks more robust here, with red stems. Leaves obovate, with rounded serrate apex. Rays 5, trichotomously then dichotomously branching. Axillary rays absent. Fruit smooth, sulcate. Seeds 2mm, dark brown, ridged and reticulate. Dec.-May. Common. (x 1/3, details enlarged). (Ma, Mi, I) FE II 221

12. *Euphorbia fontqueriana* Greuter. Decumbent or ascending blue-green perennial. Glands with short blunt horns. Capsule 5mm, smooth. Very rare. **NS**. (Illustration after Colom, *Biogeografía de las Baleares*. Palma 1957. Details from Greek specimen of *E. myrsinites* L.). Ma endemic, closely related to *E. myrsinites* – see FE II 221

13. *Euphorbia exigua* L. Dwarf Spurge. Hairless annual up to 35cm, usually much smaller, often tiny. Rays 0-3. Capsule 1.6-2mm diameter, smooth or slightly tuberculate on keels. Mar.-May. Common. (x 1, details enlarged). (Ma, Mi, I) FE II 222

Other species recorded from Mallorca:

Euphorbia serpens Kunth. Procumbent hairless annual. Leaves entire. Stipules present, often connate. Seeds more or less quadrangular, 1mm or less. Native of America. Listed for Ma by Duvigneaud and Llorens. Not BI in FE II 216

Euphorbia prostrata Aiton. A procumbent annual, resembling no 6, above. Indeed Bucknall claimed that Rodriguez' specimen of *E. chamaesyce* was this species, though Knoche disagreed. *E. chamaesyce* has a capsule 2x2mm, rather deeply sulcate, while *E. prostrata* has a capsule 1.5 x 1.5mm shallowly sulcate and sharply keeled (there are other small differences). Native of N. America. Listed for Ma by Hansen and Llorens. Not BI in FE II 216

Euphorbia squamigera Loisel. (subsp.) An African shrub, up to 120cm, with linear-lanceolate, mucronate leaves. Listed for Ma by Duvigneaud and Llorens. Not BI in FE II 220

Euphorbia lathyris L. Caper Spurge. An introduced plant, native in E. and C. Mediterranean, widely naturalized in much of Europe. A hairless, bluish-green biennial up to 150cm, glands with 2 club-shaped horns, seeds 5mm, barrel-shaped, rugulose. FE II 221

Euphorbia medicaginea Boiss. Hairless annual, easily confused with *E. segetalis* (see Plate 36). Seeds 1.5-1.75mm, white rugulose on a blackish ground. Prof. Llorens says this is common; even so, I did not find it, or perhaps did not recognise it. (Ma, Mi, I) FE II 221

Euphorbia dracunculoides Lam. subsp. *inconspicua* (Ball) Maire (recently recorded: see G. Alomar, J. Rita and J.A.Rosselló *Notas Floristicas de las Islas Baleares* (III) in *Boll. Soc. Hist. Nat. Balears* 30 (1986) pp145-154). Not BI in FE II 222

Euphorbia platyphyllos L. Duvigneaud quotes FE, which lists BI under this species. Llorens omits. Confusion may have arisen because Knoche lists '*E. platyphylla* subsp. *pubescens*', which is the same as *E. hirsuta* (no 9 above).

In other islands:

Mercurialis elliptica Lam. ?Minorca. Not BI in FE II 212
Mercurialis tomentosa L. Ibiza. FE II 212
Euphorbia margalidiana Kuhbier & Lewejohann (1978). Endemic to island Ses Margalides off the coast of Ibiza.

Plate 36

EUPHORBIACEAE (2): *EUPHORBIA* (Part 2)
RUTACEAE: *RUTA*

EUPHORBIACEAE
EUPHORBIA

1. *Euphorbia falcata* L. Hairless annual usually about 30cm. Rays 4-5. **Raylet leaves broadly triangular, aristate, with a strong mid-vein.** Glands broad, truncate, horned. Capsule smooth, ovate. Seeds pale grey or brown with transversely sulcate, darker in the depressions. May-Sept. Locally common in fields and disturbed ground. (x 1/3, raylet leaves slightly enlarged, other details x 4). (Ma, I) FE II 222

2. *Euphorbia peplus* L. Petty Spurge. Hairless annual with 2 or more basal branches and 3 rays. Leaves petiolate. **Capsule smooth, each valve with 2 dorsal wings.** Seeds pale grey, longitudinally sulcate on one side and pitted on the other, darker in the depressions. Dec.-Aug. Very common. (Small specimen x 2/3, raylet leaves slightly enlarged, other details x 4). (Ma, Mi, I) FE II 222

3. *Euphorbia segetalis* L. Annual to perennial, often up to 50cm. Primary umbel often lacking, secondary 5-rayed umbels on each of several or many axillary branches. Leaves falling in the mature plant. **Whole plant often yellowish with red stems.** Glands very variable, with or without horns. Seed ovoid, grey or reddish-brown, minutely pitted. All year. Very common. (x 1/5, raylet leaves x 1, other details x 4). (Ma, Mi, I) FE II 222

4. *Euphorbia biumbellata* Whorled Spurge. Hairless perennial. **Axillary rays present, some whorled below terminal umbel** of 8-21 rays. Glands with club-shaped horns. Seeds grey, shallowly ridged. Locally common. (upper 2/3 of plant x 1/3, raylet leaves slightly enlarged, other details x 2). (Ma, I) FE II 223

5. *Euphorbia maresii* Knoche. Hairless much-branched perennial with creeping much-branched rhizome. Leaves variable. Umbel not developed or with 2-3 rays. Glands truncate, sometimes horned. May-July. **NS.** Not seen by Duvigneaud. Very rare in shady rock crevices. (From pressed specimen x 1, including details of leaves. Capsule and glands x 2). (Ma, Mi endemic) FE II 224

6. *Euphorbia pithyusa* L. **Whole plant minutely papillose** (use lens), **leaves and bracts serrulate.** Rays 4-8. Seeds dark grey or whitish, sometimes ridged or tuberculate. Subsp. *pithyusa* of rocky shores has glands without horns, subsp. *cupanii* (Guss. ex Bertol.) A.R.Sm. has glands with much divided horns. In spite of FE both seem to have non-flowering branches, but this may be the result of the central branch often being grazed by goats. (x 1/3, leaf from middle stem x 1, glands, capsule and seeds x 2). Dec.-Aug. Common in mountains and on shore. (Ma, Mi, I) FE II 225

7. *Euphorbia paralias* L. Sea Spurge. **Bluish-green perennial, rather fleshy, with entire, regularly overlapping leaves.** Rays 3-6. Axillary rays often present. Glands notched or slightly horned. Seeds smooth, pale grey. May-Oct. Common on sandy shores. (x 1/3. Raylet leaves slightly enlarged, other details x 2) (Ma, Mi, I) FE II 225

8. *Euphorbia terracina* L. Variable hairless perennial, with **many ascending and erect flowering and non-flowering branches from base.** Rays 4-5. **Glands with 2 long slender horns.** Capsule sulcate, cinnamon brown when ripe. Seeds ovoid. Grey. Mar.-May. Common near sea. (x 1/3, raylet leaves slightly enlarged. Other details x 2). (Ma, Mi, I) FE II 226

9. *Euphorbia characias* L. Mediterranean Spurge. Robust blue-green tufted perennial up to 150cm, but here often not very densely tufted and about 60cm. Rays 10-20. Glands horned or notched. **Capsule hairy,** otherwise smooth. Dec.-Aug. Common in hilly country. (x 1/3, details x 2). (Ma, Mi) FE II 236

RUTACEAE
RUTA

Shrubby perennials. Leaves alternate, 2-3-pinnatisect. Inflorescence cymose. Flowers mostly 4-merous, sometimes 5-marous. Petals yellow. Fruit a 4 or 5 lobed capsule.

10. *Ruta montana* (L.) L. Leaf-segments linear, up to 1mm wide. Inflorescence densely glandular. **Petals undulate, without cilia.** Capsule segments rounded at apex. June-July. Occasional. (Ma) FE II 227

11. *Ruta angustifolia* Pers. Similar to 10, but terminal leaf-segments obovate-lanceolate, up to 3.5mm wide. **Petals fringed with cilia as long as width of petal.** Capsule segments pointed. May-June. Common. (Ma, Mi, I) FE II 227

12. *Ruta chalepensis* L. Almost completely hairless. Leaf segments up to 6mm wide. **Petals fringed with cilia shorter than width of petal.** Capsule segments pointed. May-June. Common. (Ma, Mi, I) FE II 227

13. *Ruta graveolens* L. Like 12, but **often bluish**, with leaf segments up to 9mm wide. **Petals not fringed,** though sometimes toothed. Capsule segments rounded. May-June. Occasional escape from cultivation. (Ma) FE II 227

Other species recorded for Mallorca:
Euphorbia sulcata De Lens ex Loisel. Annual, often much-branched from the base. Glands with horns. Capsule deeply sulcate. Seeds pale grey, ovoid-hexagonal with a longitudinal furrow on each face, darker in the furrow. Not seen by Duvigneaud. Llorens lists. (Ma, I) FE II 222
Euphorbia pinea Duvigneaud quotes FE. Llorens lists. (Ma) BI in FE II 222

Recorded from Cabrera:
Euphorbia taurinensis All. Duvigneaud lists. Llorens omits. BI in FE II 222

Plate 37

CNEORACEAE: *CNEORUM*
POLYGALACEAE: *POLYGALA*
ANACARDIACEAE: *PISTACIA*
ACERACEAE: *ACER*
AQUIFOLIACEAE: *ILEX*
BUXACEAE: *BUXUS*
RHAMNACEAE: *RHAMNUS*

CNEORACEAE
CNEORUM
1. *Cneorum tricoccon* L. Evergreen shrub up to 1m. Flowers in axillary cymes, with 3 or more usually 4-5mm yellow petals. Fruit of 3 globular 5mm 'cocci', green at first, becoming yellow then red. Common in rocky areas. (Ma, Mi, I) FE II 230

POLYGALACEAE
POLYGALA
2. *Polygala rupestris* Pourret. Small perennial. Leaves leathery, linear-lanceolate, pointed, with recurved margins. Flowers in axillary racemes, of up to 8. Wings greenish. Keel of flower with deep pink fringed crest. Mar.-Nov. Common in rocky places. (Ma, Mi, I) FE II 232
3. *Polygala monspeliaca* L. Erect annual. Leaves lanceolate, acute. Flowers in terminal racemes, greenish-white. Mar.-June. Occasional. (Ma, Mi) FE II 233
4. *Polygala vulgaris* L. Common Milkweed. Small perennial. Wings with 3-anastomosing veins. Flowers usually blue, occasionally white or pink. June. **NS.** Seen by Duvigneaud. Very local. (From British specimen). (Ma) ?BI in FE II 235

ANACARDIACEAE
PISTACIA
5. *Pistacia terebinthus* L. Turpentine Tree. Shrub or small tree, male and female flowers on separate plants. Leaves pinnate with terminal leaflet, rhachis unwinged. Flowers in dense panicles, greenish. Petals absent. Fruit a small reddish drupe, becoming brown. Rare. (From Greek specimen). Seen by Duvigneaud. (Ma) FE II 237
6. *Pistacia lentiscus* L. Gum Mastic. Shrub, male or female as above, commonly up to 2m, rarely to 10m, especially on SE coast. Leaves without a terminal leaflet, rhachis broadly winged. Inflorescence spike-like, commonly red. Mar. Common, stony scrub and higher part of shores. (Ma, Mi, I) FE II 237

ACERACEAE
ACER
7. *Acer granatense* Boiss. Small tree, rarely more than 3m here (one much larger in shelter of snow pit near peak of Massanella). May. Locally common in mountains, usual-ly inaccessible because of grazing goats. (Main illustration constructed from distant photo of mature tree and some immature leaves from a rock crevice. Single leaf from a mature branch found later). (Ma: near endemic – one small area on Spanish mainland) FE II 239

AQUIFOLIACEAE
ILEX
8. *Ilex aquifolium* L. Holly. Small shrub here. Feb.-May. Rare in rock crevices of higher mountains. **NS.** Seen by Duvigneaud. (From British specimen chosen for absence of spines, since Knoche says this is characteristic of the Mallorcan plant). (Ma) FE II 241

BUXACEAE
BUXUS
9. *Buxus balearica* Lam. Balearic Box. Evergreen shrub up to 4m. Very like Common Box, but leaves and inflorescence larger and styles longer. ?Jan.-Feb. (Not seen in flower: illustration from specimen from Cambridge University Botanic Garden). Local in mountain area, formerly much commoner. (Ma) FE II 243

RHAMNACEAE
RHAMNUS
Shrubs here. Calyx with 4 (occasionally 5) lobes, straw-coloured. Petals absent (or very small in 12). Flowers unisexual, both sexes on the same plant. Fruit a drupe with 2-4 stones.
10. *Rhamnus alaternus* L. Evergreen shrub up to 5m. Spines absent. Leaves entire or slightly toothed. Dec.-May. Common in bushy places. (Ma, Mi, I) FE II 244
11. *Rhamnus ludovici-salvatoris* Chodat. Evergreen shrub. Spines absent except for numerous small close spiny teeth on leaf-margins. Fairly common in mountain area. Mar.-May. (Ma, Mi, I: near endemic – one small area on Spanish mainland) FE II 244
12. *Rhamnus lycioides* L. Evergreen shrub to 1m, very spiny. Flowers often solitary. Fruit compressed, purple when ripe. Apr.-May. Local, mainly in higher parts of mountains. (Ma, I) FE II 244

Also in Mallorca:
Vitis vinifera L. Grape vine. Much cultivated. This and other introduced American species occasionally found in wild places. FE II 246

In other islands:
Polygala nicaeensis Risso ex Koch. Formentera. Not BI in FE II 234
Coriaria myrtifolia L. (Coriariaceae). Ibiza. FE II 236

Plate 38

MALVACEAE: *MALVA, LAVATERA, ALTHAEA*

MALVA

Annual or perennial. Leaves usually more or less pleated, sometimes palmately lobed. Flowers with 5 petals, and 5 sepals united at the base. Outside the calyx are 2-3 free sepal-like epicalyx segments. Fruit circular with seeds arranged round the edge, like a box of cheeses.

1. *Malva sylvestris* L. Common Mallow. Erect branching perennial. Sepals ovate or triangular. Peduncles with spreading hairs. **Petals 12-30mm, deep pinkish purple with darker veins.** Apr.-Sept. Common, especially in damp places. (Ma, MI, I) FE II 250
2. *Malva nicaeensis* All. Annual. Flowers in axillary clusters. **Petals 10-12mm,** pinkish white. Longest fruiting pedicels generally exceed 1cm. Common. (Ma, Mi, I) FE II 251
3. *Malva parviflora* L. Annual, usually prostrate with ascending branches. **Petals 4-5mm,** pinkish lilac, longest fruiting pedicels generally less than 1cm. Apr.-May. Common. (Ma, Mi, I) FE II 251

LAVATERA

Annual or perennial herbs or shrubs. Epicalyx segments 3, united at the base, at least in bud (but FE admits problems here: it can be difficult to tell). Otherwise very like *Malva*.

4. *Lavatera cretica* L. Very much like 1, but with **pale pink petals** with darker veins. Peduncles without spreading hairs. Apr. – Sept. (Ma, MI, I) FE II 251
5. *Lavatera arborea* L. Tree Mallow. Robust, showy perennial, commonly up to 2m. Stem stout, with large rounded, more or less lobed leaves. Flowers large, in axillary clusters. **Epicalyx segments up to 10mm, concealing calyx in flower, spreading in fruit.** Petals 15-20mm deep pinkish-lilac with darker veins and base. Mar.-Apr. Common. (Ma, Mi, I) FE II 252
6. *Lavatera maritima* Gouan. Low shrub. Flowers solitary or in pairs, **pedicels exceeding subtending petiole. Petals** generally pale pink, sometimes almost greyish, **abruptly narrowed into purple claw.** Very local. Feb.-May. (Ma, Mi, I) FE II 252

7. *Lavatera olbia* L. Short-lived shrub. Leaves and stems covered in star-shaped hairs (a feature of many of this family, but rather obvious here).**Flowers solitary long racemes, with very short pedicels,** each subtended by a leafy bract. May-June. Rare. (Illustrated from Mallorcan specimen growing in a dry rocky area dominated by *Ampelodesmos*. Bonafè quotes Garcia, collecting 1905, who found it in the same area, but Prof. Llorens considers possibly a garden escape). (Ma, Mi) FE II 252
8. *Lavatera punctata* All. Annual. **Upper leaves simple or spear-shaped.** Flowers solitary on long pedicels. June-July. **NS.** (From specimen collected by Bianor near Sóller in 1910). Not seen by Duvigneaud. Llorens lists. (Ma, MI) FE II 252
9. *Lavatera trimestris* L. **Leaves flat, not pleated, broadly ovate, cordate, the upper sometimes lobed.** Flowers solitary, pedicel often exceeding petiole of subtending leaf. Petals up to 5cm, pink. Apr.-June. Local in NW mountains. (From garden specimen: petals rather narrower in wild plant, found later).

ALTHAEA

Epicalyx segments 6-9, lanceolate, united at base.
10. *Althaea hirsuta* L. Small hairy annual, usually up to 10cm, erect or prostrate. Epicalyx segments acuminate, nearly as long as calyx. May-June. Common in scrub. (Ma, Mi, I) FE II 253

Also recorded from Mallorca:
Althaea officinalis L. Marsh Mallow. Softly grey-hairy perennial, usually about 1m. Flowers with very pale pink petals. Llorens lists. (Ma, Mi) Not BI in FE II 253

In other islands:
Lavatera triloba L. subsp. *pallescens* (Moris) Nyman. Minorca, near endemic. FE II 253
Kosteletzkya pentacarpos (L.) Ledeb. Minorca and Cabrera. FE II 256

Plate 39

THYMELAEACEAE: *DAPHNE, THYMELAEA*
GUTTIFERAE: *HYPERICUM*VIOLACEAE: *VIOLA*

THYMELAEACEAE
DAPHNE
1. *Daphne gnidium* L. Slightly bluish evergreen shrub. Flowers fragrant. June-Sept. Widespread. (Ma, Mi, I) FE II 257

THYMELAEA
2. *Thymelaea hirsuta* (L.) Endl. Shrub, up to 1m. Leaves regularly overlapping, rather fleshy, the upper surface (more or less concealed) white-tomentose. Occasional, mostly near the sea and in mountains. (Ma, Mi, I) FE II 259
3. *Thymelaea myrtifolia* (Poiret) D.A.Webb. Similar to 2, but leaves tomentose on both sides, usually larger, and not regularly overlapping. Mar.-Apr. Locally common near the sea. (Ma, Mi endemic). FE II 259
4. *Thymelaea passerina* (L.) Cosson & Germ. (probably = *Stellera pubescens* Guss. See FE). Hairy annual. Leaves linear-lanceolate, acute. Greenish flowers in clusters along straight stems, subtended by white hairs and small lanceolate bracts. **NS.** Duvigneaud records having seen 'var. pubescens'. Llorens omits. (?Ma) Not BI in FE

GUTTIFERAE
HYPERICUM
St John's Worts. Shrubs or herbs with simple opposite leaves. Sepals and yellow petals often with red or black glands. Stamens numerous, often grouped in bundles. Illustration x 1 unless stated otherwise.
5. *Hypericum hircinum* L. (including *H. cambessedesii* (Cosson) Ramos). Shrub up to 1m. Leaves sessile or nearly so, often goat-scented when crushed. Very local in mountain area beside streams. May. (From garden specimen: seen in fruit in Mallorca). (Ma) FE II 263
6. *Hypericum balearicum* L. Shrub with leathery leaves, the margins with prominent yellowish resinous vesicles. All year, chiefly May – June. Common in dry rocky places. (Ma, Mi, I endemic) FE II 263
7. *Hypericum tomentosum* L. Decumbent tomentose perennial. Sepals with marginal black glands, petals usually without. Widespread in damp places. (Ma, I) FE II 266
8. *Hypericum perfoliatum* L. Perennial herb, stems erect, leaves elongated triangular, usually amplexicaul. Sepals with numerous black glands, petals often with black streaks and dots near apex. May-June. Widespread in damp grassy places. (Ma, Mi) FE II 266
9. *Hypericum perforatum* L. Common St John's Wort. Perennial with erect usually much-branched stems. Leaves with translucent dots. Black glands absent on sepals. May-July. Common. (Main illustration reduced). (Ma, Mi, I) FE II 269

VIOLACEAE
VIOLA
10. *Viola suavis* Bieb. (including *V. barceloi* (L.) Chod.). Rhizomatous perennial with **short stout stolons**. Stipules lanceolate with long, ciliate fimbriae. Leaves at time of flowering 3-8cm, cordate, hairy. **Bracts below middle of peduncle.** Flowers fragrant, violet with a white throat, **upper 2 petals more or less erect, lateral petals not bearded.** Mar. (This one, with a yellow throat, was identified for me as *V. suavis*, and there were many plants where I found it in Mallorca. Duvigneaud and Llorens record this species, with a query, only for Ibiza. (Ma, ?I) Not BI in FE II 272
11. *Viola alba* Besser subsp. *dehnhardtii* (Ten.) Becker. Rhizomatous perennial, **stolons long and slender if any.** Stipules slightly broader than in 10. Leaves hairy. **Bracts at or above middle of peduncle.** Flowers deep violet here. **Upper petals spreading more or less horizontally, lateral petals white-bearded.** Feb.-June. Common in mountain areas. Seen by Duvigneaud and listed by Llorens. (Ma) Not BI in FE II 273
12. *Viola jaubertiana* Marès & Vigineix. Like 11, but completely hairless. Stolons stout. **Stipules broad, triangular with glandular fimbriae. Leaves shining. NS.** (From specimen in Cambridge University Botanic Garden). (Ma endemic) FE II 273
13. *Viola arborescens* L. Woody plant. Leaves ovate to linear, flowers pale violet, very variable in size. Sept.-Oct. mainly. Occasional in rock crevices. (Smaller flower illustrated is x 1, as is main illustration). (Ma, Mi, I) FE II 281

Also recorded from Mallorca:

Thymelaea tartonraira (L.) All. Duvigneaud lists for Ma, as does Llorens. Dwarf shrub 20-50cm with oblong silky leaves 10-18mm (the other 2 species, above, have leaves 10mm or less) and small yellow flowers in clusters of 2-5. Llorens lists for Ma. Not BI in FE

Viola odorata L. and related species *V. stolonifera* Rodr. (Bonafe's description of this plant seems to differ from FE description of *V. odorata* in shape of stipules (lanceolate rather than ovate) and sepals oblong and subacute rather than ovate and obtuse). Feb.-Mar. Seen by Duvigneaud. Llorens treats *V. odorata* as an alien, and omits *V. stolonifera*. FE II 272 specifically excludes BI for this species.

Viola scotophylla Jordan, is listed with a query for Ma by Llorens. Not BI in FE (see *V. alba* subsp. *scotophylla* (Jordan) Nyman). FE II 273

In other islands:
Daphne rodriguezii Texidor. (Endemic Minorca). FE II 258
Hypericum australe Ten. Minorca. FE II 268
Hypericum triquetrifolium Turra. Minorca. FE II 269

Plate 40

CISTACEAE: *CISTUS, HALIMIUM, TUBERARIA, HELIANTHEMUM, FUMANA*

CISTUS

Shrubs, usually with opposite leaves. Flowers 5-petalled, at least 2cm diameter. Sepals 3 or 5. Stamens numerous. Fruit a capsule.

1. *Cistus albidus* L. Compact greyish shrub. Leaves sessile. **Flowers large**, up to 6cm diameter. Petals crinkled like those of a poppy, deep **pink**. Sepals 5, tomentose. Common in hilly country. (Ma, Mi, I) FE II 282

2. *Cistus incanus* L. Very like 1, but leaves petiolate. Probably extinct in Mallorca, if it ever existed: Prof. Llorens believes earlier records may have referred to a variety of 1. **NS**. *Cistus incanus* definitely occurs in Minorca. (Mi) FE II 283

3. *Cistus monspeliensis* L. Sticky bush. **Leaves linear-lanceolate to linear. Flowers white**, 2-3cm diameter. **Sepals 5.** Common in hilly country, often in quite deep shade. (Ma, Mi, I) FE II 284

4. *Cistus salvifolius* L. Shrub, often procumbent. **Leaves ovate or elliptical, petiolate, rugose** on upper surface. **Flowers white**, 3-5cm diameter. Sepals 5, the two outer cordate at base. Locally common in sunny scrub. (Ma, Mi, I) FE II 284

5. *Cistus clusii* Dunal. Similar to 3, but **sepals 3**, with long white hairs. Local around Palma and the Campos area. (Ma, I) FE II 284

HALIMIUM

6. *Halimium halimifolium* (L.) Willk. **Grey-blue erect shrub**, like a **yellow-flowered *Cistus***. 'Stigma' (actually several fused stigmata) large, sessile white. Leaves opposite, those of non-flowering shoots diamond shaped. May-July. Locally common near the coast. (Ma) FE II 285

TUBERARIA

7. *Tuberaria guttata* (L.) Fourr. Spotted Rockrose. **Hairy annual**, usually 15cm or so. **Leaves** opposite, sessile, elliptical, **with 3 parallel veins. Flowers** in racemose cymes, 10-20mm, **yellow, often dark-blotched at base.** May-June. Occasional, sandy places. (Ma, Mi, I) FE II 287

HELIANTHEMUM

Dwarf shrubs. **Leaves opposite.** Flowers in raceme-like cymes. Sepals 5, the inner ovate, appressed, the outer smaller, usually linear, often partly spreading. Stamens all fertile. Style short and straight or thread-like and sigmoid.

8. *Helianthemum caput-felis* Boiss. Dwarf shrub, much-branched, with **whitish woolly leaves**. Flowers in bud like a cat's head (i.e. furry with two ears, i.e. the two spreading outer sepals: this is not distinctive, and is true of several species, especially 7). **Petals yellow with an orange crescent** at base. Very local. May-June. (Ma) FE II 287

9. *Helianthemum nummularium* (L.) Miller. Leaves oblong to lanceolate, stellate-hairy. Petiole shorter than stipules.

Inflorescence an elongated cyme. Apr.-May. Rare if at all. (From own Mallorcan specimen, which seemed distinctive). Duvigneaud quotes FE. Llorens doubts records. (?Ma) FE II 288

10. *Helianthemum appeninum* (L.) Miller. Small shrublet with (here) **pink flowers. NS.** Seen by Duvigneaud. Rare (From Mallorcan specimen). (Ma) FE II 288

11. *Helianthemum salicifolium* (L.) Miller. **Annual,** usually much-branched, the branches held horizontally, upturned at apex. Mar.-June. (From Greek specimen, but seen later, much past its prime, in Mallorca. (Ma) FE II 289

12. *Helianthemum origanifolium* (Lam.) Pers. subsp. *serrae* (Camb.) Guinea & Heywood. Dwarf procumbent or ascending shrub. Leaves **darkish green, ovate**, more or less cordate at base. Flowers 5-8mm. Apr.-May. Found W. of Can Pastilla on much trodden waste ground under flight path to aerodrome. No longer there, Prof. Llorens believes extinct. (?Ma, I endemic subsp.) FE II 290

FUMANA

Dwarf shrubs. **Leaves usually alternate.** Outer stamens sterile. Style thread-like, more or less geniculate at base.

13. *Fumana procumbens* (Dunal) Gren. & Godron. **Procumbent** with spreading branches. **Leaves** alternate, linear, mucronate, **ciliate.** Flowers 3-4, solitary in leaf-axils. Occasional, in high places. (Ma) FE II 291

14. *Fumana thymifolia* (L.) Spach ex Webb. Very variable. **Leaves opposite**, stipulate, linear with revolute margins, and small axillary shoots. (Illustrations:

14a shows flower with geniculate style, and detail of opposite mucronate leaves with bristle tipped stipules (green here) and axillary shoots (uncoloured to show stipules). These features are common to the following 3 varieties noticed.

14b is from an erect, substantial shrublet, about 30cm, typically occurring under pine trees.

14c, with enlarged detail of bud, is the commonest form, usually smaller and less woody than 14b, with flowers 10cm or more across.

14d is from a very glandular-hairy plant, under 10cm, 7mm across, locally common and quite distinctive).

15. *Fumana laevipes* (L.) Spach. Shrublet, up to 30cm, stems slender, ascending. **Leaves alternate**, stipulate, with small axillary shoots, often bluish. Apr.-May. Very local. (Ma, Mi, I) FE II 292

Also in Mallorca:

Fumana ericoides (Cav.) Gand. Seen by Duvigneaud. Llorens queries. Very like 13, and could be confused with it, indeed until someone pointed out my error 13 was labelled *F. ericoides*. The FE key could establish my plant as either or intermediate!

In Minorca:

Tuberaria lignosa (Sweet) Samp. FE II 285

Plate 41

TAMARICACEAE: *TAMARIX*
FRANKENIACEAE: *FRANKENIA*
(ELATINACEAE: *ELATINE*)

TAMARICACEAE
TAMARIX

Small trees (Tamarisks) with overlapping, scale-like leaves dotted with salt-secreting glands. Flowers 4 or 5-merous, in spike-like racemes. Petals pink or off-white, falling early – so sepals are much easier to count.

The species are quite similar in many respects. Bernard R.Baum *The Genus Tamarix* (Jerusalem 1978) is very helpful.

1. *Tamarix* species. ?*Tamarix africana* Poiret. This species, with racemes 30-80 x 5-9mm and 5-merous flowers has frequently been recorded here, at least sometimes in error for *T. boveana*. It would be interesting to know if any trees have been found here which correspond to *T. africana* as described by Baum. Trees here all seem to have at least some 5-merous flowers on each raceme. (Main illustration and unlabelled details from Mallorcan specimen originally identified as *T. africana* on account of the 5-merous flowers. a and b are details of *T. africana* after Baum's illustrations NOT from Mallorcan specimens. Unfortunately this illustration was finished from a photograph before I was aware of the problem (or of Baum's book). It would have been instructive too to see the shape of the petals). (*Tamarix africana* Poiret FE II 293)
2. *Tamarix canariensis* Willd. Bark reddish-brown. Racemes dense (buds more or less contiguous) 15-50 x 3-5mm, with papillose rhachis. Bracts entire, equalling and often exceeding calyx. Sepals very finely toothed (needs microscope). Petals 1.25-1.5mm, obovate, falling quickly. All year, especially Apr.-July. Common around the coast, often planted on beaches. (Ma, I) FE II 293
3. *Tamarix gallica* L. Bark blackish to purplish-brown. Racemes lax (green gaps between buds apparent), 25-35mm. Bracts not exceeding calyx, usually below mid-calyx. Rhachis of raceme completely hairless. Sepals almost entire. Petals 1.5-1.75mm, elliptic to slightly elliptic ovate. Apr.-Sept. Damp places near the sea: possibly commonest in the Campos area. (Ma, MI) FE II 293
4. *Tamarix boveana* Bunge. Typically has racemes 50-150 x 8-9mm, bracts exceeding calyx, and 4-merous flowers. Detail a after Baum's illustration, others from a Mallorcan specimen identified by Baum as *T. boveana*, and fitting his description in all respects except for the rather short raceme and the presence of some 5-petalled flowers (all with 4 sepals). Llorens lists. (Ma) Not BI in FE II 293

FRANKENIACEAE
FRANKENIA

Annual or perennial procumbent herbs, sometimes woody at the base. Leaves opposite, entire. Flowers sessile. Petals and sepals 5, stamens 6 in two whorls of 3, the inner longer.

5. *Frankenia pulvurulenta* L. Annual Sea-heath. Silver-haired annual. Leaves obovate, more or less inrolled. Flowers pale violet in leafy terminal and axillary spikes. May. (Ma, Mi, I) FE II 295
6. *Frankenia laevis* L. Sea-heath. Perennial. Leaves inrolled. Flowers few, solitary or in small clusters throughout upper parts main stem and branches, pink, usually facing towards tip of procumbent branches. Calyx almost hairless or puberulent. Apr.-May. (Ma, Mi, I) FE II 295
7. *Frankenia hirsuta* L. Perennial. Leaves strongly inrolled. Flowers in dense corymbiform clusters, pink, facing up to the sky. **Calyx densely covered in broad-based long white hairs.** (Ma, Mi, I) FE II 295

Also recorded from Mallorca:
Tamarix parviflora DC. This is 4-merous like *T. boveana*, but racemes are only 3-5mm diameter. Llorens treats as alien. Not BI in FE II 293
Elatine macropoda Guss. (Elatinaceae). Tiny annual aquatic herb. Leaves opposite. Flowers pedicellate. Sepals 4. Petals ovate, pale red, shorter than sepals. Llorens lists. (Ma, ?Mi) FE II 296

In Minorca only:
Elatine hydropiper L. Not BI in FE II 296

Plate 42

CUCURBITACEAE: *ECBALLIUM, (CITRULLUS)*CAC-
TACEAE: *OPUNTIA*
LYTHRACEAE: *LYTHRUM*
TRAPACEAE: *TRAPA*
MYRTACEAE: *MYRTUS, EUCALYPTUS*
PUNICACEAE: *PUNICA*

CUCURBITACEAE
ECBALLIUM
1. *Ecballium elaterium* (L.) A. Richard. Squirting Cucumber. More or less procumbent perennial herb. Whole plant fleshy and hispid. Fruit 4-5cm, green, discharging contents explosively. May-Oct. Common. (Ma, Mi, I) FE II 297

CACTACEAE
OPUNTIA
2. *Opuntia ficus-indica* (L.) Miller. Prickly Pear. Erect woody cactus, up to 5m. Joints spathulate, with groups of glochids (barbed bristles) on surface. Flowers large, bright yellow. Fruit more or less pear shaped. May-July. Native of Tropical America. Cultivated for edible fruit and as a windbreak, widely naturalized. (Ma) FE II 300

LYTHRACEAE
LYTHRUM
3. *Lythrum junceum* Banks & Solander. Hairless, straggling perennial of damp places. Petals 5-6mm, rose-coloured, stamens 12. Apr.-June. Fairly common in damp places. (Ma, Mi, I) FE II 301
4. *Lythrum hyssopifolia* L. Grass Poly. Resembles 3, but much smaller. Petals 2-3mm, stamens usually 4-6. Apr.-June. Locally common. (Ma, Mi, I) FE II 301
5. *Lythrum borysthenicum* (Schrank) Litv. Annual. Petals minute and fugaceous. Calyx broadly bell-shaped. Mar.-Apr. Rare. (From Mallorcan specimen (found withered) and a plant grown in Oxford from the seed of this specimen). Not previously recorded here, though previously recorded from Minorca. (Ma, Mi) FE II 302

TRAPACEAE
TRAPA
6. *Trapa natans* L. Water Chestnut. Annual, rooted in mud. Floating leaves rhombic, toothed, forming a rosette. **NS.** Formerly cultivated. Not seen by Duvigneaud. Llorens lists. (Ma) FE II 303

MYRTACEAE
MYRTUS
7. *Myrtus communis* L. Myrtle. Branched evergreen shrub up to 5m, usually less than 2m here. Flowers 4 or 5-petalled, sweetly scented, with numerous stamens. May-June. Fairly common. (Ma, Mi, I) FE II 303

EUCALYPTUS
8. *Eucalyptus* species. Gum Trees. Tall graceful trees with bluish pendent straight or curved lanceolate leaves. Flowers (white here) have numerous long stamens, but petals are fused in bud and fall at time of flowering. May-July. Introduced from Australia and Tasmania. *E. camaldulensis* Dehnh. River Red Gum with 5-10-flowered umbels, and *E. globulus* Labill. Tasmanian Blue Gum with solitary flowers are more or less naturalized here. Other species are planted. (Ma) FE II 304

PUNICACEAE
PUNICA
9. *Punica granatum* L. Pomegranate. Shrub or small tree. May-June. Cultivated for (fairly) edible fruit and widely naturalized (flowering and fruiting sometimes when less than 1m). Native of SW Asia. (Ma, I) FE II 305

Also recorded from Mallorca:
Lythrum thymifolia L. Llorens queries. (?Ma and ?Mi) FE II 301

In other islands:
Citrullus colocynthus (L.) Schrader. Minorca. FE II 298
Lythrum portula (L.) D.A.Webb. ?Minorca.

Plate 43

ONAGRACEAE: *OENOTHERA, EPILOBIUM*
HALORAGACEAE: *MYRIOPHYLLUM*
THELIGONACEAE: *THELIGONUM*
ARALIACEAE: *HEDERA*
UMBELLIFERAE (1): *BOWLESIA, NAUFRAGA, ERYN-GIUM, ECHINOPHORA*

ONAGRACEAE
OENOTHERA
1. *Oenothera rosea* L'Hérit. Distinguished from *Epilobium* by shape of fruit. Garden escape (naturalised at Sa Granja 1976). Introduced from North or South America. FE II 308

EPILOBIUM
2. *Epilobium hirsutum* L. Great Hairy Willow-herb. Flowers up to 2cm, petals shallowly notched. Stigma 4-lobed. May-Sept. Common in wet places. (Ma, Mi) FE II 309
3. *Epilobium parviflorum* Schreber. Small-flowered Hairy Willow-herb. Like 2, but flowers 9mm or less. Petals deeply notched. May-Aug. Damp places. (Ma, Mi, I) FE II 309
4. *Epilobium tetragonum* L. subsp. *tournefortii* (Michaelet) Léveillé. Square-stemmed Willow-herb. Stems leafy, with 4 raised lines and numerous axillary shoots. Stigma entire. May-Sept. Common in damp places. (Ma, Mi) FE II 310

HALORAGACEAE
MYRIOPHYLLUM
5. *Myriophyllum verticillatum* L. Whorled Water-milfoil. Aquatic perennial rooted in mud. Flowers in spike, held above the water, with pinnate or pectinate bracts exceeding the flowers even at apex of spike. May. **NS.** (From British specimen). Listed by Llorens and seen by Duvigneaud. (Ma) FE II 312
6. *Myriophyllum spicatum* L. Spiked Water-milfoil. Similar to 5, but upper bracts entire and shorter than the flowers. May. Common in suitable habitats. (Ma, Mi) FE II 312

THELIGONACEAE
THELIGONUM
7. *Theligonum cynocrambe* L. Leafy annual, superficially like *Parietaria* species, but hairless and slightly succulent. Flowers unisexual in axillary clusters. Perianth green, male splitting into 2-5 lobes, with 7-12 stamens, female tubular with minute teeth. Mar.-Apr. Common, shady rocks and walls. (Ma, Mi, I) FE II 312

ARALIACEAE
HEDERA
8. *Hedera helix* L. Ivy. Common here on buildings, rocks and trees, often particularly fine on shady cliffs in the mountains. (Ma, Mi, I) FE II 319

UMBELLIFERAE
BOWLESIA
9. *Bowlesia incana* Ruiz & Pavón. Procumbent annual with stellate hairs, especially on fruit and backs of leaves. **NS.** (Illustration from Duvigneaud's Mallorcan specimen, x 1, fruit enlarged). (Ma, introduced from N. or S. America) FE II 319

NAUFRAGA
10. *Naufraga balearica* Constance & Cannon. Minute perennial plant, up to 4cm. Discovered in 1967, recently found in Corsica too. **NS.** Very rare (the only patch said to be about 1 sq. metre). (Illustration from specimen from Cambridge University Botanic Garden.). (Ma) FE II 319

ERYNGIUM
11. *Eryngium maritimum* L. Sea Holly. Robust bluish spiny plant of sandy sea-shores. June-Oct. Local on the coast. (Ma, Mi, I) FE II 322
12. *Eryngium campestre* L. Field Eryngo. Like 11, but greener and more slender. Inland. (Ma, Mi, I) FE II 323

ECHINOPHORA
13. *Echinophora spinosa* L. Leaves 2-pinnate, stiff and spiny. Rays 5-8. Bracts and bracteoles 5-10, linear to lanceolate, with a terminal spine. July-Aug. **NS.** Rare, maritime sands. (Illustrated from specimen from Spanish mainland). (Ma, Mi, I) FE II 324

Plate 44

UMBELLIFERAE (2): *(ANTHRISCUS), SCANDIX, (BIFORA), SMYRNIUM, BUNIUM, PIMPINELLA, (BERULA), CRITHMUM, OENANTHE, FOENICULUM*

SCANDIX

1. *Scandix pecten-veneris* L. Shepherd's Needle. Branched annual. Leaves 2-3-pinnate, with linear lobes. Rays 1-3. Petals white, the outer enlarged and radiate. **Fruit elongated, often 60cm or more including a robust beak.** Feb.-May. Fairly common. (Ma, Mi, I) FE II 327

SMYRNIUM

2. *Smyrnium olusatrum* L. Alexanders. Hairless biennial, often up to 1m. **Leaves bright yellowish-green and shiny, 3-ternate, the segments more or less rhomboid, toothed or lobed. Rays 7-15. Bracts and bracteoles few. Flowers yellow, forming a strongly convex to almost globose umbel,** with the secondary umbels well separated. Fruit 7-8mm, broad ovoid to almost globose, black, each carpel with 3 prominent sharp ridges. Common. (Ma, Mi, I) FE II 328

BUNIUM

3. *Bunium bulbocastanum* L. Great Pignut. Hairless perennial, usually 60cm or so. Lower leaves broadly triangular, 3-pinnate with narrow segments. Stem leaves often absent, if present usually withered by flowering time. Rays 10-20. Bracts and bracteoles numerous, small, lanceolate and acute. Sepals absent or minute. Flowers white. **Pedicels minutely toothed on inner edge.** Fruit 3mm, long ovoid, dark brown with pale ridges. Apr.-May. Local. (Specimen from Spanish mainland, but found later in Mallorca). (Ma) FE II 329

4. *Bunium pachypodum* P.W.Ball. Small umbellifer, often only 10cm. **Basal leaves** 3-pinnate with linear lobes, arising from subterranean part of stem (and therefore usually **emerging from soil slightly apart from stem).** Rays 6-15 with 6-8 linear bracts. **Pedicel thickened in fruit,** almost as thick as the fruit. May-June. Occasional. (Ma) FE II 329

PIMPINELLA

5. *Pimpinella bicknelli* Briq. Perennial, usually about 50cm. **Leaves biternate with ovate pinnatisect segments, deeply toothed, and with surface deeply indented along veins.** Rays 4-8. Bracts absent, bracteoles few. Flowers white. Fruit long-ovoid (enlarged in illustration). Rather local in mountains, often with *Urtica atrovirens*. (Ma endemic) FE II 332

CRITHMUM

6. *Crithmum maritimum* L. Rock Samphire. **Leaves 1-2 pinnate, with fleshy segments more or less terete in section.** Rays usually about 8-20, stout. Bracts and bracteoles linear-lanceolate, ultimately deflexed. Flowers yellowish-green. July-Jan. Local on maritime rocks. (Ma, Mi, I) FE II 333

OENANTHE

7. *Oenanthe globulosa* L. subsp. *globulosa*. Branched hairless perennial up to 50cm. Basal leaves bipinnate, lobes oval to linear. Umbels terminal or leaf-opposed. Rays 6 or (usually here) less. Partial umbels with **pedicellate** male **flowers at the circumference** and **sessile** hermaphrodite flowers **in the middle** (petals white). **Fruit 5mm, globose, in a tight cluster** (because no pedicels). Apr.-Aug. Occasional in marshy places near the sea. (Fruit x 2). (Ma, Mi) FE II 338

8. *Oenanthe lachenalii* C.C.Gmelin. Parsley Water Dropwort. Perennial, usually about 60cm. Leaves bipinnate, the segments linear or narrowly spathulate. Umbels terminal with 5-15 rays. **Central flowers in each partial umbel with very short pedicels, peripheral, sterile flowers long pedicellate.** Fruit 3-3.5mm, with persistent styles about the same length. Apr.-Aug. Occasional in marshy places near the sea. (Fruit x 2). (Ma, Mi) FE II 339

FOENICULUM

9. *Foeniculum vulgare* Miller subsp. *piperitum* (Ucria) Coutinho. Fennel. Perennial, not infrequently 2m, but often much less. Leaf segments thread-like, upper **leaves small and rather inconspicuous in the much-branched and 'stemmy' mature plant. Umbels with up to 30 rays. Bracts and bracteoles absent. Terminal umbel often overtopped by lateral umbels. Petals yellow.** June-Aug. Very common, especially on roadsides. (Ma, Mi, I) FE II 333

Also recorded for Mallorca:

Anthriscus caucalis Bieb. Bur Chervil. Annual. Leaves 2-3-pinnate. Umbels small, rays 2-6. **Pedicels** elongating and becoming **thicker than rays in fruit.** Fruit 3mm covered in **stiff bristles.** Rare. (Ma, Mi) FE II 326

Scandix australis L. Resembles 1, but **slightly flattened beak of fruit not clearly demarcated from seed-bearing part.** Fruits tend to spread rather than remain vertical as in 1. (See Alomar, Rita & Rossello 1986). (Ma) Not BI in FE II 327

Bifora testiculata (L.) Roth and *Bifora radians* Bieb. Both listed by Llorens (? after Barceló 1867-1877) but not by Duvigneaud. (Ma) FE II 328

Bunium alpinum Waldst. & Kit. subsp. *macuca* (Boiss.) P.W.Ball. Resembles 3, but with larger leaf-lobes (5-10mm), and generally fewer rays and bracts. **Pedicels not toothed** on the inner edge. Duvigneaud queries. Llorens lists. (Ma) Not BI in FE II 329

Pimpinella tragium Vill. Small perennial. Lower leaves pinnate (or bipinnate). Rays 5-15. Bracts and bracteoles absent or few. Petals hairy on the back. Fruit ovoid, shortly tomentose. July-Aug. Very local. Not seen by Duvigneaud. Llorens lists. (Ma) FE II 331

Berula erecta (Hudson) Caville. Narrow-leaved Water-parsnip. Stoloniferous aquatic perennial with simply pinnate aerial leaves (under-water leaves more divided). Leaf-segments ovate, serrate. Umbels 3-6cm diameter, leaf-opposed. Rays 10-15, bracts and bracteoles numerous, often trilobed or pinnatisect, leaf-like. Fruit usually wider than long. May-July in shallow water. Rare. Listed but not seen by Duvigneaud. (Ma, Mi, I) FE II 333

In Minorca:
Pimpinella lutea Desf. Not BI in FE II 331

Plate 45

UMBELLIFERAE (3): *KUNDMANNIA, CONIUM, (MAGYDARIS), BUPLEURUM, APIUM, PETROSELINUM, RIDOLFIA, AMMI*

KUNDMANNIA

1. *Kundmannia sicula* (L.) DC. Hairless perennial usually about 35cm. Lobes of leaves more or less ovate, serrate. **Bracts and bracteoles numerous, long-linear, drooping. Flowers yellow.** Fruit long and narrow. Apr.-June. Locally common in agricultural areas. (Ma, Mi) FE II 342

CONIUM

2. *Conium maculatum* L. Spotted Hemlock. Almost hairless perennial, up to 2.5m. **Lower part of stem red-spotted.** Upper much branched with numerous fairly small umbels. Rays 10-20. Bracts 5-6. Bracteoles on the outer side of the partial umbel, often connate at base. May-Aug. Common. (Ma, Mi, I) FE II 342

BUPLEURUM

3. *Bupleurum lancifolium* Hornem. Hairless annual up to 75cm. **Upper leaves perfoliate.** Bracts absent. Rays 2-3. Bracteoles broad ovate, connate at base. Flowers and fruit small. Mar.-July. **NS.** Not seen by Duvigneaud. (From Italian specimen). Llorens lists. (Ma, Mi, I) FE II 346

4. *Bupleurum baldense* Turra. Hairless yellow-green annual. **Bracteoles broad and spreading,** often pinkish, much exceeding umbel. Leaves linear-lanceolate, the lower ones petiolate. Mar.-July. Common. (Ma, Mi, I) FE II 347

5. *Bupleurum semicompositum* L. Hairless **bluish annual** up to 30cm. Rays 3-6. **Bracteoles linear-lanceolate, aristate, with 3 very prominent veins.** Fruit covered in small whitish papillae. May-Sept. Occasional, mainly on dry ground, especially near the sea. (Ma, Mi, I) FE II 348

6. *Bupleurum barceloi* Cosson ex Willk. Shrublet up to 40cm. Basal leaves linear lanceolate, **stems almost leafless. Flowers yellow.** May-Aug. Fairly common in mountain areas, but usually inaccessible. (Ma, I endemic) FE II 350

APIUM

7. *Apium graveolens* L. Wild Celery. Hairless biennial up to 1m. **Leaves shining,** pinnate or bipinnate. **Umbels leaf-opposed, sessile or shortly pedunculate.** Bracts and bracteoles absent. Common in marshy ground near the sea. (Ma, Mi, I) FE II 351

8. *Apium nodiflorum* (L.) Lag. Fool's Watercress. Procumbent or ascending perennial. Stems rooting at lower nodes. **Leaves pinnate.** Peduncle usually shorter than rays. Bracts usually absent, bracteoles 5-7. May-July. Common in wet places. (Ma, Mi, I) FE II 351

PETROSELINUM

9. *Petroselinum crispum* (Miller) A.W.Hill. Parsley. Hairless biennial. Lower leaves triangular, 3-pinnate. Bracts 1-3, bracteoles 5-8, rays 8-20. Flowers yellowish-green. Fruit broadly ovoid. Escape from cultivation. (Ma, Mi, I) FE II 352

RIDOLFIA

10. *Ridolfia segetum* Moris. Hairless annual, usually around 35cm. **Leaves 3-4-pinnate with very fine segments, upper ones often reduced to sheath** only. Rays 10-60, bracts and bracteoles absent. June-Aug. Field weed, locally common. (Ma, I) FE II 352

AMMI

11. *Ammi visnaga* (L.) Lam. Annual or biennial up to 1m. Leaves 1-3-pinnate with narrow linear lobes. **Rays very numerous (up to 150).** Bracts 1-2 pinnatisect, equalling or exceeding rays. Bracteoles slender and tapering. May-June. Rare. **NS.** Not seen by Duvigneaud. (From garden specimen). Llorens lists. (Ma) FE II 353

12. *Ammi majus* L. Hairless annual. Rays 15-60. **Bracts 3-fid or pinnatisect,** bracteoles lanceolate. May-July. Common, often as a field weed. (Ma, Mi) FE II 353

Other plants recorded for Mallorca:

Magydaris panacifolia (Vahl) Lange. Very tall perennial (up to 250cm). Basal leaves simple or shallowly lobed, stem leaves pinnate or reduced to sheath. Leaves hispid on the veins below. Rays 10-20, bracts up to 30mm, deflexed, lanceolate. Bracteoles up to 20mm. Petals white. Fruit ovoid, hairy. Llorens lists. (?Ma, Mi) FE II 345

Bupleurum tenuissimum L. Resembles 5, but most umbels have only 2-3 rays. Local. Llorens lists. (Ma) Not BI in FE II 348

In other islands:

Bupleurum rigidum L. Ibiza. Not BI in FE II 349

Plate 46

UMBELLIFERAE (4): *LIGUSTICUM, (CAPNOPHYL-LUM), FERULA, PASTINACA, TORDYLIUM, LASERPITIUM, THAPSIA, TORILIS, (TURGENIA), (ORLAYA), DAUCUS, PSEUDORLAYA*

LIGUSTICUM

1. *Ligusticum lucidum* Miller subsp. *huteri* (Porta & Rigo) O. Bolòs. Almost hairless perennial. Leaves triangular, 3-5-pinnate. Lobes 2-5mm, oblanceolate to obovate, **mucronate**. Rays 11-16. Bracts usually absent, bracteoles 5-8, about half length partial umbel. Flowers white. July. **NS**. Not seen by Duvigneaud. (Ma, endemic subsp.) FE II 356

FERULA

2. *Ferula communis* L. Giant Fennel. Spectacular tall perennial, 2m or more. Leaves much divided, with linear segments. Umbels terminal and lateral, the **terminal umbel surrounded by smaller long-pedunculate umbels**. Petals yellow. May-June. Locally common. (x about 1/20). (Ma, Mi, I) FE II 359

PASTINACA

3. *Pastinaca lucida* L. Shining Parsnip. Robust perennial. **Basal leaves simple, cordate, finely serrate**. Middle leaves pinnate, with 3-7 segments, upper small, entire. Petals yellow. May-Aug. Common in mountain areas. (x about 3/4). (Ma, Mi endemic) FE II 364

TORDYLIUM

4. *Tordylium apulum* L. Annual. Rays 3-8. Bracts and bracteoles ciliate. Petals white. **Outer petal of outer flowers much enlarged, deeply bifid. NS.** Not seen by Duvigneaud. (From Greek specimen). (Ma, Mi) FE II 367

LASERPITIUM

5. *Laserpitum gallicum* L. Tall curry-scented perennial. Leaves up to 5-pinnate. Rays 20-50, bracts and bracteoles numerous, ciliate. Petals white or pink. **Fruit 6mm with 2mm wide lateral wings, and 2 narrower dorsal wings**. June-Sept. Local in mountains. **NS**. Seen by Duvigneaud. (Pinna from 3-pinnate leaf x 2/3, 4-winged fruit, from back and end-on x 1, from Spanish mainland). (Ma) FE II 370

THAPSIA

6. *Thapsia villosa* L. Hairy perennial up to 2m. (From garden specimen x 1/15, fruit x 1). Knoche records 'la forme des îles Baléares se rapproche beaucoup du *T. villosa*'. Duvigneaud lists *Thapsia villosa* subsp. Llorens omits, but records the following species, to which previous records presumably refer.

7. *Thapsia gymnesica* Rosselló & Pujadas. Stems solitary, usually 60-80cm. Basal leaves up to 50cm, 4-pinnate, segments rounded with revolute margins. **Stem leaves with sheaths only. Basal leaves absent at time of flowering**. Umbels terminal. Rays 5-10, raylets 20-30. Bracts and bracteoles absent. Petals yellow. Fruit elliptical with 2-

3mm wide lateral wings, some fruit wingless. (Ma, Mi endemic, not described in FE).

TORILIS

Annuals with white petals and **fruit with the grooves between ridges filled with spines or tubercles**.

8. *Torilis nodosa* (L.) Gaertner. Knotted Hedge-parsley. Annual, often procumbent. Leaves 2-pinnate, with deeply pinnatifid segments. Umbels leaf-opposed. Peduncle short or absent. Rays very short, concealed by flowers or fruit. Fruit at centre of umbel tuberculate, fruit at periphery of umbel with inner mericarp tuberculate, outer spiny. Mar.-May. (Ma, Mi, I) FE II 371

9. *Torilis webbii* Jury. Resembles 8, but leaves bipinnate, peduncles longer, and both mericarps spiny. Locally common. Described by S.L.Jury in *Botanical Journal of the Linnaean Society* (1987), 95: 293-299

10. *Torilis arvensis* (Hudson) Link. Field Hedge-Parsley. Erect, usually 30cm or so. Bracts 0-1. Outer petals generally longer than inner. Inner mericarp tuberculate and outer spiny. May-June. Fairly common. (Ma, Mi) FE II 371

DAUCUS

11. *Daucus carota* L. Wild Carrot. Annual or biennial, very variable (several subspecies here, not all illustrated, and different authors list different subspecies). Leaves 2-3-pinnate. Rays fairly numerous here. Bracts 1-2-pinnatisect, bracteoles of outer umbels trifid, of inner umbels simple. Flowers white, often pinkish in bud. **Fruit 2-3mm with spines on ridges**. subsp. *major* (Vis.) Arcangeli. (Main illustration). Leaves hairy. Flattish umbels become strongly contracted in fruit. Very common (Ma, Mi, I) FE II 374
Subsp. *drepanensis* (Arcangeli) Heywood. Nearly hairless, with fleshy green leaves (small segment x 1) and large globular heads (x 1/4). (Common, especially near sea).

PSEUDORLAYA

12. *Pseudorlaya pumila* (L.) Grande. Hairy annual. Resembles *Daucus* species, but rays 2-5, **fruit 7-10mm**. Apr.-May. Occasional on maritime sands. (Ma, Mi, I) FE II 375

Other species recorded for Mallorca:
Capnophyllum peregrinum (L.) Lange. Hairless annual, with 3-pinnate leaves. Rays 2-5. Bracts 0 or few. Bracteoles 4-6, shortly triangular. Petals white. Llorens lists. (Ma) Not BI in FE II 358
Torilis leptophylla (L.) Reichenb. fil. Annual, slightly resembling 8, but erect, with peduncles more than 2cm. Rays 2-3, short but easily visible. Fruit with yellowish spines. Listed but not seen by Duvigneaud. Llorens lists (Ma) FE II 371
Orlaya kochii Heywood (*Orlaya daucoides* (L.) Greuter). Listed by Llorens. (Ma, Mi) Not BI in FE II 372

In Ibiza:
Elaeoselinum asclepium (L.) Bertol. FE II 368
Thapsia garganica L. FE II 370

Plate 47

PYROLACEAE: *MONOTROPA*
ERICACEAE: *ERICA, ARBUTUS*
PRIMULACEAE: *PRIMULA, CYCLAMEN, ASTEROLI-NON, (GLAUX), ANAGALLIS, SAMOLUS, CORIS*

PYROLACEAE
MONOTROPA

1. *Monotropa hypopitys* L. Yellow Bird's Nest. Saprophytic plant, wholly pinkish-yellow. May-Sept. Very local. (Ma) FE III 5

ERICACEAE
ERICA

2. *Erica arborea* L. Tree Heath. Tall branched shrub. Feb.-May. Occasional in sheltered places in the mountains. (Ma, Mi, I) FE III 7
3. *Erica multiflora* L. Branched shrub, usually less than 1m. Some flowers usually present, main flowering Aug.-Sept. Common in dry rocky places. (Ma, Mi, I) FE III 7

ARBUTUS

4. *Arbutus unedo* L. Strawberry Tree. Tree or shrub (flowering when only about 1m). Oct.-Jan. Common in hilly areas. (Ma, Mi, I) FE III 11

PRIMULACEAE
PRIMULA

5. *Primula vulgaris* Hudson subsp. *balearica* (Willk.) W.W.Sm. & Forrest. Mallorcan Primrose. Very like the common primrose, which does not occur here, but flowers nearly white, and more scented. Under side of leaf almost hairless. Very local in the mountains. **NS.** (From photograph kindly loaned by Mr W.F.Taylor). (Ma endemic)

CYCLAMEN

6. *Cyclamen balearicum* Willk. Flowers pure white. Flowering probably throughout year, especially Apr.-May. Common in rocky places. Not endemic in spite of name, occurs also in S. of France. (Ma, Mi, I) FE III 25

ASTEROLINON

7. *Asterolinon linum-stellatum* (L.) Duby. Hairless annual with opposite leaves. Corolla white, less than 2mm, much exceeded by calyx. Small and easily overlooked. Occasional in dry stony places. (Ma, Mi, I) (FE III 27)

ANAGALLIS

8. *Anagallis tenella* (L.) L. Bog Pimpernel. Stems creeping, rooting at nodes. Leaves usually opposite, suborbicular. Apr.-Sept. **NS.** Rare in marshy places. (From British specimen). Seen by Duvigneaud. (Ma) FE III 28
9. *Anagallis arvensis* L. Scarlet Pimpernel. Annual. Flowers blue or red. Flowering stems usually longer than subtending leaves. **Petals fringed with hairs with globose tip** (use lens). Maritime plants often rather fleshy. Apr.-May. Common. (Ma, Mi, I) FE III 28
10. *Anagallis foemina* Miller. Blue Pimpernel. Very like 9, but flowering stems usually shorter than subtending leaves. Petals with **few marginal hairs without a globose tip or none**, always blue. Rather rare. Duvigneaud saw this plant. Llorens queries. (My plant was quite distinctive as a whole, as well as in diagnostic details). (Ma, ?Mi, I) FE III 28
11. *Anagallis monelli* L. Perennial. **Stem terete** (stem in 9 and 10 is quadrangular). Flowers blue. **NS.** Duvigneaud lists as seen. Llorens omits. (?Ma, ?I) Not BI in FE III 28

SAMOLUS

12. *Samolus valerandi* L. Brooklime. Perennial hairless herb. Inflorescence racemose, usually branched. Corolla white, 2-3mm. May-June. Common in wet places. (Ma, Mi, I) FE III 29

CORIS

13. *Coris monspeliensis* L. Perennial herb up to 30cm. Flowers in dense, head-like racemes, pink or purple. Corolla tubular, deeply divided into 5 bifid lobes. May. Local in sandy places. FE III 29

In Minorca:
Erica scoparia L. FE III 8
Lysimachia minoricensis Rodr. FE III 26
Anagallis minima (L.) E.H.L.Krause. FE III 28

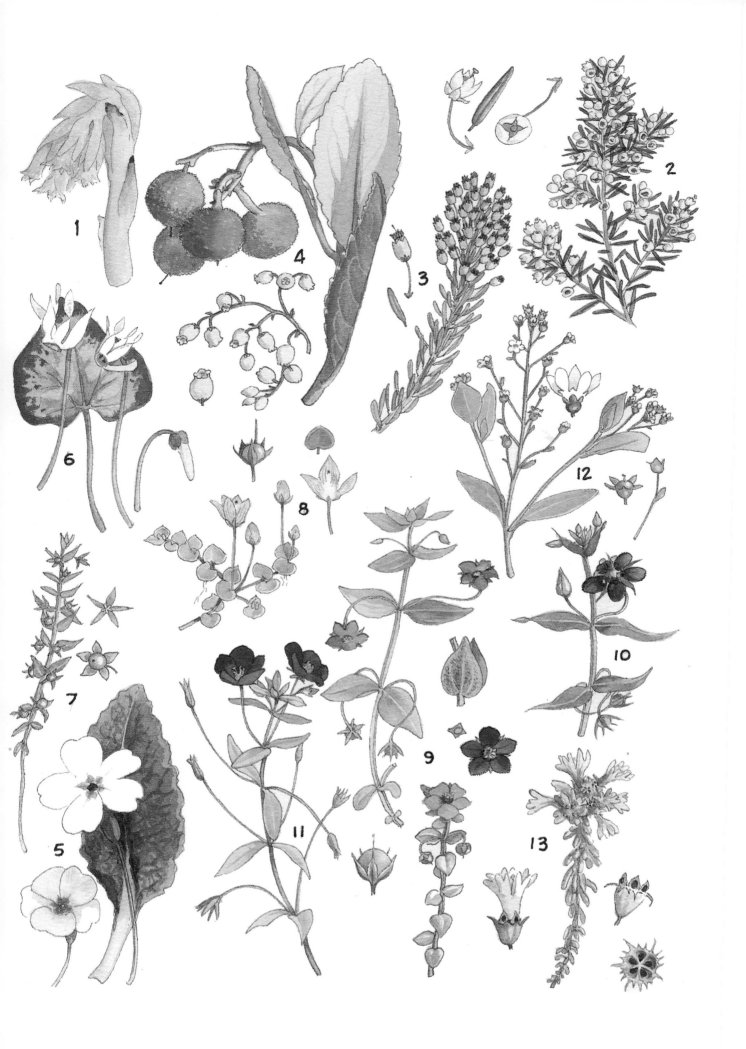

Plate 48

PLUMBAGINACEAE: *LIMONIUM*

This is a very difficult genus: many of the plants are hybrids persisting by apomixis. Upwards of 30 species are recorded for Mallorca, many of them endemic to Mallorca or the Balearic Islands; others occur only in Minorca, Ibiza or the smaller islands (even these have their endemics). The classification is constantly being revised, and it is not generally possible to give an exact FE equivalent for Knoche's names, or for the names used by M. Erben in his recent classification, used here (see bibliography: essential reading for any serious study of this genus).

The plants are mostly perennials. The shape of the basal leaves is important for identification, also the general form and pattern of branching of the inflorescence, including nonflowering branches with a single reduced scale at the tip (see B1, bottom right), and sterile branches which have overlapping reduced scales at the tip (B2). The branches of the inflorescence usually have a small scale at the base, and the shape and size of the largest of these is sometimes helpful in identification.

The inflorescence is a panicle with terminal spikes of 1-5-flowered spikelets. The number of spikes per centimetre and the form of the bracts are important. Each spikelet is enveloped by 3 bracts. The middle one is often hidden, but the inner bract is longer than the outer, and both of these are easily seen. The relative lengths of these bracts and their anatomy in terms of size and shape, width of hyaline border, arrangement of nerves and whether these stop short of the edge of the bract or run out beyond the edge are important.

The plants illustrated here have been identified by M. Erben, and the names are the names he uses. The illustrations are intended to give some idea of the variation in form within this genus, and are not adequate for identification, for which Erben's papers should be consulted. The specimens were chosen to show a wide range of forms, and characteristically 2 out of 5 are hybrids. (All illustrations x 3/4 to 1, details x about 4).

1. *Limonium minutum* (L.) Chaz. x *L. virgatum* (Willd.) Fourr. Leaves small, papillose-hairy, in rosettes at apex of short woody branches. Spikelets 1-3-flowered, hardly curved. Aug.-Sept. Rocky places by the sea.

2. *Limonium camposanum* Erben spec. nov. x *L. pseudoebusitanum* Erben. Plant has numerous long broad 1-veined spathulate leaves with short mucro. Branches all fertile, up to 7cm, with 7-9 spikelets per centimetre, each with 2-4 flowers. Tip of coloured part of bract running out nearly to edge of membranous margin. Aug.-Sept. Rocks in Campos area.

3. *Limonium virgatum* (Willd.) Fourr. Leaves are linear to spathulate with one vein. Numerous sterile branches present. Spikelets about 4 per centimetre, curved, with 1 or 2 flowers. Inner bract has reddish-brown margin, more or less hyaline towards apex. Aug.-Sept. Common in sandy saline soils. (Compare *L. oleifolium* Miller, FE III 46)

4. *Limonium connivens* Erben. A fairly compact plant with few stems. Leaves slightly incurved, mostly 1-veined, but the larger ones may have a few pinnately arranged smaller veins. Branching starts near the base of the stem, rather short straight branches coming off in a regular zig-zag arrangement at an angle of 50-70°. There are 4-6 2-4-flowered spikelets per centimetre (i.e. spikelets more or less contiguous). Long curved teeth of calyx in fruit are striking. Aug.-Sept. Mainly on E. coast. (Compare *L. duriusculum* (Girard) Fourr. FE III 46)

5. *Limonium echioides* (L.) Miller. This species at least is easily identified, and its specific name derives from Linnaeus' name (though the genus was then *Statice*, not *Limonium*). A bushy much-branched annual, with small curved spikelets, 1-2 per centimetre. The inner bract is tuberculate. Apr.-May. Fairly common on beaches. FE III 50

Plate 49

OLEACEAE: *(JASMINUM), FRAXINUS, OLEA, PHILLYREA*
GENTIANACEAE: *BLACKSTONIA, CENTAURIUM*

OLEACEAE
FRAXINUS

1. *Fraxinus angustifolia* Vahl. Narrow-leaved Ash. Tree resembling *Fraxinus excelsior* L., the common ash of Northern Europe, but with brown rather than black buds. Locally common. (x 1/2). (Ma, introduced) FE III 54

OLEA

2. *Olea europaea* L. Olive. Tree up to 15m. **Underside of leaves scaly.** Flowers in axillary panicles. Petals white. Stamens 2. Drupe green. Introduced, common in cultivation. Plants established in the wild with spiny lower branches may also be found. May-June. (Ma, Mi, I) FE III 55

PHILLYREA

Evergreen shrubs. Leaves opposite, simple, **underside without scales.** Corolla with 4 lobes. Stamens 2. Fruit a bluish-black drupe.

3. *Phillyrea angustifolia* L. Up to 2.5m. Leaves with 4-6 pairs of rather obscure veins, the lower running a long way up leaf. **Calyx with rounded lobes. Immature drupe ovoid**, becoming globose. Mar.-June. Fairly common. (x 2/3, details x 5). (Ma, Mi, I) FE III 55

4. *Phillyrea latifolia* L. Shrub or tree up to 15m. Juvenile leaves ovate, toothed or serrate. Mature leaves lanceolate with 7-11 pairs of distinct veins. **Calyx-lobes triangular. Fruit globose** at all stages. Mar.-June. Not common. Seen, but illustration from garden specimen. (Ma, I) FE III 55

GENTIANACEAE
BLACKSTONIA

5. *Blackstonia perfoliata* (L.) Hudson. Yellow-wort. Hairless blue-green annual. Leaves opposite, stem leaves usually connate at base. Corolla lobes 6-12, bright yellow. All four subspecies described in FE occur here. They differ mainly in size of flowers and number of petals. Jan.-Sept. Common. (Ma, Mi, I) FE III 56

CENTAURIUM

6. *Centaurium erythraea* Rafn. Common Centaury. Hairless biennial, often exceeding 30cm. Rosette leaves present at time of flowering. Flowers in corymbiform cyme, the **calyx 1/2-3/4 x corolla-tube.** Corolla lobes bright pink. Apr.-Aug. Locally common. (Ma, Mi) FE III 57

7. *Centaurium pulchellum* (Swartz) Druce. Hairless annual, with no basal rosette at flowering time. **Stem with 2-4 internodes**, usually dichotomously **branched from below middle.** Flowers in a cyme, branching repeatedly and regularly, with a flower at the point of branching. **Calyx nearly equalling corolla-tube.** Corolla usually deep reddish-pink or (not uncommonly) white. Apr.-May. Fairly common. (Ma, Mi, I) FE III 59

8. *Centaurium tenuiflorum* (Hoffmanns. & Link) Fritsch. Hairless annual, sometimes with weak leaf-rosette at flowering time. **Stem with 5-9 internodes, branched above.** Branches strict. **Calyx nearly equalling corolla-tube.** Apr.-May. Very common, especially near the sea. (Ma, Mi, I) FE III 59

(Descriptions after FE: but angles of divarication of branches vary between 15° (?strict) and about 30°. These do not seem to show any regular correspondence with the number of internodes, or branches above or below middle of stem. Possibly hybrids?).

9. *Centaurium spicatum* (L.) Fritsch. Hairless annual or biennial. Stem often branched from base or middle. Inflorescence a spike or very short-stalked raceme. June-Oct. Local in saline habitats. (Ma, Mi, I) FE III 59

10. *Centaurium maritimum* (L.) Fritsch. Hairless annual or biennial. **Flowers yellow** (less common) or **pinkish-yellow** (var. *erubescens* Willk.). Dry places near the sea. (Ma, Mi) FE III 59

(Upper illustration here probably *C. bianoris* (Sennen) Sennen, whose status is uncertain, possibly *C. maritimum* x *C. tenuiflorum.* Common endemic plant of Mallorca and Ibiza).

Other species recorded for Mallorca:
Jasminum fruticans L. Rare in Arta region. Llorens lists. (Ma) Not BI in FE III 53
Centaurium quadrifolium López & Jarvis subsp. *barrelieri* (Duf.) López. Llorens lists. Not described in FE

In Minorca, or recorded for BI unspecified:
Cicendia filiformis (L.) Delarbre. Minorca. FE III 56
Centaurium enclusense O. Bolòs, Molinier & P. Monts. (Mi endemic) FE III 58
Centaurium linariifolium (Lam.) G. Beck. Smythies records from BI. D quotes FE. ?BI in FE III 59

Plate 50

APOCYNACEAE: *NERIUM, VINCA*
ASCLEPIADACEAE: *GOMPHOCARPUS, CYNAN-CHUM, VINCETOXICUM*
RUBIACEAE (1): *SHERARDIA, CRUCIANELLA, ASPE-RULA*

(APOCYNACEAE and ASCLEPIADACEAE both have regular 5-merous flowers, often with a corona or scales near the base of the petals. In Apocynaceae the petals tend to be asymmetrical, one edge more strongly curved than the other, producing a Catherine-wheel like effect. Leaves are simple and usually opposite in both).

APOCYNACEAE
NERIUM
1. *Nerium oleander* L. Oleander. Shrub, here up to about 2m. Formerly native in Mallorca, now probably only planted, though occasionally in wild situations. Still wild in Ibiza. (?Ma, I) FE III 68

VINCA
2. *Vinca difformis* Pourret. Periwinkle. Creeping perennial. Dec.-July. Common in hedgerows in cultivated areas. (Ma, Mi, I) FE III 69

ASCLEPIADACEAE
GOMPHOCARPUS
3. *Gomphocarpus fruticosus* (L.) Aiton fil. Bristly Silkweed. June-July. Not common. Introduced from S. Africa. Naturalized in waste places. (Ma) FE III 70

CYNANCHUM
4. *Cynanchum acutum* L. Stranglewort. Woody climber. June-Aug. Shrubby places. Uncommon. **NS.** (From Greek specimen). (Ma, Mi, I) FE III 71

VINCETOXICUM
5. *Vincetoxicum nigrum* (L.) Moench. Twining perennial. Flowers blackish-purple. May-Aug. Fairly common in northern mountain area. (Ma, Mi) FE III 71
6. *V. hirundinaria* Medicus subsp. *intermedium* (Loret & Barradon) Markgraf. Perennial herb up to 1m, sometimes twining. Flowers greenish-white. May-July. Occasional in mountains. (Main illustration from Mallorcan specimen, detail from garden specimen, possibly a different subsp.). (Ma, Mi) FE III 72

RUBIACEAE
These are mainly herbs with regular 4 or 5-merous small flowers with an inferior ovary. Leaves are entire, simple, commonly in whorls, sometimes opposite. The fruit is dry, usually with 2 mericarps.

SHERARDIA
7. *Sherardia arvensis* L. Field Madder. Procumbent annual. Mar.-July. Very common. In open grassy places and field margins. (Ma, Mi, I) FE IV 3

CRUCIANELLA
8. *Crucianella maritima* L. Woody perennial up to 50cm, usually less. May-Oct. Locally common on higher parts of seashore. (Ma, Mi, I) FE IV 4
9. *Crucianella angustifolia* L. Hairless annual. Lowermost leaves linear-lanceolate. Corolla 3-5mm long, pale yellow, exceeded by free bract, which is long-pointed and lanceolate. Bracteoles easily visible. May – July. Occasional. **NS.** (From garden specimen). (Ma, I) FE IV 4
10. *Crucianella latifolia* L. Annual. Stems slightly hairy. Lowermost leaves obovate-elliptical. Bracts slightly connate, concealing bracteoles. Corolla 5-7.5mm long, yellowish-purple, exceeding bract. May-June. Widespread in rocky places. (x 1/2). (Ma, I) FE IV 4

ASPERULA
11. *Asperula laevigata* L. Scrambling perennial. Stems weak, hairless. Leaves elliptical to ovate, rounded at apex, in whorls of four. Flowers 4-merous. Apr.-July. Occasional in damp places. (Ma, Mi) FE IV 12
12. *Asperula arvensis* L. Annual. Rare. (From garden specimen. Found later as street weed, or perhaps garden escape in Puerto Alcudia, looking similar but more robust, with many more flowers). (Ma, Mi, I) FE IV 13

Another possible species in Mallorca:
Asperula cynanchica L. Knoche quotes Barceló (1867-1877). Llorens lists. (Ma, I) FE IV 10

In Ibiza only:
Asperula paui Font Quer (cf. *A. aristata* FE IV 6)

Plate 51

RUBIACEAE (2): *GALIUM, VALANTIA, RUBIA*

GALIUM

Herbs. Leaves in whorls of 4 or more. **Flowers 4-merous** in cymes or panicles. Mericarps of fruit generally paired (except 12 here). Nos 1-5 are perennial, the others annual.

1. *Galium elongatum* C.Presl. **Stems** straggling, **with downward pointing prickles on the 4 angles.** Leaves 25-30 x 2.5-5mm, in whorls of 4 or 6. Inflorescence pyramidal. Corolla white, 3-4mm diameter. Fruit 2.5-3.5mm, smooth or tuberculate. May-June. Local in wet places. (x 1, detail x 3). (Ma, Mi, I) FE IV 21

2. *Galium lucidum* All. Stoloniferous **perennial. Stems terete, hairless or with a few short hairs**, branching only in the upper part. Leaves 10-30 x 1-2mm inrolled. Inflorescence dense, ovoid. Corolla white. Apr.-June. Occasional in hilly areas. (Part of inflorescence slightly enlarged, details x 3). (Ma, I) FE IV 25

3. *Galium cinereum* All. Resembles 2, but **bluish-green** and without stolons. Leaves 8-15mm. Apr.-June. Locally common in mountain area. (Upper and lower part of stem x 1, 5 internodes between omitted). (Ma) FE IV 25

4. *Galium crespianum* J.J.Rodr. Erect or ascending almost hairless. **Leaves bright green, shining, downwardly curved**, the longest 3-4cm. Flowers ochre to yellow (not white, in spite of FE description), in a dense pyramidal inflorescence. May-Sept. Locally common in rocky places. (x 1, details x 3). (Ma, I endemic) FE IV 25

5. *Galium balearicum* Briq. **Mat-forming** perennial. Stems usually about 6cm. **Leaves dark green**, ovate to shortly lanceolate, **up to 5mm long**, in whorls of 5-6. Flowers few. Corolla purplish-red, not apiculate. Very local in mountains. (x1, detail of flower x 6, and of plant as seen from above x 2). (Ma endemic) FE IV 30

6. *Galium setaceum* Lam. Very slender annual. **Leaves in whorls of 6-8, narrow linear to thread-like.** Flowers minute, purple. **Fruit less than 1mm, densely covered in fine bristles.** Apr.-May. Local in dry rocky places. (x 1, detail of flower x 4). (Ma) FE IV 34

7. *Galium aparine* L. Goose-grass, Cleavers. Annual. Leaves in whorls of 6-8, the margins with prickles pointing towards the 4-angled main stem, which also has downward pointing prickles on the angles. Flowers white. **Fruit 3-5mm, with dense hooked bristles.** Mar.-Apr. Common in cultivated ground. (x 1, flower x 4). (Ma, Mi, I) FE IV 35

8. *Galium tricornutum* Dandy. Rough Corn Bedstraw. Vert much like 7. Stem also has downward pointing prickles on the angles. Flowers usually in 3s, the central hermaphrodite and the lateral male. **Fruit 3-5mm, with numerous papillae, but no bristles**: male flowers often develop vestigial fruit. Mar.-Apr. Common in cultivated ground. (x 1, detail enlarged). (Ma, Mi, I) FE IV 35

9. *Galium verrucosum* Hudson. Rather like 8, including flowers in 3s as above. Margins of leaves with bristles pointing towards leaf-tip. **Fruit 4-6mm, strongly verru-** cose. Mar.-Apr. Common in cultivated ground. (x 1, detail enlarged). (Ma, Mi, I) FE IV 35

10. *Galium parisiense* L. Slender annual. Stems with prickles directed downwards. Inflorescence strongly divaricate. **Peduncles 1-3 x length pedicels.** Corolla 0.5-1mm, the lobes erect, greenish inside and reddish outside. **Fruit up to 1mm, finely papillose**, with or without hairs, **pedicels not deflexed in fruit.** Locally common, especially at roadsides. (x 1, corolla and fruit x 3). (Ma, Mi) FE IV 35

11. *Galium divaricatum* Pourret ex Lam. Slender annual. Lower stem with sparse downwardly directed prickles, upper stem nearly smooth. Flowers minute, red or yellow. **Fruit up to 0.7mm, finely papillose, pedicels deflexed in fruit.** Apr.-May. Local in dry rocky places. (x 1: upper detail showing deflexed pedicels slightly enlarged, lower details x 10). (Ma, Mi) FE IV 36

12. *Galium murale* (L.) All. Small annual, up to 20cm, usually much less. **Fruit cylindrical**, mericarps separate from each other, **with hooked bristles mainly near the apex.** Mar.-Apr. Common on walls and rocks. (x 1, details x 6). (Ma, Mi, I) FE IV 36

VALANTIA

Annuals with 3-flowered axillary cymes of small yellow flowers. Peduncles and pedicels become thickened, deflexed and coalesced to enclose the fruit of central hermaphrodite flower (outer two are male).

13. *Valantia hispida* L. Usually erect. Fruit has 15-25 soft hyaline bristles at apex. Apr.-May. Common, walls and rocky places. (x 1, details x 2). (Ma, I) FE IV 38

14. *Valantia muralis* L. Differs from 13 in having a hard bristly horn projecting from the top of the fruit, which is otherwise without bristles. On sea shores there is a distinctive prostrate form with a rosette of stems with very regular overlapping fleshy leaves like a large edition of *Selaginella denticulata* (Plate 1). Apr.-May. Common, walls and dry sandy places. (x 1, details x 2). (Ma, Mi, I) FE IV 38

RUBIA

15. *Rubia peregrina* L. Climbing, usually prickly, perennial. Leaves ovate-elliptical, dark and shining, in whorls of 4-8. **Flowers 5-merous.** Corolla yellowish. Fruit a black berry. Apr.-Sept. Common on walls and in thickets. (Left x 1/2, and lower flower x 2). (Ma, Mi, I) FE IV 38

16. *Rubia angustifolia* L. Resembles 15, but has curved linear leaves, prickly on both sides, and with revolute margins. Common, in similar places. (Right, x 1/2, and upper flower x 2). (Ma, Mi, I) FE IV 38

Another possible species for Mallorca:
Galium debile Desv. Llorens omits. ?BI in FE IV 21

Possibly in Ibiza:
Galium corrudifolium Vill. BI in FE IV 25

Plate 52

CONVOLVULACEAE: *CUSCUTA, CRESSA, CALYSTE-GIA, CONVOLVULUS, IPOMOEA*
BORAGINACEAE (1): *HELIOTROPIUM*

CONVOLVULACEAE
CUSCUTA

Annual parasites with clusters of small flowers along twining leafless stem.

1. *Cuscuta campestris* Yuncker. Stems stout, yellowish. Flowers 2-3mm in 10-12mm globular clusters. Stigma capitate. **NS.** Listed by Hansen and Duvigneaud. Llorens lists. (From Greek specimen, though originally North American). (Ma, Mi, ?I) FE III 75

2. *Cuscuta epithymum* (L.) L. subsp. *kotschyi* (Desmoulins) Arcangeli. Flowers about 2.5mm, usually pinkish, in 5-6mm globular clusters. Calyx-lobes keeled, fleshy. Stigmas elongate. Apr.-May. Common, mainly on dwarf shrubs. (slightly enlarged). (Ma, Mi, I) FE III 77

3. *Cuscuta epithymum* (L.) L. subsp. *epithymum*. Flowers 3-4mm, usually white, globular clusters 7-10mm, Calyx-lobes acute or acuminate, membranous. Stigmas elongate: stigmas and styles together much longer than ovary. Common, often on Leguminosae. (Slightly enlarged). (Ma, Mi, I) FE III 77

CRESSA

4. *Cressa cretica* L. Branched greyish hairy shrublet. Leaves lanceolate to ovate, sessile, passing gradually into bracts. Flowers 3-5mm, pale pinkish, with 5 spreading lobes. Apr.-May. Local in sandy saline areas. (Ma, I) FE III 78

CALYSTEGIA

5. *Calystegia soldanella* (L.) R.Br. Sea Bindweed. Perennial rhizomatous plant, not climbing. Leaves kidney-shaped, slightly fleshy. Corolla 30-50mm, funnel-shaped, pink with white markings. Occasional. Maritime sands. (Ma, Mi, I) FE III 78

6. *Calystegia sepium* (L.) R.Br. Bellbine. Climbing perennial. Leaves sagittate. Bracteoles scarcely overlapping the calyx. Corolla funnel-shaped, 30-70mm, white. Common. (Ma, Mi, I) FE III 78

CONVOLVULUS

7. *Convolvulus lineatus* L. Silvery slightly bushy perennial with **silky appressed** hairs. Leaves linear to elliptical, basal leaves widened and scarious at the base. Corolla 12-25mm, pale pink or whitish. May. **NS.** Not seen by Duvigneaud. Llorens lists. (From garden specimen). (Ma, Mi) FE III 81

8. *Convolvulus cantabrica* L. Shrubby perennial with **spreading hairs at least below.** Leaves linear to oblanceolate, basal leaves widened and scarious at the base Corolla 15-25mm, pink. May-Oct. Locally common, mainly on sandy or stony soils. (Ma, Mi) FE III 81

9. *Convolvulus tricolor* L. Erect herbaceous annual or perennial. **NS.** Probably not recorded recently. FE III 81

10. *Convolvulus siculus* L. Annual or perennial. Stems trailing, rarely twining. Leaves lanceolate to ovate, cordate at base. Corolla 7-12mm, blue. Mar.-June. Rather rare. (From Cretan specimen: detail added from Mallorcan specimen found later). (Ma, Mi, I) FE III 81

11. *Convolvulus arvensis* L. Bindweed. Corolla 10-25mm white to pink. Very common. (Ma, Mi, I) FE III 81

12. *Convolvulus althaeoides* L. Mallow-leaved bindweed. 2 subsp. here, one with mostly patent hairs and leaves with broad lobes, one with almost only appressed hairs and narrow leaf-lobes (detail on right). Both have a 25-40mm bright pink corolla. Mar.-July. Both common. (Ma, Mi, I) FE III 81

IPOMOEA

13. *Ipomoea sagittata* Poiret. Climbing or creeping perennial. Sepals rounded or notched with terminal mucro. July-Sept. **NS.** Seen by Duvigneaud. Introduced from America, like other species of *Ipomoea* (Morning Glory) which are commonly cultivated here. This species has been recorded as naturalised, climbing on *Arundo*. (Ma, Mi, I) FE III 82

BORAGINACEAE
HELIOTROPIUM

14. *Heliotropium europaeum* L. Heliotrope. Much-branched annual. Leaves ovate to elliptical, wedge-shaped at base, greyish with appressed hairs. Flowers 2-4mm, white with yellow centre, in terminal scorpioidal cymes. May-Oct. Locally common, sometimes a street weed. (Ma, Mi, I) FE III 85

15. *Heliotropium curassavicum* L. Hairless, fleshy procumbent perennial, rather dark blue-green. Flowers as 14. May-Sept. Fairly common in saline places near the sea. Introduced from N. America. (Ma, Mi, I) FE III 85

Other species recorded for Mallorca:
Cuscuta planiflora Ten. Flowers 1.5-2.5mm, white. Calyx lobes swollen, nearly semicircular in section. Seen by Duvigneaud. Llorens lists. (Ma) FE III 77

Cuscuta approximata Bab. Flowers 3-4mm. Calyx tube golden-yellow, shiny and reticulate when dry, the lobes with a terminal fleshy appendage. Duvigneaud lists as seen. Llorens queries. Not BI in FE

Calystegia silvatica (Kit.) Griseb. Dubious. Llorens omits. BI in FE III 79

Convolvulus pentapetaloides L. Annual or short-lived perennial. Corolla 7-10mm, blue with yellow centre. Seen by Knoche. Not seen by Duvigneaud. Llorens lists. (Ma, I) FE III 81

In other islands:
Convolvulus valentinus Cav. Ibiza. Not BI in FE III 81
Heliotropium supinum L. Minorca. FE III 86

Plate 53

BORAGINACEAE (2): *LITHOSPERMUM, NEATOS-TEMA, BUGLOSSOIDES, ALKANNA, ECHIUM, NONEA, (SYMPHYTUM), ANCHUSA, BORAGO, (MYOSOTIS), (LAPPULA), CYNOGLOSSUM*

LITHOSPERMUM

1. *Lithospermum officinale* L. Gromwell. Erect perennial. Leaves lanceolate, with conspicuous lateral veins. Corolla tubular, yellowish-white, with 5 longitudinal folds inside, limbs 5, spreading. **Nut shining white.** May-Aug. **NS.** (Seen by Duvigneaud). (From British specimen). (Ma) FE III 86

NEATOSTEMA

2. *Neatostema apulum* (L.) I.M.Johnston. Yellow Gromwell. Bristly annual. **Corolla yellow, the lobes of limb glandular-puberulent on both surfaces.** May-Aug. Occasional. (Ma, I) FE III 86

BUGLOSSOIDES

3. *Buglossoides arvensis* (L.) I.M.Johnston. Corn Gromwell. Small hairy annual resembling 1. Corolla with 5 longitudinal bands of hairs inside. **Nut brownish.** Occasional. (Ma, Mi, I) FE III 87

ALKANNA

4. *Alkanna lutea* DC. Hispid annual, bristles with white-bulbous bases. **Corolla yellow, hairless on outside** (differentiating from 2), with cylindrical tube and funnel-shaped limb. May-June. Occasional. (Ma, Mi, I) FE III 96

ECHIUM

Hispid herbs, usually biennial here. Flowers in bracteate cymes, usually pinkish or blue. Calyx lobed almost to base. Corolla funnel-shaped, usually with oblique limb.

5. *Echium asperrimum* Lam. Rough Bugloss. Intricately branched more or less **domed** plant with rather stinging bristles. Flowers flesh pink, **stamens long-exserted with red filaments.** May-Sept. Rather rare. (Small illustration x 1/25 of plant in rubbish-tip near Arenal shows habit, larger illustration shows detail slightly reduced). (Ma, Mi, I) FE III 98

6. *Echium italicum* L. Pale Bugloss. Inflorescence branched, **pyramidal**, up to 1m. Corolla white, pale blue or pale pink. **Stamens long-exserted**, usually with blue filaments. (x 1/25, detail slightly reduced). May-Sept. Common. (Ma, Mi, I) FE III 98

7. *Echium plantagineum* L. Purple Viper's Bugloss (the infamous Paterson's Curse of Australia). Tall, much-branched plant, **softly hairy. Corolla** 18-30mm, deep blue, reddish or purple, **with hairs on the veins and margins. Two stamens usually exserted.** Apr.-July. Common. (Ma, Mi, I) FE III 99

8. *Echium sabulicola* Pomel. (Sometimes perennial). Easily mistaken for small plants of 7, but **bristly. Corolla** 12-22mm, **uniformly hairy. One or two stamens usually exserted.** Apr.-July. Common in sandy places near the sea. (Ma, Mi, I) FE III 99

9. *Echium parviflorum* Moench. Plant usually erect. Corolla 10-13mm, **all stamens included. Calyx** 6-8mm at time of flowering, **up to 15mm in fruit x 3-6mm wide at base.** Mar.-June. Common. (Ma, Mi, I) FE III 100

10. *Echium arenarium* Guss. Plant ascending. Corolla 6-11mm, **all stamens included. Calyx** up to 7mm at time of flowering, **up to 10mm in fruit x 2-3mm wide at base.** Common on sandy ground near the sea. (Ma, I) FE III 100

NONEA

11. *Nonea vesicaria* (L.) Reichenb. Hispid and glandular-hairy annual or biennial. **Corolla funnel-shaped, brownish-purple**, lobes erect, not spreading. Calyx much enlarged in fruit. Apr.-May. **NS.** (Seen by Duvigneaud). (From Portuguese specimen). Llorens lists. (Ma, I) FE III 103

ANCHUSA

12. *Anchusa azurea* Miller. Blue Alkanet. Tall perennial, with **regular corolla** with straight tube and spreading limbs, deep blue to violet with white scales at throat. Calyx lobed almost to base. Common field weed. May-Aug. (Ma, Mi, I) FE III 108

BORAGO

13. *Borago officinalis* L. Borage. Hispid annual, distinguished from *Anchusa* by the very short **corolla** tube, **with pointed lobes** and short white basal scales, and **fused blackish anthers.** May-Sept. Common. (Ma, Mi, I) FE III 109

CYNOGLOSSUM

14. *Cynoglossum creticum* Miller. Blue Hound's Tongue. Biennial. Corolla regular with a short tube, white or pale blue with darker blue reticulate venation. Mar.-May. Common. (Ma, Mi, I) FE III120

15. *Cynoglossum cheirifolium* L. Leaves silvery-tomentose on both surfaces. Corolla red or purplish. Locally common, often in grazed turf. (Ma, Mi, I) FE III 120

Other species recorded for Mallorca:

Echium creticum L. Knoche records 'forme maritimum', probably = *E. plantagineum*. Duvigneaud quotes FE. Llorens lists for Ma. BI in FE III 99

Symphytum tuberosum L. Bonafè gives one location. Llorens lists for (Ma, Mi) FE III 104

Anchusa undulata L. Very like 12, but **calyx lobed to not more than 2/3**, leaves often with rounded teeth and undulate. Bonafè gives two locations.Llorens lists for (Ma, Mi) FE III 107

Myosotis arvensis (L.) Hill. Common Forget-me-not. Bonafè gives one location. Duvigneaud quotes FE. Llorens lists. (Ma) FE III 112

Myosotis ramosissima Rochel. Early Forget-me-not. Many earlier records. Not seen by Duvigneaud. Llorens lists. (Ma) FE III 112

Lappula squarrosa (Retz.) Dumort. Knoche quotes Bianor (1914-1917). Duvigneaud queries. Llorens lists. (Ma) ?BI in FE III 118

In Minorca:
Cerinthe minor L. FE III 94

Plate 54

VERBENACEAE: *VITEX, VERBENA, LIPPIA*
CALLITRICHACEAE: *CALLITRICHE*
LABIATAE (1): *TEUCRIUM*

VERBENACEAE
VITEX
1. *Vitex agnus-castus* L. Chastity Bush. Shrub, usually up to 3m here. Leaves with 5-7 digitate leaflets. Flowers in a terminal panicle. With blue or occasionally pink flowers. Aug.-Oct. Local in stream beds. (Ma, Mi, I) FE III 122

VERBENA
2. *Verbena officinalis* L. Vervain. Slender perennial. Leaves opposite. Flowers small, mauve, in a terminal spike, 10-25cm, sometimes branched. May-Oct. Fairly common. (Ma, Mi, I) FE III 122

LIPPIA
3. *Lippia nodiflora* (L.) Michx. Creeping perennial, with procumbent rooting stems and ascending flowering stems with opposite leaves. Flowers 2mm, white, in a dense terminal spike. May-Sept. **NS.** Seen by Duvigneaud. (From garden specimen). (Ma, Mi, I) FE III 122
4. *Lippia canescens* Kunth. As above, but woody at base: flowers 3mm, lilac. July-Aug. **NS.** Seen by Duvigneaud. (Specimen from Spanish mainland, though plant originates in America. (Ma) FE III 122

CALLITRICHACEAE
CALLITRICHE
The morphology of this genus varies with habitat. Only aquatic forms are shown here, but these too are variable.
5. *Callitriche stagnalis* Scop. Water Starwort. Plant of fresh water rooting in mud, with floating rosettes of leaves. Submerged leaves elliptical, stalked. Flowers axillary, minute. Fruit with erect or spreading styles. Mar.-Sept. **NS.** Seen by Duvigneaud. (From British specimen). (Ma, Mi) FE III 125
6. *Callitriche brutia* Petagna. Submerged leaves linear, often notched at apex. Floating rosettes with elliptical or obovate leaves. Styles deflexed, appressed to sides of fruit. **NS.** Seen by Duvigneaud. (Specimen from Spanish mainland). (Ma, Mi) FE III 125

LABIATAE
Herbs or shrubs, stems usually quadrangular in section. Leaves opposite or occasionally whorled, usually simple. Stipules absent. Calyx of 5 variously united sepals, corolla tubular, often two lipped, occasionally actinomorphic or almost so. Stamens 2 or 4. Ovary superior.

TEUCRIUM
Flowers in axils of more or less leaf-like bracts. **Corolla without upper lip:** lower lip 5-lobed. Flowers pale or deeper pink unless otherwise stated. 7-13 have lax inflorescences: 14-16 have flowers in dense heads.
7. *Teucrium asiaticum* L. Dwarf shrub with distinctive **foul carrion smell. Leaves narrow and toothed**, up to 30cm. Inflorescence lax. Flowers mostly solitary in axils of leaf-like bracts, diminishing upwards. Apr.-Sept. Common in mountain areas. (Ma, Mi endemic) FE III 132
8. *Teucrium scordium* L. Water Germander. Hairy perennial, garlic-scented when crushed. **Leaves ovate**, toothed, bracts similar and only slightly smaller. Flowers mostly single or in pairs in axil of each bract. May. **NS.** Not seen by Duvigneaud. (Ma, Mi) FE III 132
9. *Teucrium botrys* L. Cut-leaved Germander. Small annual. **Leaves 1-2-pinnatisect.** Occasional in hilly country. (Ma) FE III 132
10. *Teucrium chamaedrys* L. Wall Germander. Rhizomatous dwarf shrub. **Leaves** oblong-ovate, **deeply toothed, paler and hairy** beneath. Flowers in whorls. Fairly common in hilly country. (Ma, Mi) FE III 132
11. *Teucrium flavum* L. Shrubby perennial. Leaves more or less heart shaped, crenate, velvety or hairless (2 subsp.). **Flowers yellow.** May-August. Rather uncommon in hilly districts. (Seen in Mallorca, but not in flower. Illustration from garden specimen). (Ma, I) FE III 132
12. *Teucrium marum* L. Cat Thyme. Small shrub. Leaves linear-lanceolate rhombic, grey-tomentose beneath. Flowers few, purplish in axils of leaf-like bracts. **NS.** Duvigneaud quotes FE. Llorens gives ?Ma, ?MI. FE III133
13. *Teucrium subspinosum* Pourret ex Willd. Prickly shrublet forming a neat hemispherical 'hedgehog' up to 60cm in higher parts of mountains, much smaller in lower parts. Leaves tiny, greyish, inrolled triangular. May-July. Common in hilly areas and in mountains. (Ma, Mi) FE III 133
14. *Teucrium cossonii* D.Wood. Dwarf shrub. Stem and leaves greyish with branched hairs. **Leaves** narrowly oblanceolate, revolute, **with up to 3 crenations on each side. Flowers in terminal and lateral heads, pinkish-red. NS.** Seen by Duvigneaud. (From garden specimen). First described in 1972. (Ma endemic). FE III 134
15. *Teucrium polium* L. subsp. *polium*. Woolly compact shrublet, greyish, **leaves** narrowly oblong **with** revolute margins and **up to 5 crenations on each side. Flowers in a simple terminal head, pinkish-red or white** (otherwise very like *T. cossonii*). May-July. Locally common in sandy places near sea, including beaches. (Ma) FE III 134
16. *Teucrium polium* subsp. *capitatum* (L.) Arcangeli. Differs from 15 mainly in the **compound heads.** May-July. Locally common in sandy places near sea, and sometimes inland. (Ma) FE III 134

Also recorded from Mallorca:
Verbena supina L. Shortly bristly annual, usually **procumbent. Flower spikes up to 8cm.** Duvigneaud lists Mi only. Llorens gives (Ma, Mi) FE III 123
Teucrium campanulatum L. Knoche quotes Barceló (1867-1877). Not seen by Duvigneaud. Llorens lists (Ma) FE III 131

In other islands:
Callitriche truncata Guss. Minorca. Not BI in FE III 124

Plate 55

LABIATAE (2): *AJUGA, SCUTELLARIA, PRASIUM, MARRUBIUM, SIDERITIS, PHLOMIS, LAMIUM, MOLUCCELLA, BALLOTA*

AJUGA

1. *Ajuga iva* (L.) Schreber. Small (up to 20cm, usually much less) tufted perennial, woolly-haired, often woody at base. Leaves linear, (usually narrower than in upper illustration) entire or lobed. Corolla yellow or pinkish. May-Oct. Common in dry places. (Ma, Mi, I) FE III 129

2. *Ajuga chamaepitys* (L.) Schreber. Ground Pine. Annual or short-lived perennial. Leaves tripartite with linear segments. Corolla usually yellow sometimes with purplish markings or entirely purple. Rare. **NS.** (from garden specimen). Not seen by Duvigneaud. Llorens lists. (Ma) FE III 129

SCUTELLARIA

3. *Scutellaria balearica* Barc. Slender decumbent perennial. Leaves ovate to deltoid, crenate. Calyx with erect dorsal scale (typical of genus). Flowers few, small, in axillary pairs. May. Rather local in moist shady places in mountains. (Ma endemic) FE III 136

PRASIUM

4. *Prasium majus* L. Small shrub with shining hairless leaves. Flowers in terminal racemes. Calyx with 5 more or less equal broad leafy lobes. Corolla white. Nuts black. May. Rather rare. (Ma, Mi) FE III 137

MARRUBIUM

5. *Marrubium vulgare* L. Aromatic woolly-haired perennial, up to 45cm. Verticillasters globose, with many small white flowers. Stamens included in corolla tube. Apr.-Sept. Common in waste places. (Ma, Mi, I) FE III 138

SIDERITIS

6. *Sideritis romana* L. Hairy annual, erect or decumbent. Calyx 2-lipped, upper tooth much broader than the 4 other lanceolate teeth, all with straight prickly apex. Flowers white. Apr.-Aug. (Ma, Mi, I) FE III 143

PHLOMIS

7. *Phlomis italica* L. Stellate-woolly shrub, usually about 1m. Leaves sage-like. Corolla usually dirty-pinkish, occasionally with deep red lower lip. May-June. Common in mountain area. (Ma, Mi endemic) FE III 145

LAMIUM

8. *Lamium amplexicaule* L. Henbit. Annual. Flowers in dense verticillasters subtended by more or less amplexicaul, shallowly-lobed bracts. Corolla tube 10-14mm, straight. Feb.-Oct. Common in recently cultivated ground. (Ma, Mi) FE III 148

MOLUCCELLA

9. *Moluccella spinosa* L. Bells of Ireland. This is inappropriately included here. This is one of the first plates I finished in the early stages of this book, when I hoped to include everything ever recorded in Mallorca! This was probably a garden escape when recorded by Barceló (1867-1877)! FE III 149

BALLOTA

10. *Ballota nigra* L. Black Horehound. Slightly unpleasant smelling perennial herb, usually less than 1m. Calyx infundibuliform, regular, with mucronate teeth. May-Sept. Fairly common. (Ma, Mi) FE III 150

Also recorded from Mallorca:

Ballota hirsuta Bentham. Similar to 10, but calyx campanulate, irregular, with 10 or more teeth. Not seen by Knoche or Duvigneaud. Listed by Llorens for (Ma, I) FE III 150

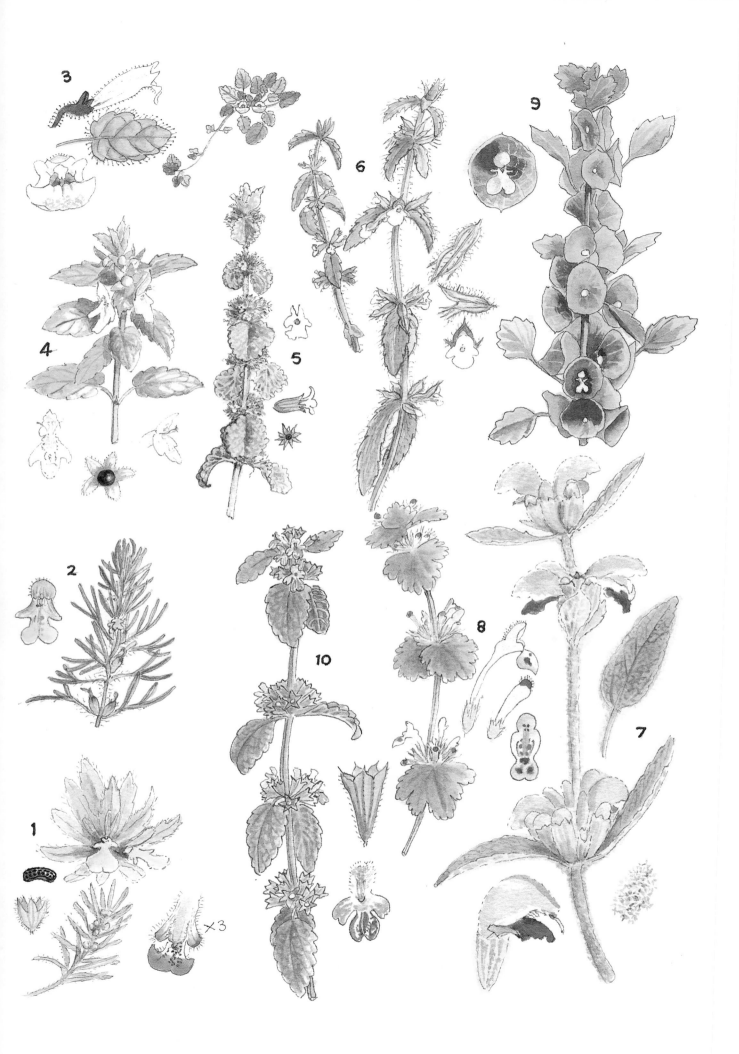

Plate 56

LABIATAE (3): *STACHYS, (NEPETA), PRUNELLA, (MELISSA), (ACINOS), CALAMINTHA,(SATUREJA), MICROMERIA, (ORIGANUM),THYMUS, MENTHA, ROSMARINUS, LAVANDULA, SALVIA*

Main illustration x 1 unless otherwise stated.

STACHYS

1. *Stachys germanica* L. Downy Woundwort. White hairy perennial usually up to about 60cm. Most leaves truncate or cordate at base. Knoche's account suggests that corolla is usually white here (elsewhere pink or purple). Apr.-Aug. **NS.** Seen by Duvigneaud. (From garden specimen, less hairy than usual). Llorens lists. (Ma) FE III 153
2. *Stachys ocymastrum* (L.) Briq. Erect hairy annual, up to 50cm. Corolla white or pale yellow with deeper yellow lower lip. Mar.-June. Common. (Ma, Mi, I) FE III 157
3. *Stachys arvensis* (L.) L. Annual. Corolla white or pale pink, scarcely exceeding calyx. Mar.-May. Occasional, but not common. (Lobed upper lip in this specimen unusual). (Ma) FE III 157

PRUNELLA

4. *Prunella laciniata* (L.) L. White Self-heal. Perennial, usually small. Typically leaves are laciniate, but in the small population from near peak of Teix from which this specimen is taken all leaves were entire. Corolla creamish-white. July. Very local. (Ma) FE III 162

CALAMINTHA

5. *Calamintha sylvatica* Bromf. subsp. *ascendens* (Jordan) P.W.Ball. Common Calamint. Stoloniferous perennial. Calyx with 13 veins, lower two teeth up to 3.5mm, long-ciliate. (Details of calyx, side view and below, x 2). Aug.-Oct. Locally common in mountain areas. (Ma, Mi, I) FE III 166
6. *Calamintha nepeta* (L.) Savi subsp. *glandulosa* (Req.) P.W.Ball. Resembles 5, but calyx shorter with the two lower teeth 1-2mm, rarely ciliate. **NS.** Not seen by Duvigneaud. Probably dubious here. Llorens queries. (Calyx only from Italian specimen). (?Ma, ?Mi) FE III 166

Calamintha rouyana (Briq.) Rouy. Strong smelling hairy herb, appearing in FE index as one of the two above. Main distinctive feature seems to be a bright blue corolla. Knoche mentions that the leaves are often reddish beneath. **NS.** Seen by Knoche and Duvigneaud. Llorens lists as Ma endemic. Not illustrated.

MICROMERIA

7. *Micromeria filiformis* (Aiton) Bentham. Dwarf shrub, prostrate or ascending. **Leaves ovate-triangular, up to about 4mm**, usually less, the **lower cordate at base**. Flowers white, often in pairs, sometimes in pedunculate cymes of up to 4 flowers. A very variable plant, common in dry stony places. (Ma, Mi, I) FE III 168
8. *Micromeria microphylla* (D'Urv.) Bentham. Very much like 7, but usually erect or ascending. **Lower leaves rounded or wedge-shaped at base**. Whorls of 6 or 7 purplish flowers in lax inflorescence. May-June. Local. (Ma) FE III 168
9. *Micromeria nervosa* (Desf.) Bentham. Like 7 and 8, but larger. **Leaves up to 1cm, ovate**. Whorls with 4-20 flowers. **Calyx with long dense spreading hairs** (x 1/2). Apr.-June. Occasional. (Ma, I) FE III 169

THYMUS

10. *Thymus capitatus* (L.) Hoffmans. & Link. Shrub, usually about 35cm. Leaves gland-dotted, linear or rather broader. Flowers in conical heads. **Calyx-tube strongly flattened, 2 lipped** (front and back x 6). June-Oct. Rather local. FE III 174
11. *Thymus richardii* Pers. subsp. *richardii*. Much-branched shrublet. Resembles familiar *Thymus praecox* Opiz, but larger in all its parts: leaves ovate, 7-12 x 3-6mm, corolla 7-9mm. Very rare. **NS.** Not seen by Knoche or Duvigneaud. Llorens lists as Ma endemic subsp. (FE III 180 gives also W. Jugoslavia).

MENTHA

12. *Mentha pulegium* L. Penny-royal. Creeping perennial, with characteristic scent. Lower two calyx-teeth longer and narrower than upper 3. Whorls of flowers dense, each subtended by leaf-like bracts protruding well beyond flowers. Apr.-Aug. Common, especially where water stands seasonally. (Ma, Mi) FE III 184
13. *Mentha aquatica* L. Water Mint. **Flowers in a dense terminal head**, often with dense whorls below. **Bracts inconspicuous**. July-Oct. Occasional. (From British specimen, though seen in Mallorca). FE III 185
14. *Mentha suaveolens* Ehrh. Apple-scented Mint. **Leaves more or less rounded, rugose**, usually softly tomentose. **Flowers usually very pale violet** or whitish. Whorls closely crowded together at tip of inflorescence, more widely spaced below. Bracts usually inconspicuous. May-Oct. Occasional, probably usually as escape from cultivation. (Ma, Mi, I) FE III 185
15. *Mentha spicata* L. Spearmint. **Leaf-length usually twice width**, not rugose. Whorls of flowers usually more widely spaced than in 14, with conspicuous bracts, and **corolla more deeply coloured**. (Ma, I) FE III 186

ROSMARINUS

16. *Rosmarinus officinalis* L. Rosemary. Shrub, erect or trailing, up to 2m, but flowering when only a few cm. Jan.-Mar. Common in rocky areas. (Ma, Mi, I) FE III 187

LAVANDULA

17. *Lavandula dentata* L. Grey tomentose shrub. Leaves oblong-linear, very regularly and closely crenate. Flowers small, purple in long-pedunculate head with dark purple bracts. Jan.-May. Local in dry rocky places. (Ma, I) FE III 188

SALVIA

18. *Salvia verbenaca* L. Lower leaves deeply lobed or pinnatifid. Bracts in inflorescence much smaller than leaves and shorter than calyx. Whorls distant. Some flowers cleistogamous. Corolla blue-lilac. Feb.-June. Common. (Ma, Mi, I) FE III 192

Other records for Mallorca:
Likely, but mostly rare:

Nepeta cataria L. Catmint. Stems up to 100cm. Leaves ovate, cordate at base and grey-tomentose beneath. Inflorescence spike like, with the lower whorls distant. Flowers 7-10mm, white with small purple spots. Llorens lists. (Ma, Mi) FE III 159

Prunella vulgaris L. Self-heal. As 4, but leaves always entire, flowers smaller, pinkish to bluish purple, more numerous. Llorens lists. (Ma, Mi, I) FE III 162

Acinos arvensis (Lam.) Dandy. Hairy annual. Whorls 3-8-flowered, corolla deep violet with white marks on lower lip. Llorens lists. (Ma) FE III 166

Micromeria graeca (L.) Bentham ex Reichenb. Resembles 7 and 8, but the small leaves are linear in the inflorescence. Llorens lists. (Ma, I) FE III 169

Micromeria inodora (Desf.) Bentham (= *Satureja barceloi* (Willk.) Pau). Flowers in winter – which tends to overlooking. Ericoid dwarf shrub, with crowded, erect branches. Leaves 2-3 x 0.5mm, rigid, evergreen. Corolla 8-10mm, purple. Listed but not seen by Duvigneaud. Llorens lists. (Ma, I) FE III 170

Origanum virens Hoffmanns. & Link. Genus recognised by regularly overlapping 2-ranked bracts in inflorescence – in this species twice as long as calyx, pale green. Llorens lists. (Ma) FE III 171

Thymus herba-barona Loisel. Fairly recent new record for Mallorca. (Formerly only Corsica and Sardinia). Not BI in FE III 180

Lavandula stoechas L. Resembles 17, but leaves linear, entire. See Rita J. et al. (1985). (Ma, Mi, I) FE III 187

Salvia viridis L. Annual. Stems erect, with whorls of pink or violet flowers, often with conspicuous bicoloured bracts. Llorens lists. (Ma). Not BI in FE III 192

In other islands:
Stachys brachyclada De Noë ex Cosson. Ibiza. FE III 157
Nepeta nepetella L. Minorca. FE III 160
Thymus vulgaris L. Ibiza. FE III 176
Thymus richardii Pers. subsp. *ebusitanus* (Font Quer) Jalas. (Ibiza, endemic subsp.). FE III 180

Plate 57

SOLANACEAE: *LYCIUM, HYOSCYAMUS, WITHANIA, SOLANUM, LYCOPERSICON, (MANDRAGORA), DATURA), NICOTIANA*

LYCIUM

1. *Lycium intricatum* Boiss. A very spiny small shrub. Corolla pinkish-purple, narrowly funnel-shaped with 5 small lobes. Very local. (Ma) Not BI in FE III 194

HYOSCYAMUS

2. *Hyoscyamus albus* L. White Henbane. Annual to perennial sticky herb up to about 50cm. Common in waste places. (Ma, Mi, I) FE III 195

WITHANIA

3. *Withania somnifera* (L.) Dunal. Grey stellate-tomentose shrub up to 1.2m. Flowers in clusters of 4-6, patent on short pedicels; corolla about 5mm, yellowish-green. Apr.-Aug. Occasional. (Specimen from Spanish mainland). (Ma, Mi, I) FE III 195

4. *Withania frutescens* (L.) Pauquy. Hairless shrub up to 1.8m. Flowers usually solitary, nodding, corolla 8-15mm. Rare. **NS**. (Specimen from Spanish mainland). Knoche records from Ibiza only. Apr.-Aug. (Ma, Mi, I) FE III 195

SOLANUM

5. *Solanum nigrum* L. Black Nightshade. Annual up to 70cm, variably hairy. Mar.-May. Common in waste places. (Ma, Mi, I) FE III 197

6. *Solanum luteum* Miller. Very like 5, but with red berries. Mar.-May. Common. (Ma, Mi, I) FE III 197

7. *Solanum ducamara* L. Woody Nightshade. Scrambling perennial. Apr.-June. Rare. **NS**. (From British specimen). (Ma, I) FE III 198

8. *Solanum bonariense* L. Shrub to 3m, spectacular in flower. May-Aug. Commonly cultivated, more or less naturalised in places. (S. America). (Ma) FE III 199

9. *Solanum sodomeum* L. Prickly shrub to 3m or more, with very poisonous yellow 'tomatoes'. Common near sea. Introduced (Africa). (Ma, I) FE III 199

LYCOPERSICON

10. *Lycopersicon esculentum* Miller. Tomato. Common casual. FE III 199

NICOTIANA

11. *Nicotiana glauca* R.C.Graham. Shrub Tobacco. Hairless, blue-green shrub or small tree to 6m. May-Oct. Introduced from S. America, widely naturalised, especially in the South. (Ma, I) ?BI in FE III 201

Other species recorded from Mallorca:

Lycium europaeum L. Barceló (1867-1877) records. Llorens treats as alien. BI in FE III 194

Solanum sublobatum Willd. = *S. ottonis* Hyl., which Llorens records for Ma. Not BI in FE III 197

Mandragora autumnalis Bertol. Bianor (1910-1914). No recent records. ?BI in FE III 200

Datura stramonium L. Llorens records for Ma and I. BI excluded in FE III 200

In Ibiza only:

Datura innoxia Miller. Not BI in FE III 200
Nicotiana rustica L. ?Ibiza. ?BI in FE III 201

Plate 58

SCROPHULARIACEAE (1): *VERBASCUM, SCROPHU-LARIA, ANTIRRHINUM, MISOPATES, CHAENOR-RHINUM*

VERBASCUM

1. *Verbascum creticum* (L.) Cav. Tall greyish biennial. Inflorescence unbranched. **Flowers solitary in the axil of each bract.** Upper petals with reddish blotch at base. Stamens 4, unequal, the lower with decurrent anthers. **NS.** Seen by Duvigneaud. (Specimen from Spanish mainland). (Ma, Mi, I) FE III 209

2. *Verbascum thapsus* L. subsp. *crassifolium* (Lam.) Murb. Tall greyish biennial. Inflorescence unbranched. Bracts and upper leaves long-decurrent. Flowers in clusters in axils of at least lower bracts, sometimes solitary above. **Stamens 5, filaments of upper stamens with white hairs,** lower two sometimes hairless. May-July. Locally common. (x 1/10, details x 1). (Ma) FE III 211

3. *Verbascum boerhavii* L. Tall woolly biennial. Inflorescence **usually unbranched.** Flowers in clusters. **Stamens 5, with violet-haired filaments.** May-July. Local and occasional. (x 1/10, details x 1). (Ma) FE III 211

4. *Verbascum sinuatum* L. Grey woolly biennial, with **wavy-edged** round-lobed pinnatifid basal **leaves. Inflorescence much-branched,** up to 100cm. Flowers in clusters. **Stamens 5, with violet-haired filaments.** Apr.-Oct. Common, roadsides and waste places.(Plant x 1/20, leaf from rosette x 1/4, part of inflorescence x 1/2). (Ma, Mi, I) FE III 213

SCROPHULARIA

5. *Scrophularia peregrina* L. Annual. Leaves irregularly saw-toothed. **Bracts mostly leaf-like.** Apr.-July. Locally common. (Ma, Mi, I) FE III 218

6. *Scrophularia auriculata* L. Water Betony, Water Figwort. Perennial, up to 100cm. **Stem 4-angled, the angles winged.** Leaves simple, crenate. Apr.-July. Occasional in damp places. (Ma, Mi, I) FE III 219

7. *Scrophularia ramosissima* Loisel. Shrubby perennial up to 50cm. Stems very numerous, densely and intricately branched, the branches patent and ascending. Persistent dead branches hard and prickly, but not actually spiny. Leaves pinnate or bipinnate, dark green and shining. Flowers crimson or crimson and white, up to 4mm. Apr.-July. Local on beaches. (Ma, Mi) FE III 220

8. *Scrophularia canina* L. Perennial, up to 1m. Up to 10 stems, usually many fewer, the stems sparingly branched. Flowers more than 4mm, crimson with broad white margin. (? subsp. *bicolor* (Sibth. & Sm.) W.Greuter, described in FE for SE Europe). (Ma, Mi, I) FE III 220

ANTIRRHINUM

9. *Antirrhinum majus* L. Snapdragon. Perennial. Apr.-May. Llorens treats as garden escape. Sometimes in waste places. (Ma) FE III 223

MISOPATES

10. *Misopates orontium* (L.) Rafin. Weasel's Snout. Annual, like a small pink Snapdragon. Apr.-May. Common, walls and roadsides. (Ma, Mi, I) FE III 224

CHAENORRHINUM

11. *Chaenorrhinum origanifolium* (L.) Fourr. subsp. *origanifolium.* Perennial, up to about 35cm. Leaves entire, opposite above. Racemes lax, of 9-20mm blue-violet flowers, with the tube produced into a straight spur. May-July. **NS.** Seen by Duvigneaud. (From garden specimen). (Ma) FE III 225

12. *Chaenorrhinum rubrifolium* (Robill. & Cast. ex DC.) Fourr. subsp. *rubrifolium.* Annual. Leaves ovate, the lowest red beneath and usually forming a basal rosette. Corolla resembles that of 11, but with yellow palate and lower lip. Apr.-July. **NS.** Not seen by Duvigneaud. Rare in sandy places. (Illustration after line drawing in Knoche's Flora Balearica, coloured after his description: corolla slightly enlarged, seed x 2). (Ma) FE III 226

Also recorded for Mallorca:

Verbascum blattaria L. Biennial. Flowers solitary, corolla yellow or white. **Stamens 5: filament hairs of 3 upper stamens white and purple, of two lower purple only.** Llorens lists. (Ma) Not BI in FE III 208

In Ibiza:

Chaenorrhinum origanifolium (L.) Fourr. subsp. *crassifolium* (Cav.) Rivas Goday & Borja. FE III 225

Chaenorrhinum rubrifolium (Robill. & Cast. ex DC.) Fourr. subsp. *formenterae* (Gand.) R. Fernandes. (Ibiza and Formentera endemic subsp.). FE III 226

Plate 59

SCROPHULARIACEAE (2): *LINARIA, CYMBALARIA, KICKXIA*

LINARIA

1. *Linaria triphylla* (L.) Miller. Hairless, bluish green annual, usually up to about 25cm. Leaves entire, elliptical or obovate, in whorls, some usually opposite or alternate. Corolla 20-30mm, white, yellow or violet, with yellow boss and violet spur. Apr.-May. Common, fields and waysides. (Slightly enlarged). (Ma, Mi, I) FE III 230

2. *Linaria chalepensis* (L.) Miller. Hairless green annual. Corolla 12-16mm, white. Apr. **NS.** Seen by Duvigneaud. (From Greek specimen x 2/3). (Ma, Mi, I) FE III 231

3. (*Linaria repens* (L.) Miller. Hairless perennial. Leaves more or less linear, whorled, sometimes alternate above. Corolla 8-15mm, white with violet veins. Presence here dubious. (From British specimen). ?BI in FE III 231

4. *Linaria pelisseriana* (L.) Miller. Hairless blue-green annual. Corolla 15-20mm, purple violet, often with white palate. Apr.-May. **NS.** Seen by Duvigneaud. (Specimen from Spanish mainland). (Ma, Mi) FE III 232

5. *Linaria aeruginea* (Gouan) Cav. subsp. *pruinosa* (Sennen & Pau) Chater & Valdés. Ascending blue-green perennial. Leaves linear, with revolute margins, whorled below, alternate above. Racemes with 1-6 flowers. Calyx with reddish stalked glands. Corolla 15-27mm, shades of orange-brown and reddish, with darker stripes. Apr.-July. Occasional in higher parts of mountains. (Slightly enlarged). (Ma, endemic subsp.) FE III 233

CYMBALARIA

6. *Cymbalaria muralis* P.Gaertner, B.Meyer & Scherb. Ivy-leaved Toadflax. Trailing perennial. Leaves with 5-9 lobes, hairless at maturity. Corolla up to 15mm, bluish violet with yellow palate. Apr.-Aug. Fairly common on walls. (Ma, Mi, I) FE III 237

7. *Cymbalaria aequitriloba* (Viv.) A.Cheval subsp. *aequitriloba*. Resembles 6, but leaves hairy at maturity 3-5-lobed. Palate always white. Apr.-July. Common in damp shady places in mountains. (Rather variable. Lower specimen x 1, upper from a different site, much more robust, x 1 1/2). (Ma, Mi) FE III 237

KICKXIA

8. *Kickxia cirrhosa* (L.) Fritsch. Annual, stems very slender, trailing. Leaves narrow spear-shaped, acute. Flowers axillary, on long very slender pedicels, 4-6mm, violet. May-June. Sandy places near the sea, not common. (Main illustration x 1, details x 3). (Ma, Mi) FE III 238

9. *Kickxia commutata* (Bernh. ex Reichenb.) Fritsch. Procumbent perennial. Leaves broadly ovate below, with arrow-or spear-shaped base in peripheral parts of plant. Pedicels long, hairless except just below flower. Corolla 11-15mm, whitish, with white or slightly yellowish lower lip and purple-spotted palate. Occasional in grassy places. (Ma, Mi, I) FE III 238

10. *Kickxia spuria* (L.) Dumort subsp. *integrifolia* (Brot.) R.Fernandes. Glandular hairy annual. Leaves with rounded or cordate base, petiole very short. Flowers 10-15mm, deep yellow with purple upper lip. Spur curved. (Ma, Mi, I) FE III 239

11. *Kickxia lanigera* (Desf.) Hand.-Mazz. Procumbent densely villous annual. Leaves broadly ovate, usually cordate in distal part of stem. Corolla 8-11mm, bluish-white with violet upper lip. Pedicels very hairy, longer or shorter than corolla. May-Sept. Occasional in grassy places. (Ma, I) FE III 239

Other species recorded for Mallorca:

Linaria arvensis (L.) Desf. Blue-green annual. Stem erect. Flowers 2.5-9mm in dense terminal raceme. Spur 1.5-3mm, strongly curved. Listed but not seen by Duvigneaud. Llorens lists. (Ma) FE III 236

Linaria simplex (Willd.) DC. Similar to *L. arvensis*, but spur straight 2-3.5mm, corolla pale yellow, sometimes with violet veins. Not seen by Duvigneaud. Llorens lists. (Ma, I) FE III 236

Linaria micrantha (Cav.) Hoffmanns. & Link. Also similar to *L. arvensis*, but corolla 2.5-5mm lilac-blue, spur 1mm. Listed but not seen by Duvigneaud. Llorens lists. (Ma) FE III 236

Kickxia elatine (L.) Dumort. Similar to 10 above, but with spear-shaped leaves. Llorens lists. (Ma, I) FE III 238

In other islands:

Linaria pedunculata (L.) Chaz. Formentera. Not BI in FE III 228

Cymbalaria aequitriloba subsp. *fragilis* (Rodr.) D.A.Webb. (Minorca: endemic subsp.). FE III 237

Plate 60

SCROPHULARIACEAE (3): *DIGITALIS, ERINUS, VERONICA, SIBTHORPIA, PARENTUCELLIA, BELLARDIA*

DIGITALIS

1. *Digitalis dubia* Rodr. Balearic Foxglove. Rather like *Digitalis purpurea* L., but generally smaller, fewer-flowered and with long soft hairs on leaves and stems and on outside of corolla. May-July. Locally common in rock crevices. (Ma, Mi) FE III 240

ERINUS

2. *Erinus alpinus* L. Fairy Foxglove. Small hairy, cushion-forming perennial with erect stems, usually less than 10cm, with racemes of small irregular 5-petalled pink flowers. May-June. Very local in the mountains. (Specimen from Spanish mainland, not differing significantly from plant found later in Mallorca). (Ma) FE III 241

VERONICA

Annual or perennial herbs. Leaves opposite at least below, often alternate in inflorescence. Flowers in terminal or axillary racemes. Calyx and corolla with 4 lobes, the corolla lobes usually blue and unequal. Stamens 2. Fruit usually a more or less heart-shaped capsule.

3. *Veronica anagalloides* Guss. Annual. Stem usually about 50cm, sometimes with long branches from the base. Flowers in long axillary **racemes, up to 6 x as long as subtending leaves. Leaves** linear-lanceolate, **sessile**, more or less serrate. Corolla 3-5mm, lilac or whitish according to FE, but in this specimen definitely blue. Capsule elliptical, not notched except when beginning to open. Occasional, in wet mud. (Ma, Mi, I) FE III 248

4. *Veronica anagallis-aquatica* L. Water-Speedwell. Usually perennial. Upper leaves sessile, more or less amplexicaul, **lower leaves often stalked.** Flowers in long axillary **racemes, up to 3 x as long as subtending leaves. Corolla 5-10mm**, bluish-violet with darker veins. Capsule orbicular, egg-shaped or elliptical. Calyx erect in fruit. Apr.-Sept. Fairly common in wet places. (Main illustration x 1/2, details x 3). (Ma, Mi, I) FE III 248

5. *Veronica catenata* Pennel. Pink Water-Speedwell. Like 4, but all leaves sessile and **corolla** 3-5mm, **pink** with darker veins. Capsule wider than long, emarginate. **NS.** (From British specimen, corolla x 4. Possibly dubious here). FE III 248)

6. *Veronica arvensis* L. Wall Speedwell. **Erect annual.** Leaves ovate, crenate, the upper sessile and lower petiolate. **Flowers solitary in leaf-axils. Corolla** 2-3mm, all **lobes deep blue.** Capsule flat heart-shaped, usually hairless apart from marginal cilia. (Ma, I) FE III 249

7. *Veronica verna* L. Spring Speedwell. Resembles 6, but **upper leaves pinnatifid** with narrow lobes. Capsule kidney-shaped, flat, glandular-hairy. (Garden specimen from British seed). Possibly dubious here. Not BI in FE III 249)

8. *Veronica polita* Fries. Grey Field Speedwell. Procumbent annual. Flowers solitary axillary. **Calyx lobes usually overlapping. Corolla** 4-8mm, **blue**, the upper lobe usually darker. **Capsule rounded, not flattened**, with glandular and eglandular hairs. Dec.-June. Fairly common. (Ma, Mi, I) FE III 250

9. *Veronica persica* Poiret. Buxbaum's Speedwell. Procumbent annual. **Flowers** solitary in leaf-axils, **with long pedicels much exceeding the subtending leaf, recurved in fruit.** Corolla 8-12mm, blue. Capsule with very divergent lobes, flattened and strongly keeled. Mar.-May. Very common in cultivated ground. (Ma, Mi, I) FE III 250

10. *Veronica hederifolia* L. subsp. *hederifolia.* Ivy-leaved Speedwell. Slightly fleshy annual, with numerous procumbent stems. Flowers solitary in leaf-axils, pedicels not or hardly exceeding subtending leaf. **Flowers** small, 6-9mm, **pale blue with a white centre.** Calyx strongly ciliate. **Capsule shallowly 4-lobed, not compressed,** hairless. (Ma, Mi, I) FE III 250 (subsp. *triloba* (Opiz) Celak, with dark blue flowers also occurs in Mallorca).

11. *Veronica cymbalaria* Bodard. Procumbent annual, rather like 10, but with leaves more lobed, pedicels longer and **flowers white.** Calyx lobes blunt, spreading in fruit. **Capsule shallowly 4-lobed, not compressed.** Jan.-Apr. Common in cultivated areas. (Ma, Mi, I) FE III 250

SIBTHORPIA

12. *Sibthorpia africana* L. Creeping perennial. Leaves kidney-shaped to round, crenate, hairy. Flowers 4-7mm, tubular at base, with 5 equal yellow lobes. Jan.-Sept. Common on damp rocks in shady places. (Ma, Mi, I, endemic) FE III 252

PARENTUCELLIA

13. *Parentucellia viscosa* (L.) Caruel. Yellow Bartsia. Erect sticky annual. Leaves opposite, sessile more or less lanceolate, coarsely serrate. Bracts like the leaves, becoming smaller above. Corolla 16-24mm, 2-lipped, bright yellow, upper lobe entire and lower 3-lobed. Apr.-July. Common in grassy places. (Ma, Mi, I) FE III 269

14. *Parentucellia latifolia* (L.) Caruel. Very sticky annual. Leaves triangular-lanceolate, very deeply toothed. Corolla 8-10mm, red, pink or white or with various combinations of these. Mar.-May. Not very common, sandy places often under pine. (Ma, Mi) FE III 269

BELLARDIA

15. *Bellardia trixago* (L.) All. Annual, resembling 13. Corolla 20-25mm, usually with pink upper lip and white lower lip, lower lip rarely pale yellow. Apr.-July. Common in grassy places. (Ma, Mi, I) FE III 269

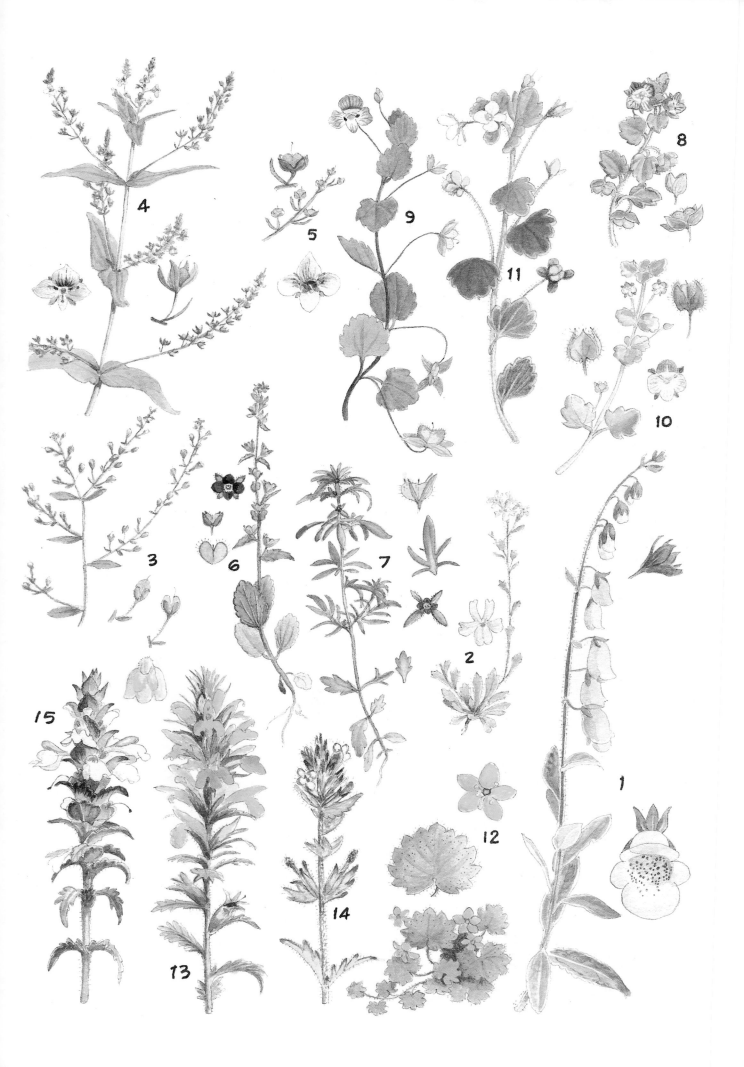

Plate 61

GLOBULARIACEAE: *GLOBULARIA*
(ACANTHACEAE): *ACANTHUS*
OROBANCHACEAE: *OROBANCHE*

GLOBULARIACEAE
GLOBULARIA

1. *Globularia cambessedesii* Willk. Herbaceous perennial. Heads 3.5cm in diameter. Apr.-May. Local in rock crevices of Nothern mountains. (Ma endemic) FE III 282
2. *Globularia alypum* L. Small shrub. Heads up to 2.5cm. Corolla usually blue, sometimes white with a pink base. Oct.-Apr. Locally common in dry scrub. (Ma, Mi, I) FE III 283

OROBANCHACEAE
OROBANCHE

These are difficult to identify and variable. For clear identification fresh specimens should be used with a key. Illustrations here offer only tentative identification.

3. *Orobanche ramosa* L. Three rather ill-defined subspecies are recorded here. Main illustration (x 1) and upper detail are subsp. *nana* (Reuter) Coutinho, which seems fairly common here, lower details are from a much-branched plant with numerous flowers ? subsp. *mutelii* (F.W. Schultz) Coutinho or *ramosa*. Apr.-Oct. Subsp. *nana* at least common here: Duvigneaud records having seen this subsp. Bonafè lists all three subsp. in the text of his book, but not in his *Tabulae Plantarum* Appendix II. Llorens does not differentiate between subsp. (Ma, Mi) FE III 288
4. *Orobanche rosmarina* G. Beck. Possibly not previously recorded. Found by F. Rumsey and illustrated from his photographs. **NS**. Rare. (Ma) Not BI in FE III 288
5. *Orobanche crenata* Forskål. Bean Broomrape. Corolla 20-30mm, opening out at mouth, with large rounded and frilled lobes, white or pale pinkish-purple with darker markings. Stigma white, yellow or pinkish. Apr.-June. Common, parasitic on leguminous crops, especially Broad Bean. (Ma, Mi, I) FE III 290
6. *Orobanche loricata* Reichenb. Long bracts often conspicuous. Spike rather pointed until top flowers open. Corolla 14-22mm, white or yellowish tinged and veined with violet. Upper lip emarginate or bifid. Stigma purple. Occasional. Parasitic on species of Compositae, also on *Daucus carota* L. (Ma) FE III 291
7. *Orobanche minor* Sm. Resembles 6, though top of stem with unopened buds usually dome-shaped rather than spire-like, and bracts less conspicuous. Flowers relatively small (corolla 10-18mm), pale yellow tinged with dull violet distally. Stigma purple, rarely yellow. June-Sept. Occasional. Llorens lists. (Ma) Not BI in FE III 291
8. *Orobanche ?clausonis* Pomel. (See Foley M.J.Y. (1996) *Anales Jard. Bot. Madrid* 54: 319-326: he refers to 'A single, rather inadequate specimen from the Balearics [Majorca, 1985. Beckett (RNG)]'). An odd-looking plant almost uniformly yellowish-ochre, which was tentatively identified as this species by F. Rumsey. (Illustrated from this plant). Not previously recorded here. FE III 292
9. *Orobanche hederae* Duby. Ivy Broomrape. Spike rather lax, corolla 10-22mm, dull cream tinged with purple. Stigma yellow. Common, parasitic on Ivy. (Main illustration x 1 from Mallorcan specimen, detail from British specimen). (Ma, Mi, I) FE III 292
(*Orobanche balearica* Sennen & Pau is 9 according to Med-Checklist, though Knoche treats as separate species).
10. *Orobanche gracilis* Sm. Corolla yellow outside, shining bright red inside. Stigma yellow. May-July. Rare. **NS**. (From Greek specimen x 3/4). Seen by Duvigneaud. Parasitic on Leguminosae and *Cistus* species. (Ma, ?I) FE III 293

Also recorded from Mallorca:

Acanthus mollis L. Bear's Breeches. Tall herbaceous perennial slightly resembling a large *Orobanche*, though it has green leaves. May-July. Common relic of garden cultivation. (Ma, Mi) FE III 283

Orobanche purpurea Jacq. Whole plant glandular-puberulent, with greyish tinge. Corolla 18-25mm, narrowly campanulate, white below and bluish-violet distally with purple veins. Stigma white or pale blue. Smythies lists this species, though Bonafè adds 'a verificar'. Llorens omits. ?BI in FE III 289

Orobanche foetida Poiret. Corolla dark purplish-red outside, shining dark red inside. Seen by Knoche. Listed by Llorens. BI in FE III 293

In other islands:
Orobanche ramosa subsp. *mutelii* Ibiza. FE III 288
Orobanche lavandulaceae Reichenb. Ibiza. FE III 288
Orobanche latisquama (F.W.Schultz) Batt. Ibiza. FE III 292
Orobanche sanguinea C. Presl. Minorca. FE III 293

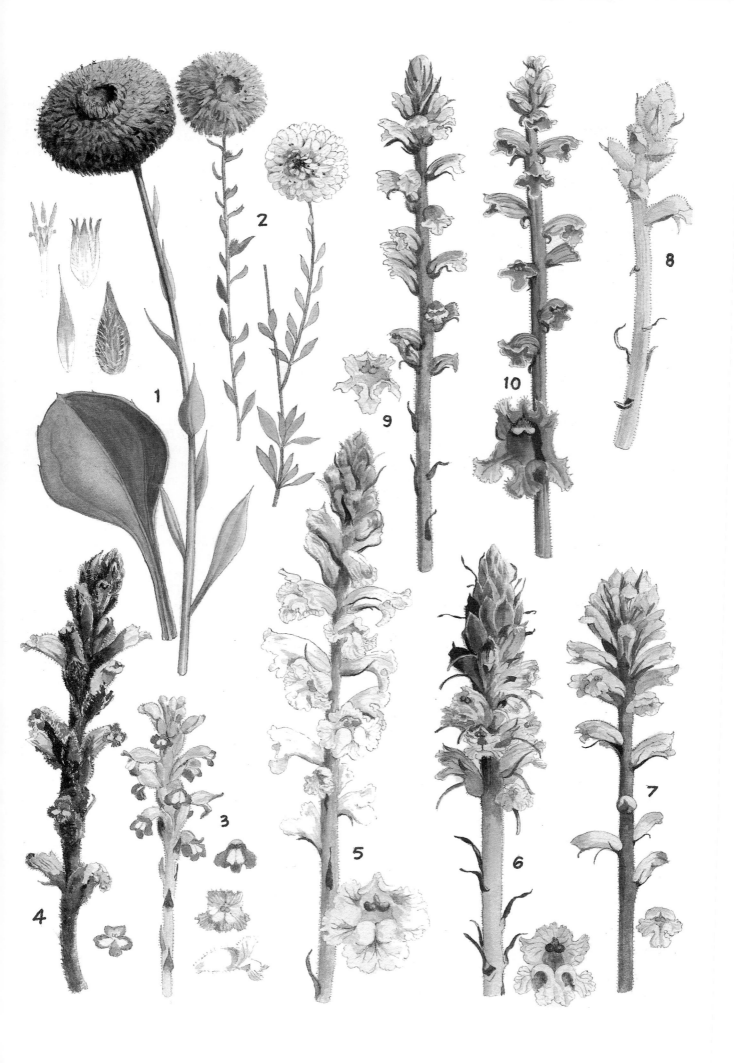

Plate 62

PLANTAGINACEAE: *PLANTAGO*
CAPRIFOLIACEAE: *SAMBUCUS, VIBURNUM, LONICERA*

PLANTAGINACEAE
PLANTAGO

Herbs. All leaves in a basal rosette (except in 8). Flowers small, 4-merous in pedunculate spikes. Sepals connate at base. Petals scarious. Main illustrations x 1, details enlarged.

1. *Plantago major*. L. Plantain. **Leaves broad, abruptly contracted into stalk. Spike usually much exceeding peduncle.** Apr.-Nov. Very common. (Small specimen: one specimen found here had spike about 60cm without the peduncle!). (Ma, Mi, I) FE IV 39
2. *Plantago coronopus* L. subsp. *coronopus*. Buck's horn plantain. **Leaves linear to lanceolate, hairy, pinnate. Spike usually much exceeding peduncle.** Bract subtending flower with broad base and long narrow apex. Apr.-Oct. Common near the sea. (Ma, Mi, I) FE IV 40
   Subsp. *purpurascens*, with purplish spikes and ovate subacute bracts also occurs here. Not common. **NS.** Not seen by Duvigneaud. (Ma endemic subsp.)
3. *Plantago crassifolia* Forskål. **Leaves linear, fleshy, hairless or slightly hairy, usually with a few small teeth. Spike usually much exceeding peduncle.** Bracts subtending flower short, rounded. Apr.-Oct. Damp saline soils. Common in this habitat. (Ma, Mi, I) FE IV 40
4. *Plantago lanceolata* L. Ribwort Plantain. Perennial. **Spike very dense, much shorter than peduncle. Bracts and calyx hairless or shortly hairy.** Anterior sepals connate for most of length. Corolla hairless. Common in grassy places. (Ma, Mi, I) FE IV 42
   FE describes this plant as very variable: certainly the Mallorcan plant, which Llorens names var. *sphaerostachya* Mart. & Koch, looks distinctly unlike the British plant. Usually with a larger, more elliptical head.
5. *Plantago lagopus* L. Rather like 4, but sometimes annual. **Bracts and calyx densely villous with long hairs.** Unopened apex of spike softly greenish-white hairy. Apr.-May. Common. (Ma, Mi, I) FE IV 43
6. *Plantago albicans* L. Perennial. **Leaves densely silvery-haired often wavy-edged.** Spike longer or shorter than peduncle. **Stamens long-exserted** (4-7mm) with whitish anthers. Apr.-June. Local. (Ma, Mi, I) FE IV 43

7. *Plantago bellardii* All. Hairy annual, bright green. **Spike much shorter than peduncle** (usually about 1cm or less), short ovoid. **Corolla white** (all others here more or less straw-coloured). Calyx-lobes and bracts pointed. May-June. Local in dry stony or sandy ground. (Ma, Mi, I) FE IV 43
8. *Plantago afra* L. Annual, glandular hairy above. Differs from the others in having a **branched stem and no basal rosette.** Flowers in pedunculate axillary spikes. (Ma, Mi, I) FE IV 44

CAPRIFOLIACEAE
SAMBUCUS

9. *Sambucus ebulus* L. Danewort. Stout perennial usually about 1m. Inflorescence corymbose, flowers white, about 1cm diameter. Fruit globose, black. (Upper part stem much reduced, flower slightly enlarged, fruit x 1). Locally common (especially around Lluc, where it appears to be a troublesome weed). (Ma, Mi, I) FE IV 44

VIBURNUM

10. *Viburnum tinus* L. Laurustinus. Evergreen shrub with hairless, dark green ovate leaves. Mature flowers in corymbs, white, buds pinkish. Dec.-Mar. Occasional in rocky places in mountain areas. (Ma) FE IV 45

LONICERA

11. *Lonicera pyrenaica* L. subsp. *majoricensis* (Gand.) Browicz. Small shrub. Leaves leathery narrow obovate, in opposite pairs. Flowers in pedunculate pairs. Corolla 12-15mm, tube much longer than limb, white or pinkish. Berries globose, red. June. Rare in mountains. (Ma, endemic subsp.) FE IV 46
12. *Lonicera implexa* Aiton. Minorca Honeysuckle. Climbing shrub, sweetly scented. Differs from *L. periclymenum* L. (common Honeysuckle) mainly in the connate pairs of leaves in the upper parts of twigs and connate bracts encircling the inflorescence. (Ma, Mi, I) FE IV 47

In Minorca:
Plantago macrorhiza Poiret. Not BI in FE IV 40

Plate 63

VALERIANACEAE: *VALERIANELLA, FEDIA, CENTRANTHUS*
DIPSACACEAE: *CEPHALARIA, DIPSACUS, SCABIOSA, (KNAUTIA)*
CAMPANULACEAE: *CAMPANULA, LEGOUSIA, TRACHELIUM, LAURENTIA*

VALERIANACEAE
VALERIANELLA

Small, often very similar, dichotomously branched annual herbs, flowering here in April to May. Leaves are opposite. Flowers, with 5 slightly unequal corolla lobes and more or less developed calyx in terminal clusters, sometimes solitary in dichotomies of inflorescence. The ovary is inferior, 3-locular with 2 loculi sterile and sometimes small. Ripe fruit is needed to distinguish between species, and particular attention should be paid to the persistent calyx on top of the fruit (sometimes absent).

1. *Valerianella discoidea* (L.) Loisel. Petals 5, blue. Calyx longer than densely hairy fruit, with 8-15 hooked teeth. (Ma, Mi, I) FE IV 50
2. *Valerianella eriocarpa* Desv. Petals 5, blue. Fruit and tiara-like calyx slightly hairy. Calyx almost as long as fruit with 5 or 6 short teeth. (*V. muricata* (Steven ex Bieb.) J.W.Loudon (left hand detail) has fewer or no teeth. It is not a distinct species). Both common in waste places. (Ma, Mi, I) FE IV 51
3. *Valerianella microcarpa* Loisel. Petals 4, pink. Calyx an indistinct rim. Common in waste places. (Ma, Mi, I) FE IV 51

FEDIA

4. *Fedia cornucopiae* (L.) Gaertner. Hairless slightly succulent annual. Flowers in terminal paired heads, 8-16mm, with a long tube and 5 unequal pinkish-purple lobes with deep red markings at the base of the lower 3. Apr.-June. Mainly in the South. **NS.** Seen by Duvigneaud. (From Portuguese specimen). (Ma) FE IV 52

CENTRANTHUS

5. *Centranthus ruber* (L.) DC. Dustman's Breeches. Robust perennial. Leaves undivided, the upper amplexicaul. Flowers in cymose inflorescence with dense terminal heads. Corolla red, pink or white, tube 7-10mm with a basal spur, and 5 unequal lobes. One stamen. Apr.-Sept. Common, usually as a garden escape. (Ma, I) FE IV 55
6. *Centranthus calcitrapae* (L.) Dufresne. Annual. Upper leaves pinnatifid, lower variable. Inflorescence as 5, but smaller. Corolla pink, spur minute and difficult to see. Apr.-July. Very common, and very variable in size, flowering when tiny. (Ma, Mi) FE IV 56

DIPSACACEAE
CEPHALARIA

7. *Cephalaria squamiflora* (Sieber) W. Greuter, subsp. *balearica* (Willk.) W.Greuter. Robust scabious like perennial with white flowers. Aug. Rare in mountains. Seen by Duvigneaud. (Ma, I endemic subsp.) FE IV 57

DIPSACUS

8. *Dipsacus fullonum* L. Teasel. Tall prickly biennial with ovoid heads and long upward-curving involucral bracts. May-July. Fairly common. (Ma, I) FE IV 59

SCABIOSA

9. *Scabiosa cretica* L. Large woody-based perennial. Leaves entire, obovate-lanceolate with appressed silky hairs. Heads 35-50mm diameter held well above the leaves on long stems. Florets pale purplish-pink, marginal florets larger than central. Fruiting head globular, white. Corona in fruit white with darker veins. May-July. Occasional in rocky places. (Ma, Mi, I) FE IV 69
10. *Scabiosa atropurpurea* L. Tall (commonly 1m) straggling biennial, with branched leafy stems. Upper leaves pinnatifid. Flowers pinkish-purple. Fruiting head green, ovoid. Corona short, exceeded by calyx bristles. Common. (Ma, Mi, I) FE IV 71

CAMPANULACEAE
CAMPANULA

11. *Campanula erinus* L. Small annual. Stem dichotomously branched. Flowers blue, bell-shaped, 3-5mm, surrounded by spreading calyx. May-June. Fairly common, walls and dry places. (Ma, Mi, I) FE IV 88

LEGOUSIA

12. *Legousia falcata* (Ten.) Fritsch. Pubescent annual. Leaves obovate, sessile above, shortly stalked below. Flowers singly or in pairs in leaf axils, spike occupying at least half the stem. Corolla 5-lobed, violet, about 1/3 length of patent or recurved calyx lobes. Apr.-May. Fairly common in the mountain area. (Ma) FE IV 94
13. *Legousia hybrida* (L.) Delarbre. Venus's Looking-Glass. Rather like 12, but flowers in terminal corymbs, corolla about 1/2 length calyx-lobes. Apr.-May. Occasional. (Ma, Mi) FE IV 94

TRACHELIUM

14. *Trachelium caeruleum* L. Throatwort. Superficially rather like 5, but corolla blue, without spurred tube, and with 5 stamens. May-Sept. Locally common garden escape. (Ma) FE IV 94

LAURENTIA

15. *Laurentia tenella* A. DC. Very small perennial with obovate to spathulate leaves in a basal rosette. Flowers solitary on long pedicels. Corolla lilac, with a narrow tube and 5 unequal lobes, the upper two smaller than the lower three. Mar.-Apr. Rather rare. **NS.** Seen by Duvigneaud. (From garden specimen). (Ma) FE IV 102
16. *Laurentia gasparinii* (Tineo) Strobl. Resembles 15, but annual with blue corolla. Mistakenly included in illustration. Occurs in Minorca and Ibiza, not Mallorca. FE IV 102

Other plants recorded for Mallorca:
Valerianella species:
The following key includes all those known to have been recorded in Mallorca:

1. Calyx absent. *V. costata* (Steven) Betcke. (Ma, possibly only very old records).
1. Calyx present.
2. Calyx in fruit not or hardly toothed. *V. microcarpa* Loisel. (Ma, Mi, I) (No 3 above).
2. Calyx in fruit toothed.
3. Calyx much narrower than length of fruit.
4. Calyx reduced to an indistinct tooth at the apex of each horn. *V. echinata* (L.) DC. (Ma, possibly only very old records).
4. Calyx obliquely truncate with unequal teeth. *V. rimosa* Bast. (Ma, possibly only very old records).
3. Calyx in fruit almost length of fruit or longer.
5. Calyx longer than fruit, crown-like, densely hairy inside, with 8-15 teeth. *V. discoidea* (L.) Loisel. (Ma, Mi, I) (No 1).
5. Calyx almost as wide as fruit length, tiara-like, oblique, almost hairless to densely hairy, with 6 teeth. *V. eriocarpa* Desv. (Ma, Mi, I)

V. coronata (L.) DC and *V. carinata* Loisel., both BI in FE, probably do not occur here.

Knautia integrifolia (L.) Bertol. Duvigneaud queries. Llorens lists. BI in FE IV 67

Scabiosa stellata L. A pubescent annual scabious with pale bluish florets, the outer enlarged. Corona 6-9.5mm, slightly exceeded by the 5 calyx setae and excurrent veins. Possibly old records only. FE IV 70

Scabiosa monspeliensis Jacq. Resembles *S. stellata*, but marginal florets not or hardly enlarged, and calyx setae at least twice as long as corona. Recently recorded. (Rita J. et al. 1985). Not BI in FE IV 71

In Ibiza only:
Campanula dichotoma L. FE IV 84

Plate 64

COMPOSITAE (1): *EUPATORIUM, SOLIDAGO, BEL-
LIS, BELLIUM, ASTER, ERIGERON, CONYZA, FILA-
GO, LOGFIA*

EUPATORIUM

1. *Eupatorium cannabinum* L. Hemp Agrimony. Perennial, usually more than 1m, with opposite palmately divided leaves. Florets all tubular in heads of 5-6 arranged in dense corymbs. May-July. **NS.** Not seen by Duvigneaud. Llorens treats as alien. (From British specimen). (Ma) FE IV 109

SOLIDAGO

2. *Solidago virgaurea* L. Golden Rod. Perennial herb with more or less oblanceolate toothed leaves. Inflorescence a loose panicle with straight erect branches, subtended by bracts resembling the leaves. Heads 6-10mm, with 6-12 ligules. October. **NS.** (Possibly dubious here). Not seen by Duvigneaud. (Ma, I) FE IV 110

BELLIS

3. *Bellis annua* L. Annual Daisy. Resembles the familiar *Bellis perennis* L. (which curiously does not occur here, although almost throughout Europe). Leaves, however, are not in a basal rosette, stem leaves becoming smaller further up the stem. Ligules commonly become pale violet as they age. Oct.-May. Very common. (Ma, Mi, I) FE IV 111

4. *Bellis sylvestris* Cyr. Perennial, like a very large *Bellis perennis* L., with heads 20-40mm diameter. All leaves basal. Oct.-Mar. Widespread, but nowhere common. (Ma, Mi) FE IV 112

BELLIUM

5. *Bellium bellidioides* L. Perennial. Leaves all basal, elliptical, narrowed to a petiole longer than the lamina. Involucral bracts in one row. Apr.-Sept. Common. (Ma, Mi, I) FE IV 112

ASTER

6. *Aster squamatus* (Sprengel) Hieron. Annual or biennial up to 100cm. Leaves linear-lanceolate, entire, sessile. Heads small, very numerous in symmetrical cone-shaped panicle. Involucral bracts in 3 rows, green with a purplish serrulate apex, tapering to a point. Ligulate florets violet blue in more than 1 row, more numerous than the tubular florets. Aug.-Sept. Common on saline soils, especially in the Campos area. (x 1/20, top left detail x 2/3, other slightly enlarged). Native of S. America, introduced. (Ma, Mi, I) FE IV 115

7. *Aster tripolium* L. subsp. *pannonicus* (Jacq.) Soó. Sea Aster. Fleshy annual or perennial, usually up to about 60cm. Leaves linear-lanceolate, sessile above. Ligules bluish-lilac. Sept.-Nov. Common in brackish marshes. (Ma, Mi, I) FE IV 115

ERIGERON

8. *Erigeron karvinskianus* DC. Perennial with lax leafy branches. Leaves entire or 3-lobed. Involucral bracts in several rows, with long fine points. Ligules white, becoming reddish-purple. May-Oct. (Native of Mexico, occasional garden escape). (Ma) FE IV 117

CONYZA

9. *Conyza canadensis* (L.) Cronq. Canadian Fleabane. Branched leafy annual, commonly up to 60cm, in some respects resembling 6, but with very short, 0.5-1mm, more or less erect inconspicuous purplish ligules. Heads less than 1cm wide. June-July. Fairly common. (Part of inflorescence x 1). (Ma, Mi, I) FE IV 120

10. *Conyza bonariensis* (L.) Cronq. Similar to 9, but more densely hairy, and often taller, also generally a much darker green. Heads often more than 1cm wide. Involucral bracts often purple-tipped, ligules up to 0.5mm, shorter than the pappus. All year. Common in waste places. (Native of central America, introduced). (Ma, Mi, I) FE IV 120

(The variant *C. floribunda* Kunth, with a narrow cylindrical inflorescence and very short branches is also common here: lower detail shows flower with greenish involucral bracts).

FILAGO

11. *Filago vulgaris* Lam. Cudweed. Greenish-white to greyish densely tomentose annual, usually erect. **Leaves widest in lower half.** Heads 5 x 1.6mm, in dense globose **clusters of 20-40** terminating main stem and branches. Involucral bracts with fine yellow arista. Apr.-June. **NS.** Seen by Duvigneaud. (From British specimen). (Ma, Mi, I) FE IV 121

12. *Filago pyramidata* L. Annual, much-branched from the base, stems prostrate ore ascending. **Leaves widest in upper half.** Involucre 5-angled. Involucral bracts with short recurved arista. Heads in **clusters of 8-20**, often overtopped by subtending leaves. Apr.-June. Dry waysides and sandy places, common and rather variable. (Ma, Mi, I) FE IV 122

LOGFIA

13. *Logfia gallica* (L.) Cosson & Germ. Narrow Cudweed. Plant greyish, with slender branched erect stems. **Leaves linear to filiform**, acute. Heads 5-angled in **clusters of 2-14. Involucral bracts** not aristate, **spreading to form a star in fruit. NS.** Seen by Duvigneaud. (Ma, Mi, I) FE IV 124

Also in Mallorca:

Conyza sumatrensis (Retz.) E.Walker. Llorens lists. (Ma, Mi, I) Not in FE

Filago congesta Guss. ex DC. Resembles 12, but heads usually in clusters of 3-6, very numerous. Involucral bracts hairy only on the margin, inner bracts obtuse. Mar.-June. Trampled places, mainly in the South. **NS.** Seen by Duvigneaud. (Ma, I) FE IV 122

In Formentera:

Filago fuscescens Pomel. Not BI in FE IV 122

Plate 65

COMPOSITAE (2): *EVAX, BOMBYCILAENA, GNAPHA-LIUM, HELICHRYSUM, PHAGNALON*

EVAX

1. *Evax pygmaea* (L.) Brot. subsp. *pygmaea*. Annual, green or silvery, with short lateral branches terminated by rosettes of leaves 5-15 x 2-5 (-8)mm, which enclose one, or clusters of several heads of small greenish florets, surrounded by narrow brownish aristate involucral bracts. Apr.-May. Common in dry places. (Ma, Mi, I) FE IV 124

2. *Filago petro-ianii* Rita & Dittrich (sp. nov. 1989). Very small annual. Stem short, with or without procumbent axillary branches. Stem leaves linear, 4 x 0.5mm. Rosette leaves about 6mm long with an enlarged rhomboid apical part with an acuminate tip with inrolled margins. Heads about 4mm diameter, solitary or forming a flat cushion-shaped cluster with 3-5 peripherally inserted heads. Rare and local. **NS.** (Ma new endemic). Not in FE – see Dittrich M. and Rita J. in Kit Tan (ed.) *Plant Taxonomy, Phytogeography and Related Subjects. The Davis and Hedge Festschrift* pp 1-9, Edinburgh University Press (1989). Illustration x 3.

BOMBYCILAENA

3. *Bombycilaena ?erecta* (L.) Smolj. Erect silvery-white annual. Heads small, in terminal and axillary clusters. Inner involucral bracts pouched, each enclosing one of the peripheral florets. Rare in mountains. (Plant illustrated here was collected near one of the higher peaks. It appears to be *B. erecta*, lacking the brownish-yellow colouration of the heads of *B. discolor* (Pers.) Laínz. The leaves are undulate. Knoche records *Micropus erectus* L. var *bombycinus* Lag. FE equates *M. bombycinus* Lag. with *Bombycilaena discolor*. Llorens lists only *B. discolor* (Ma, Mi, I), and FE gives only *B. discolor* for Balearic Islands.

GNAPHALIUM

4. *Gnaphalium luteo-album* L. Silvery green annual. Clusters of heads yellowish, terminal. April. Uncommon. (From garden specimen: later found in Mallorca, where it looked much the same). (Ma, Mi, I) FE IV 128

HELICHRYSUM

5. and 6. and possibly 7 (see below) *Helichrysum stoechas* (L.) Moench. A very variable small shrub up to 50cm, usually less. Densely white-woolly to green and almost hairless. Leaves sometimes aromatic. Heads egg-shaped just before flowering. 5 is the commonest form, 6. seems close to *H. decumbens* Camb. (whose status is uncertain, see FE). (Ma, Mi, I) FE IV 129

7. Was originally identified as *H. rupestre* (Rafin.) DC., but Llorens considers this species absent from Mallorca. Knoche and Duvigneaud both record it from Mallorca. The FE key does not distinguish unambiguously between this species and *H. stoechas*. (?Ma, I) FE IV 129

8. *Helichrysum ambiguum* (Pers.) C.Presl is a fine robust plant up to 60cm or more in flower, with spathulate basal leaves at least 7mm wide at the widest part. Apr.-May. Local in mountain areas. (Ma, Mi endemic) FE IV 130

9. *Helichrysum italicum* (Roth) G.Don fil. Curry Plant. Heads are cylindrical to bell-shaped just before flowering. Outer involucral bracts are coriaceous (scarious in other species here). Always curry-scented. Apr.-May. Uncommon (but found exactly where Knoche recorded it in the early 1920s). (Ma) FE IV 130

PHAGNALON

Dwarf shrubs. All grow on walls or other dry rocky situations.

10. *Phagnalon sordidum* (L.) Reichenb. Leaves linear, inrolled, densely woolly on both surfaces. Heads in terminal clusters of 2-6. May-June. Locally common. (Ma, Mi, I) FE IV 133

11. *Phagnalon rupestre* (L.) DC. Leaves oblanceolate to obovate, woolly beneath, hairless or slightly hairy above, with wavy slightly inrolled margins. Heads solitary. Outer involucral bracts with flat margins, appressed. Apr.-May. (Ma, Mi, I) FE IV 133

12. *Phagnalon saxatile* (L.) Cass. Leaves as in no 11. Heads solitary. Middle involucral bracts with undulate margin, spreading. May-June. Locally common, especially in the South. (Ma, I) FE IV 133

Plate 66

COMPOSITAE (3): *INULA, DITTRICHIA, PULICARIA, JASONIA, PALLENIS, ASTERISCUS, AMBROSIA, XANTHIUM*

INULA

1. *Inula conyza* DC. Ploughman's Spikenard. Perennial. Lower leaves serrulate, upper entire, serrulate, wedge-shaped at base. Heads cylindrical, ligules absent or very small. Outer and middle involucral bracts with recurved, leaf-like apex. May-Aug. **NS.** Not seen by Duvigneaud. Llorens treats as alien. (Ma) FE IV 136

2. *Inula crithmoides* L. Golden Samphire. Fleshy shrub. Leaves linear or linear lanceolate, entire or occasionally toothed at apex. May-July. Common on saline soils. (Ma, Mi, I) FE IV 136

DITTRICHIA

3. *Dittrichia viscosa* (L.) W.Greuter. Tall, resin-scented perennial. Leaves above acute, semiamplexicaul. Flowers ligulate in a pyramidal many-flowered inflorescence. Involucre 6-8mm. Aug.-Oct. Common. (Ma, Mi, I) FE IV 137

4. *Dittrichia graveolens* (L.) W.Greuter. Annual. Ligules hardly exceeding the involucre. Aug.-Oct. Uncommon. (Ma, Mi, I) FE IV 137

PULICARIA

5. *Pulicaria odora* (L.) Reichenb. Perennial. Stems sparingly branched usually about 50cm. Stem leaves amplexicaul, with small auricles. Flowers usually solitary. July-Oct. Common in damp places. (Ma, Mi, I) FE IV 137

6. *Pulicaria dysenterica* (L.) Bernh. Fleabane. Perennial. Stems much-branched, white-woolly. Leaves clasping stem with pronounced auricles. Heads in dense clusters. June-Oct. Common in damp places. (Ma, Mi, I) FE IV 137

7. *Pulicaria vulgaris* Gaertner. Annual. Leaves lanceolate to elliptical, margins wavy. July-Oct. **NS.** Seen by Duvigneaud. (Ma, Mi) Not BI in FE IV 137

8. *Pulicaria sicula* (L.) Moris. Annual. Leaves in middle and upper part of stem linear, not wavy. July-Oct. Not common. In places flooded in winter. (Ma, Mi) FE IV 137

JASONIA

9. *Jasonia glutinosa* (L.) DC. Small sticky perennial. Stems 10-45cm. Inner involucral bracts scarious except for green mid-vein. Ligules absent. Florets yellow. July. **NS.** Seen by Duvigneaud. (Specimen from Spanish mainland). (Ma) FE IV 138

PALLENIS

10. *Pallenis spinosa* (L.) Cass. Perennial. Stem rigid. Stem leaves sessile and slightly amplexicaul. Heads terminate branches, with long patent spine-tipped outer involucral bracts exceeding the ligules. Ligulate florets in 2 rows. Apr.-June. Common. (Ma, Mi, I) FE IV 139

ASTERISCUS

11. *Asteriscus aquaticus* (L.) Less. Annual, usually without a stem or with a very short one, but occasionally up to 50cm with a branched stem. Ligules short, sometimes hardly spreading. Outer involucral bracts with a long leaf-like apex exceeding the ligules, which are in two rows as in *Pallenis*. Fairly common, and very variable in size, the whole plant sometimes minute. Apr.-June. Widespread in dry sandy places (both x 1). (Ma, Mi, I) FE IV 139

12. *Asteriscus maritimus* (L.) Less. Perennial. Stems woody, much-branched. Ligules broad, and longer than involucral bracts. Fairly common on maritime sands. (Ma, Mi, I) FE IV 139

AMBROSIA

13. *Ambrosia maritima* L. Wormwood. Dark greyish-green annual. Leaves petiolate, pinnatifid. Heads unisexual. (Terminal part of 40cm specimen, slightly reduced. Male heads x 2). Sept.-Oct. Not listed by Duvigneaud or Llorens: this from a Mallorcan specimen. Bonafè quotes Bianor and adds 'A verificar'. (Ma) Not BI in FE IV 142

XANTHIUM

14. *Xanthium strumarium* L. Cocklebur. Annual. Leaves long-petiolate, more or less diamond-shaped, coarsely serrate. Heads terminal and in axillary clusters, unisexual. Fruit ellipsoid, yellowish-green, densely covered in hooked spines. June-Aug. Local in disturbed ground and river beds. (Ma, Mi) FE IV 143

15. *Xanthium spinosum* L. Spiny Cocklebur. Annual with long rust-coloured 3-pronged spines at the base of each leaf. Fruit resembles that of 14, but smaller, with small straight spines. June-Sept. Occasional ruderal. (Ma, Mi, I) FE IV 143

Also recorded from Mallorca:
Tagetes minuta L. Erect pungent annual. Involucre cylindrical, of 3 bracts. Ligules 1-3mm. Achenes 4-6mm, linear, black, with pappus of 5 small scales. (Ma) FE IV 144 (A.A.Butcher, private communication). Not BI in FE IV 144

Plate 67

COMPOSITAE (4): *SANTOLINA, ANTHEMIS, ACHILLEA, CHAMAEMELUM, (ANACYCLUS), (OTANTHUS), CHRYSANTHEMUM, COTULA, GYMNOSTYLES, ARTEMISIA*

SANTOLINA

1. *Santolina chamaecyparissus* L. Lavender Cotton. Whitish grey aromatic shrub. Leaves closely and finely pinnatisect. Heads about 1cm wide, with very numerous pale yellow tubular florets. Apr.-Aug. Very local near the sea, commoner in mountains. (x 1, head x 2, detail of floret x 6). (Ma, Mi) FE IV 145

ANTHEMIS

2. *Anthemis maritima* L. Perennial. Leaves pinnatifid, fleshy. Involucral bracts with broad scarious margins. Ligules often rather short and broad. May-Aug. Local near sea. (Slightly reduced, involucral bract x 3). (Ma, Mi, I) FE IV 151

3. *Anthemis arvensis* L. Corn Chamomile. Annual or biennial. Leaves pinnatisect, sometimes bipinnatisect, with acute mucronate lobes. Receptacular scales with short stiff point subtending florets all over conical receptacle. Achene with prominent ribs. Apr.-June. Common. (Detail of receptacle with achenes removed x 1, of achene x 6, other details x 2). (Ma, Mi) FE IV 153

4. *Anthemis cotula* L. Stinking Mayweed. Annual, superficially like 3. Receptacle without scales in the lower part, scales in the upper part very narrow. Ribs of achenes tuberculate. May-Sept. Occasional, roadsides and waste places. (Detail of receptacle with some achenes removed x 2, of disc floret and receptacular scale x 4, achene x 6). (Ma, Mi, I) FE IV 155

ACHILLEA

5. *Achillea ageratum* L. Perennial, woody at base. Stems usually simple. Upper leaves narrow ovate, serrate, sessile, lower more or less pinnatifid, petiolate. Flowers all tubular, in a corymbose inflorescence with up to 15 heads. May-Sept. Local in hilly areas. (Ma, I) FE IV 164

CHAMAEMELUM

6. *Chamaemelum mixtum* (L.) All. Pubescent annual. Leaves 1-pinnate. Heads much as 3. Involucral bracts with wide scarious margin. Tube of disc florets sac-like at base, enclosing apex of achene. Uncommon. **NS.** Not seen by Duvigneaud. (Specimen from Spanish mainland: detail of involucral bract x 2, tubular florets, achenes and receptacular scale x about 4). Llorens lists. (Ma, Mi) Not BI in FE IV 165

CHRYSANTHEMUM

7. *Chrysanthemum segetum* L. Corn Marigold. Hairless, often bluish annual. **Leaves fleshy, toothed**, the upper sessile, more or less amplexicaul. Head pedunculate, solitary, 25-50mm diameter. Involucral bracts with brown marginal band and scarious apex. Ligules broad, overlapping, bright yellow. Apr.-June. **NS.** Seen by Duvigneaud. (From British specimen). (Ma, Mi) FE IV 168

8. *Chrysanthemum coronarium* L. Crown Daisy. Hairless or slightly hairy annual. **Most leaves bi-pinnatisect.** Inner involucral bracts with broad scarious apical appendage which covers bud. Ligules uniformly bright yellow or pale yellow peripherally and deep yellow in the central 1/3 or so. Mar.-July. Very common. (Details x 1 1/2). (Ma, Mi, I) FE IV 169

COTULA

9. *Cotula coronopifolia* L. Hairless annual. Leaves linear with or without a few teeth at apex. Heads 5-10mm diameter, terminal or axillary, pedunculate, bright yellow. Outer florets without a corolla. Involucral bracts in 2 rows. Apr.-Aug. Local in wet places. Native of S. Africa, naturalized here. (Ma) FE IV 177

GYMNOSTYLES

10. *Gymnostyles stolonifera* (Brot.) Tutin. Woolly annual with procumbent stems rooting at nodes. Leaves pinnatisect. Heads 5-8mm diameter, sessile in axils of leaves. Outer florets without a corolla. Achenes villous, with a transversely sulcate thick wing. Style persistent. Native of S America, naturalized here, specimen from Spanish mainland, leaf x 2, achene x 5. (Ma, Mi) FE IV 178

ARTEMISIA

11. *Artemisia arborescens* L. Shrubby Wormwood. Aromatic whitish perennial up to 1m. Stems woody below. Leaves 1-2 pinnatisect. **Heads 6-7mm across, hemispherical**, in a large paniculate inflorescence. Apr.-June. Local, inland. **NS.** Seen by Duvigneaud. (Small branch flowering stem x 1, detail x 2, specimen from Spanish mainland). Llorens treats as garden escape. (Ma, Mi, I) FE IV 180

12. *Artemisia caerulescens* L. Grey-green aromatic shrub. Flowering stems woody for most of their length, sparsely pubescent or becoming hairless at time of flowering. Lower leaves entire or trifid or 1-pinnatisect. **Heads narrow ovoid, 2.5-5mm.** June-Oct. Common in saltmarshes. (Ma, Mi) FE IV 181

Others recorded for Mallorca:

Anacyclus clavatus (Desf.) Pers. Distinguished from *Anthemis* species by broadly 2-winged outer achenes. Possibly not seen recently. Llorens lists. (Ma, I) FE IV 168

Otanthus maritimus (L.) Hoffmans. & Link. Densely white-tomentose perennial with slightly conical inflorescence without ligulate florets. Tubular florets have 2 spurs at base which partially enclose ovary. Possibly not seen recently. (Ma, I) FE IV 168

Cotula australis (Sieber ex Sprengel) Hooker fil. Resembles 9, but hairy. Leaves usually bi-pinnatifid, not or hardly fleshy. Capitula usually smaller. (Native of Australia and New Zealand). Llorens lists. (Ma) FE IV 177

In Ibiza:

Leucanthemum paludosum (Poiret) Bonnet & Barratte. FE IV 177

Plate 68

COMPOSITAE (5): *SENECIO, CALENDULA, ARCTOTHECA, GAZANIA, CARLINA, ATRACTYLIS, XERANTHEMUM, ARCTIUM, STAEHELINA*

SENECIO

Herbs or small shrubs with alternate leaves. Heads usually in corymbs. Involucral bracts mainly in one row, often with a few small supplementary bracts.

1. *Senecio bicolor* (Willd.) Tod. subsp. *cineraria* (DC.) Chater. Dusty Miller. Densely white-tomentose shrubby perennial. Leaves usually pinnate, often further divided. Heads with yellow ligules 12-15mm in dense compound corymbs. May-June. Cultivated and widely naturalised. (Ma, Mi) FE IV 194

2. *Senecio leucanthemifolius* Poiret subsp. *crassifolius* Willd. Leaves fleshy, shining, often purple beneath, sometimes turning entirely red or purple. Ligules yellow. Mar.-May. Abundant on at least one area of rocky coast. (Ma, I) Ibiza only in FE IV 203.

3. *Senecio leucanthemifolius* Poiret subsp. (or var.) *rodriguezii*. Leaves fleshy, bluish green with faint white markings. Ligules pale violet, disc florets deep reddish-violet. Jan.-July. Widespread in rocky places near the coast. (Ma, endemic subsp.) FE IV 203

4. *Senecio vulgaris* L. Groundsel. Annual. Involucral bracts black-tipped. Heads usually without ligules. Feb.-June. Common weed of cultivated ground. (Ma, Mi, I) FE IV 204

CALENDULA

5. *Calendula arvensis* L. Field Marigold. Annual, often more or less white-woolly. Leaves entire or slightly toothed, sessile, sometimes amplexicaul. Heads 1-2cm diameter. Involucral bracts usually in one row, often red-tipped. Ligules and tubular florets orange. Achenes curved and toothed with a long beak alternating with others more or less boat-shaped, strongly curved. Very common. (Ma, Mi, I) FE IV 207

ARCTOTHECA

6. *Arctotheca calendula* (L.) Levyns. Annual. Ligules bicoloured yellow above, greenish-purple below. May-June. South African native, locally naturalised. (Ma) Not BI in FE IV 208

GAZANIA

7. *Gazania rigens* (L.) Gaertner. Perennial. Stems decumbent. Leaves greyish, sparsely floccose above, and densely white-tomentose beneath. Ligules bright orange, with a basal black patch with a white spot on it. May-July. Another South African native, much-planted and occasionally naturalised. (Ma, Mi) Not BI in FE IV 208

CARLINA

Annual or perennial herbs. Leaves alternate, pinnatisect, spiny-toothed. Involucral bracts in several rows, the outer like the upper leaves, the inner entire, scarious, shining, radiate when dry (often coloured and looking like ligules). Ligules absent.

8. *Carlina corymbosa* L. Perennial. Heads solitary on short branches, often forming a dense corymb. Inner involucral bracts bright brownish-yellow above. June-Oct. Very common. (Heads often larger than those in illustration). (Ma, Mi, I) FE IV 209

9. *Carlina lanata* L. Annual. Heads often solitary. Inner involucral bracts purplish-red on both surfaces. May-Aug. Less common than 8, but fairly widespread. (Ma, Mi, I) FE IV 211

ATRACTYLIS

10. *Atractylis cancellata* L. Annual, slender or fairly robust. Leaves linear-lanceolate, spiny. Outer involucral bracts erect, spiny, almost as long as head in flower, incurved to cover the head in bud. Apr.-June. Common in rocky places. (Ma, Mi, I) FE IV 211

XERANTHEMUM

11. *Xeranthemum inapertum* (L.) Miller. Annual. Stem erect, up to 40cm. Leaves alternate, entire. Heads long pedunculate, florets concealed by erect inner involucral bracts, which are pinkish-red. June-July. **NS.** Not seen by Duvigneaud. (From Greek Specimen). (Ma) FE IV 212

ARCTIUM

12. *Arctium tomentosum* Miller. Woolly Burdock. Erect biennial usually about 1m. Leaves entire, broadly ovate, cordate at base, petioles solid. Inflorescence much branched. Heads more or less globular, with purple florets and arachnoid-tomentose involucre, each bract terminating in a hooked spine. (Ma) FE IV 215

STAEHELINA

13. *Staehelina dubia* L. Shrubby perennial. Leaves narrow, green above and white-tomentose beneath, sometimes with rounded teeth. Heads long and narrow, 15-20 x 3-5mm. Involucral bracts green with reddish apex. Florets all tubular with purplish-pink corolla. June-Aug. Not common. (Ma, Mi, I) FE IV 217

Also recorded for Mallorca:
Arctium minus Bernh. Petioles hollow. Inflorescence racemose. Llorens lists. FE IV 215

In other islands:
Senecio gallicus Chaix. ?Ibiza FE IV 203
Senecio lividus L. Cabrera and Minorca. FE IV 204
Senecio viscosus L. Minorca. FE IV 204
Calendula tripterocarpa Rupr. Ibiza. FE IV 207
Atractylis humilis L. Minorca and Ibiza. FE IV 211

Plate 69

COMPOSITAE (6): *CARDUUS, CIRSIUM, PICNOMON, NOTOBASIS, GALACTITES, TYRIMNUS, ONOPORDUM*

CARDUUS

Annual or perennial thistles with spiny-winged stems. Pappus of many rows of bristles, united at the base into a ring.

1. *Carduus tenuiflorus* Curtis. Sea Thistle. Annual or biennial up to 75cm. Leaves with 6-8 pairs of lobes. Heads cylindrical in compact clusters of 3-8. Stem with continuous prickly wing. Apr.-May. Common. (Ma, Mi, I) FE IV 231

2. *Carduus pycnocephalus* L. Annual up to 80cm. Leaves with 2-5 pairs of lobes. Heads cylindrical, solitary (usually) or in clusters of 2-3. Wing of stem absent below heads. Fairly common. (Ma, Mi, I) FE IV 231

CIRSIUM

Spiny, usually perennial herbs. Pappus of several rows of plumose setae, sometimes with simple setae in the outermost row.

3. *Cirsium echinatum* (Desf.) DC. Perennial thistle up to 40cm. Middle leaves decurrent on stem for up to 1cm, upper rather less, stem otherwise unwinged. Heads in corymb overtopped by 2-8 subtending leaves. Involucre up to 4cm., more or less globular June-Aug. Common in mountain areas. (Ma) FE IV 237

4. *Cirsium vulgare* (Savi) Ten. Spear Thistle. Middle leaves at least decurrent for whole internode. Heads more or less pear-shaped. May-Oct. Common. (Ma, Mi, I) FE IV 237

5. *Cirsium arvense* (L.) Scop. Creeping Thistle. Perennial up to 1m, with creeping rootstock. May-Sept. Common weed of cultivation. (Ma) FE IV 242

PICNOMON

6. *Picnomon acarna* (L.) Cass. (*Cirsium acarna* (L.) Moench). Greyish woolly-haired annual, up to 50cm, Heads almost concealed by upper leaves. Florets purple. Rare. **NS**. (From Cretan specimen x 1/2). Knoche quotes Bianor (1910-1914), not seen, though listed, by Duvigneaud. Llorens lists. (Ma) FE IV 242

NOTOBASIS

7. *Notobasis syriaca* (L.) Cass. Annual, up to 1m or more. Uppermost stem leaves surrounding and often exceeding heads. May-June. Not common. (x 1/4, detail of head x 1). (Ma, Mi, I) FE IV 242

GALACTITES

8. *Galactites tomentosa* Moench. Annual thistle. Leaves white-veined and variegated. Outer florets large, spreading. Mar.-July. Common. A major field weed (but beautiful nonetheless!). (Ma, Mi, I) FE IV 244

TYRIMNUS

9. *Tyrimnus leucographus* (L.) Cass. Annual up to 60cm. Leaves white-veined above, grey woolly below. Heads solitary on long peduncles. June-July. Rare. **NS**. Seen by Duvigneaud but not by Knoche. (Specimen from Spanish mainland). (Ma) FE IV 244

ONOPORDUM

10. *Onopordum illyricum* L. Biennial, up to 150cm, with densely spiny white-woolly stem. Leaves with at least 8 pairs of lobes. Heads much enlarged in fruit. June-July. Locally common. (x about 1/10, details x 1). (Ma) FE IV 247

Also recorded from Mallorca:

Onopordum macracanthum Schousboe. Differs from 10 in sparsely spiny stem and leaves with 5-7 pairs of lobes. Listed by Duvigneaud and Llorens. Not BI in FE IV 247

In Ibiza only:

Carduus bourgeanus Boiss. & Reuter. Not BI in FE IV 229

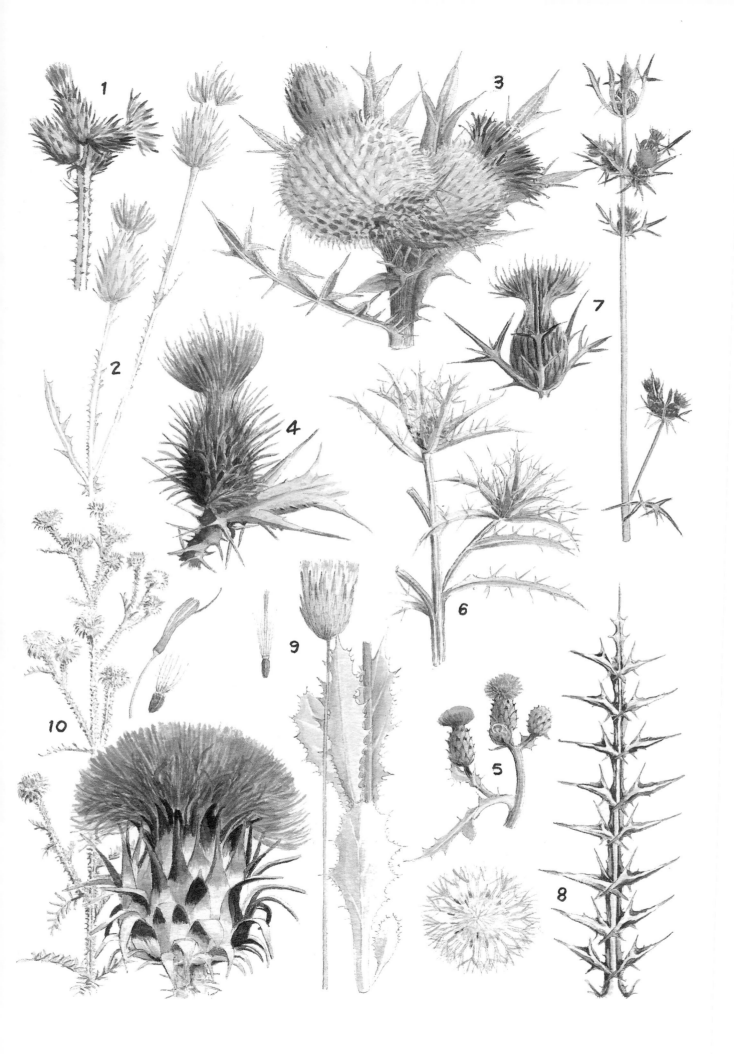

Plate 70

COMPOSITAE (7): *CYNARA, SILYBUM, CHEIROLO-PHUS, LEUZEA, MANTISALCA, CENTAUREA, CRUPINA, CARTHAMUS*

CYNARA

1. *Cynara cardunculus* L. Cardoon. Very robust prickly perennial. Heads about 50mm diameter. Involucral bracts narrowed into a stiff purplish spine with yellow margins and tip. Corolla blue. Local, commoner in the South. (Ma, Mi, I) FE IV 248

SILYBUM

2. *Silybum marianum* (L.) Gaertner. Milk Thistle. Annual or biennial up to 1.5m. Leaves green variegated with white along the main veins. Heads up to 4cm. Outer and middle involucral bracts with toothed appendage ending in a channelled spine. Corolla pinkish purple. Common in waste places. (Ma, Mi, I) FE IV 249

CHEIROLOPHUS

3. *Cheirolophus intybaceus* (Lam.) Dostál. Perennial. Lower leaves lyrate with linear segments, upper entire, linear-lanceolate, acuminate. Involucre 12-16mm, bracts with semilunar shortly fringed appendages. Florets purple. June-Aug. **NS**. Seen by Duvigneaud. (Ma, I) FE IV 250

LEUZEA

4. *Leuzea conifera* (L.) DC. Perennial. Stem woolly, leaves white tomentose beneath. Involucre up to 4cm diameter, ovoid. Involucral bracts reddish-brown, with more or less laciniate papery appendages. Florets few, purple. May-Aug. Locally common. (Ma, Mi) FE IV 253

MANTISALCA

5. *Mantisalca salmantica* (L.) Briq. & Cavall. Biennial or perennial. Leaves pinnately lobed below, toothed or pinnatisect above, decreasing in size upwards. Heads 10-15mm, ovoid. Bracts blackish at the tip with a single slender spine, often recurved. Apr.-Oct. **NS**. Listed but not seen by Duvigneaud. (From Portuguese specimen). Llorens lists. (Ma) FE IV 254

CENTAUREA

Annual to perennial herbs. Involucral bracts often with a fringed or spiny appendage, the main means of distinguishing between them.

6. *Centaurea calcitrapa* L. Star Thistle. Heads 6-8mm diameter with purple florets. Involucral bracts green, leathery, with a pale margin and a 10-18mm channelled spine (with straw coloured margins and tip) at the apex, usually with short basal spines. May-Sept. Common. (Ma, Mi, I) FE IV 282

7. *Centaurea aspera* L. Rough Star Thistle. Much-branched perennial. Heads 15-25mm with purple florets, the outer spreading. Involucral bracts with small spreading or deflexed appendages with 3 (sometimes 5) palmately arranged short spines. May-Sept. Common. (Ma, Mi, I) FE IV 284

8. *Centaurea melitensis* L. Maltese Star Thistle. Perennial. Heads solitary or in groups of 2-3, 8-12mm diameter, with yellow florets. Bracts with apical spine 5-8mm, with 1-3 short lateral spines on each side. May-June. Locally common. (Ma, Mi, I) FE IV 285

9. *Centaurea diluta* Aiton. Tall perennial. Stems up to 100cm, erect, branched. Heads 8-12mm diameter, ovoid. Appendage white, membranous, arising from upper half of bract, and nearly as long body of bract, with a terminal rigid spine slightly exceeding the appendage. May-June. Head only, from Mallorcan specimen). Not previously recorded. (Ma) FE IV 285

CRUPINA

10. *Crupina* species (cf *C. vulgaris* Cass. and *C. crupinastrum* (Moris) Vis.). Tall slender branched annual, up to 100cm. Heads about 10cm diameter, long ovate in bud. Florets 15 or more, but in plants examined only one achene developing in each head. Pappus with outer row of blackish scabrid hairs, and inner row of dark lanceolate scales. (Between 2 species described in FE). May-June. Locally common, chiefly in the South. (Ma) FE IV 301

CARTHAMUS

11. *Carthamus lanatus* L. Glandular annual with white arachnoid indumentum at least around ovoid capitula, sometimes more. Corolla yellow. Outer and middle involucral bracts with long green spiny channelled appendages. May-Sept. Common. (Two very different plants occur here, one with spreading branches with solitary flowers, and one a tall spike-like inflorescence with numerous nearly sessile flowers). (Ma, Mi, I) FE IV 303

In other islands:
Centaurea collina L. Ibiza. ?BI in FE IV 263
Centaurea balearica Rodr. (endemic Mi). FE IV 273
Centaurea hyalolepis Boiss. Ibiza. FE IV 282
Centaurea seridis (Dufour) Dostál. Ibiza. (?BI in FE IV 283)
Centaurea cyanus L. Minorca. Not BI in FE IV 300

Plate 71

COMPOSITAE (8): *CARDUNCELLUS, SCOLYMUS, CICHORIUM, CATANANCHE, TOLPIS, HYOSERIS, HEDYPNOIS, RHAGADIOLUS*

CARDUNCELLUS

1. *Carduncellus pinnatus* (Desf.) DC. Perennial, without a stem or with a very short one. Leaves pinnate, spiny-toothed. Heads about 15mm diameter, with many rows of imbricate, spiny involucral bracts. **Corolla bluish-purple**, **pappus bristles reddish-brown**, plumose, 3-4 x length achene. Apr.-May. **NS.** Seen by Duvigneaud. Llorens lists. (Ma, I) FE IV 303

2. *Carduncellus caeruleus* (L.) C.Presl. More or less cottony haired perennial with unbranched stem up to 50cm. Leaves simple and toothed, or pinnatisect, with margin and apex spiny. Outer involucral bracts leaf-like, exceeding the inner. Peripheral **florets blue**, central white or blue. **Pappus scales ciliate, whitish**, 1.5-2 x length achene. Apr.-May. Local, field margins and grassy places. (Ma, Mi, I) FE IV 304

From here on plants are subfamily CHICORIOIDEAE, which have only ligulate florets – ASTEROIDEAE (above) always have some florets at least without ligules. CHICORIOIDEAE also nearly always have latex, a milky juice exuded when a part of the plant is broken.

SCOLYMUS

3. *Scolymus maculatus* L. Annual, up to 90cm. Stems with continuous toothed and spiny wings with thickened white margin. Florets bright yellow in small panicles. Pappus absent. **NS.** Not seen by Duvigneaud. Llorens lists. (Ma, Mi) FE IV 304

4. *Scolymus hispanicus* L. Spanish Oyster Plant. Robust biennial or perennial up to 80cm. Stems with interrupted spiny wings, not much thickened at the margin. June-July. Locally common. (Ma, Mi, I) FE IV 304

CICHORIUM

5. *Chicorium intybus* L. Chicory. Perennial. Leaves mostly basal. Stems up to 1m or so, with stiff patent to ascending branches. Flowers terminal and axillary, with blue ligules. Widespread in grassy places – small stemless 1-flowered plants occur occasionally in dry pastures. Apr.-Sept. Common. (Ma, Mi, I) FE IV 304

CATANANCHE

6. *Catananche caerulea* L. Cupidone. Perennial. **NS.** Probably inappropriately here! Seen once by Knoche on Puig Major in 1912. Llorens omits. (From garden specimen). (?Ma) FE IV 305

TOLPIS

7. *Tolpis barbata* (L.) Gaertner. Annual. Leaves toothed, hairy, mainly in basal rosette. Heads usually numerous on much-branched inflorescence. Ligules usually exceeded by long curved outer involucral bracts. Outer ligules pale yellow, inner deep yellow or purplish. **NS.** Not seen by Duvigneaud. (From garden specimen, wild flower about 1/2 this diameter). Llorens lists. (Ma, Mi) FE IV 306

HYOSERIS

Annual or perennial herbs. Leaves pinnatifid, all basal. Involucral bracts in 2 rows, the outer much shorter than the inner. Ligules yellow.

8. *Hyoseris scabra* L. Annual. Stem pinkish red, swollen, usually procumbent from the middle of basal rosette. Heads solitary, with rather few florets, usually about 1cm across in flower. Inner and middle achenes with pappus of pale linear scales, inner with pappus of short hairs. Mar.-May. Fairly common. (Ma, Mi, I) FE IV 307

9. *Hyoseris radiata* L. Perennial. Leaves with lobes overlapping like roof tiles. Heads usually more than 1cm across in flower with numerous ligules, the outer with a purplish stripe on the back. Inner involucral bracts enlarge and develop a purplish swelling near the base in fruit. All achenes with pappus of both rigid hairs and scales. Common. (Ma, Mi, I) FE IV 307

HEDYPNOIS

10. *Hedypnois cretica* (L.) Dum.-Courset Variable annual, stems branched or simple. Heads small in flower, becoming much-enlarged with thickened pedicel in fruit. Involucral bracts in 2 rows, the inner becoming incurved and enclosing the outer achenes in fruit. Achenes linear, blackish, often curved. Pappus of outer achenes usually a corona, of inner narrow aristate scales. May-June. Common. (Ma, Mi, I) FE IV 307

RHAGADIOLUS

11. *Rhagadiolus stellatus* (L.) Gaertner. Star Hawkbit. Annual. Stems usually solitary, branched. Heads in flower small and narrow with a few erect yellow ligules. Involucral bracts in 2 rows, the outer very small, the 5 inner becoming enlarged and spreading to form a star in fruit. Achenes narrow cylindrical, pappus absent. (Ma, Mi, I) FE IV 308

In Ibiza only:
Carduncellus monspelliensium All. FE IV 303
Carduncellus dianius Webb. ?BI in FE IV 304

Plate 72

COMPOSITAE (9): *UROSPERMUM, HYPOCHAERIS, LEONTODON, PICRIS, SCORZONERA, TRAGOPOGON*

UROSPERMUM

1. *Urospermum dalechampii* (L.) Scop. ex F.W.Schmidt. Perennial with pubescent stem and slightly hispid leaves. Lower leaves sometimes pinnatifid, stem leaves entire, amplexicaul. Heads solitary, up to 5cm wide. Involucral bracts broad, in one row, connate at base. Ligules pale yellow, with red stripe on outer face and 5 tiny black-tipped teeth, which give a black centre to the immature head. Achene blackish, tuberculate, with long scabrid beak and a very pale reddish pappus (colour often only noticeable against white paper). Apr.-June. Common. (Ma, Mi, I) FE IV 308

2. *Urospermum picroides* (L.) Scop. ex F.W.Schmidt. Annual. Stem usually branched. Leaves prickly at least on veins beneath, and usually on margins, stem leaves very variable, amplexicaul. Involucral bracts broad, in one row, connate at base. Ligules bright yellow, with slightly greyish stripe beneath. Achene resembles achene of 1, but smaller and with a white pappus. (Achene x 2). Common. (Ma, Mi, I) FE IV 308

HYPOCHAERIS

3. *Hypochaeris achyrophorus* L. Annual. Stem hispid at least above, often sparingly branched, but small apparently scapose plants are very common. Involucral bracts in several rows, hispid. Fully open head very characteristic, with very numerous florets in many rows with short imbricate ligules. Achenes beaked, with pappus in two rows, the outer much shorter than the inner. Apr.-June. Very common. (Achene x 2). (Ma, Mi, I) FE IV 309

LEONTODON

4. *Leontodon tuberosus* L. Tuberous rooted perennial. Stems simple, with rigid simple, or long stalked bifid or trifid hairs. Leaves toothed or pinnatifid, gradually narrowed to petiole. Involucral bracts hairless or with bifid hairs, often confined to the midline. Ligules bright yellow. Achenes minutely transversely ridged, the outer curved with a pappus of very short hairs, the inner straight with a long beak and a pappus of longer plumose hairs. May-June. Occasional. (Achenes x 2). (Ma, Mi, I) FE IV 315

5. *Leontodon taraxacoides* (Vill) Mérat. Lesser Hawkbit. Resembles 4, but not tuberous rooted. Heads usually drooping in bud. Outer ligules greyish-violet on outer face. Outer achenes with pappus of short scales, inner more or less beaked with pappus of hairs. **NS.** Seen by Duvigneaud. Locally common. (From British specimen, achenes x 2). (Ma, Mi, I) FE IV 315

PICRIS

6. *Picris echioides* L. Bristly Ox-tongue. Bristly annual or biennial. Stems much-branched. Heads numerous, with broad heart-shaped outer involucral bracts. Ligules bright orange-yellow. Achenes (outer curved, inner straight) with minute transverse ridges and beak equalling body and pappus of two rows of white hairs. May-Sept. Common. (Achene slightly enlarged). (Ma, Mi, I) FE IV 316

SCORZONERA

7. *Scorzonera laciniata* L. Annual to perennial. Basal leaves pinnatisect. Stems branched. Cauline leaves usually entire, linear. Ligules equalling involucral bracts or half as long again, yellow. Achenes up to 17mm, with pappus hairs the same length, producing a white globe of 6mm or more in fruit. Apr.-June. Occasional. (Flowering head from garden specimen; fruiting heads from Mallorca, slightly reduced). (Ma, Mi, I) FE IV 318

TRAGOPOGON

8. *Tragopogon porrifolius* L. Salsify. Tall biennial. Leaves broadly linear. Peduncles inflated below head. Ligules violet or purple. Achenes with a long beak with an annulus separating it from the pappus. Apr.-June. Cultivated for the edible roots, commonly escaping. (Ma, Mi, I) FE IV 323

9. *Tragopogon hybridus* L. Hairless annual. Flowering head resembles that of 8, but ligules pinkish-lilac, and achenes without an annulus, the inner with a pappus of mostly plumose hairs, the outer with a pappus of long rigid hairs. (Head only plus achenes x 4/5 beside illustration of 8, whose achenes are not illustrated). (Ma, Mi) FE IV 325

In Minorca:
Hypochaeris glabra L. FE IV 309

Plate 73

COMPOSITAE (10): *REICHARDIA, LAUNAEA, AETHE-ORHIZA, SONCHUS, LACTUCA*

REICHARDIA

Stem leaves usually amplexicaul. Involucral bracts in several rows, the outer at least with scarious margins. At least the outer achenes 4-5 angled and transversely ridged.

1. *Reichardia tingitana* (L.) Roth. Hairless annual, immediately recognizable by the reddish-black bases of central ligules and the heart-shaped involucral bracts. Mar.-May. Common. (Ma, Mi, I) FE IV 325
2. *Reichardia picroides* (L.) Roth. Much like 1, but without purple bases to ligules. Heart shaped bracts with narrow (up to 0.5mm) scarious border resemble the small bracts on the peduncle. (Ma, Mi, I) FE IV 325

LAUNAEA

3. *Launaea cervicornis* (Boiss.) Font Quer & Rothm. Spiny dwarf shrub, very much branched. May-June. Exposed rocky ground near sea. Common, especially in the North. (Ma, Mi endemic)

AETHEORHIZA

Rhizomatous perennial herbs. Involucral bracts in 3 rows.

4. *Aetheorhiza bulbosa* (L.) Cass. subsp. *bulbosa* Stems with solitary flowers, with blackish stalked glands on involucre and upper part of stem. Involucral bracts linear-lanceolate, gradually narrowed to a pointed apex. May-June. Fairly common in grassy places. (Ma, Mi, I) FE IV 326
5. *Aetheorhiza bulbosa* (L.) Cass. subsp. *willkommii* (Burnat & Barbey) Rech. fil. Resembles 4, but a smaller, often mat-forming plant. May-June. Fairly common in rocky places in the mountain area. (Ma, I endemic) FE IV 326

SONCHUS

Weak annual to perennial herbs with copious latex (Milkthistles). Stems usually branched. Leaves finely toothed to pinnatisect, the stem leaves amplexicaul. Achenes flattened, narrowed above and below, with truncate apex. Pappus of two kinds of hairs.

6. *Sonchus asper* (L.) Hill. Spiny Milk-or Sow-thistle. Weedy hairless annual usually up to about 1m, stem-leaves with characteristic rounded auricle. Heads with very numerous small bright yellow ligules. Occasional, waste places. May-June. (Ma, Mi, I) FE IV 327
7. *Sonchus tenerrimus* L. Very variable annual, biennial or perennial. At least upper leaves pinnatisect with many lobes, which are either linear or strongly contracted at the base. Amplexicaul auricles of upper leaves are usually broad and wavy. May-June. Very common, especially in waste places in towns. (Ma, Mi, I) FE IV 327
8. *Sonchus oleraceus* L. Sow Thistle. Resembles 6 and 7. Auricles of upper stem-leaves pointed, not rounded. Heads with very numerous pale yellow ligules. May-June. Common especially in waste places in towns. (Ma, MI, I) FE IV 327
9. *Sonchus maritimus* L. Rhizomatous perennial of damp places. Stems sparingly branched or unbranched. Subsp.

maritimus (illustrated here) (of saline habitats) has large bright orange heads with ovate outer involucral bracts. Subsp. *aquatilis* (Pourret) Nyman (of fresh water habitats) is usually more branched with smaller yellower heads and lanceolate involucral bracts. June-Oct. Occasional. (Ma, Mi, I) FE IV 327

LACTUCA

Weak annual to perennial herbs with copious latex and much-branched stems. Leaves entire to pinnatifid, often prickly. Flowers usually rather small and numerous, ligules yellow or blue. Achenes compressed and beaked, pappus of simple hairs.

10. *Lactuca viminea* (L.) J. & C.Presl. Hairless perennial. Stems numerous, with narrow leaves with long-decurrent linear auricles. Stems much-branched. Inflorescence with numerous small yellow heads usually with only 5 florets. Achenes black, the beak equalling the body or shorter. June-Sept. Dry rocky places and near sea. Occasional. (Leaf, small part of inflorescence and achenes x 1). (Ma) FE IV 329
11. *Lactuca serriola* L. Prickly Lettuce. Compass Plant. Annual or biennial, up to 2m. Usually a single stem with a few axillary branches below. Stem leaves entire or occasionally pinnatifid, with prickles on margins and back of central vein, often held flat in a NS plane. Inflorescence much-branched, with small heads usually with 7-15 florets. Achenes 6-8mm, greyish, with beak about as long as the body. (Ma, Mi, I) FE IV 330
12. *L. tenerrima* Pourret. Perennial up to 50cm, usually less. Heads relatively large, with 12-20 florets with 12-20 florets with bluish lilac ligules. Achenes obovate, dark blackish-brown with beak rather longer than body. May-Aug. Occasional in mountain scrub. (Ma) FE IV 331

Other species recorded in Mallorca:

Reichardia intermedia (Sculz Bip.) Coutinho = Knoche's *Picridium intermedium* Willk. Knoche states that it is the commonest plant in the Balearic islands, which throws some doubt on his identification since it certainly isn't common. Llorens lists this species for Ma only. It resembles *R. picroides,* but the scarious margins of the outer involucral bracts are up to 1.25mm wide, and the bracts are larger. FE IV 325

Lactuca saligna L. Upper leaves linear, lower pinnate with narrow segments. Florets 6-15, ligules pale yellow. Achenes pale brown, 7-8-ribbed, with beak 1-3 x length body. Knoche and Duvigneaud record from Mi only: Llorens lists for Ma and Mi. FE IV 330

Lactuca virosa L. Leaves toothed to pinnatifid with wide lobes. Inflorescence pyramidal. Ligules yellow. Beak equalling blackish 5-ribbed fruit. Llorens lists for Ma, and Knoche quotes Bianor (1910-1914). ?BI in FE IV 330

Recorded from Minorca:
Sonchus arvensis. Not BI in FE IV 330

Plate 74

COMPOSITAE (11): TARAXACUM, CHONDRILLA, LAPSANA, CREPIS, ANDRYALA, HIERACIUM

TARAXACUM

Taraxacum species. Dandelion. Fleshy perennial herbs with a tap-root, basal leaves and latex. Leaves entire or toothed. Stems few to many, hollow, with solitary head, more or less flat-topped at time of flowering. Involucral bracts in 2 rows, the inner erect and more or less linear, the outer shorter, usually wider and often curving outwards. Bracts may have a small appendage on the outer surface just below the apex. Ligules yellow, often with a dark stripe on the outside. Achenes with a slender beak and a pappus of many rows of (usually) white hairs. Some plants of this genus produce little or no pollen, and set viable seed asexually (apomixis), which perpetuates mutations. Others reproduce sexually. The many species recorded here are outside the scope of this book. One common species is illustrated here to represent them all.

1. *Taraxacum* sp. (Ma) see FE 332 et seq.

CHONDRILLA,

2. *Chondrilla juncea* L. Slightly shrubby biennial or perennial with grey-green arching branches from (usually) a single stem. Branches rush-like, with few, linear or lanceolate more or less toothed leaves, and sessile or shortly pedunculate heads, solitary or in small groups. Heads with 9-12 florets. Involucral bracts in two rows, the outer much shorter. Occasional in scrub. (x 1). (Ma, Mi) FE IV 343

LAPSANA

3. *Lapsana communis* L. Nipplewort. Annual herb. Lower leaves with large terminal and small lateral lobes. Inflorescence branched with numerous small heads. Involucral bracts in 2 rows, the outer small and scale like. May. Rare. (From British specimen x 1/4. Details x 1: but a larger specimen was later collected in a neglected garden in Mallorca). (Ma) FE IV 344

CREPIS

Annual to perennial. Stems usually branched. Heads (here) numerous. Involucral bracts in 2 rows. Achenes usually with white pappus.

4. *Crepis triasii* (Camb.) Nyman. Handsome perennial. **Leaves** mostly basal, **with yellowish hairs**, oblanceolate, attenuate at base. Stem leaves few. Stems usually numerous in mature plants. Heads large (for this genus), in corymbose inflorescence. Involucral bracts linear to linear-lanceolate, acute, tomentose, the outer 1/3-1/2 length inner. May-June. Locally common in rock crevices in mountain area. (Main illustration x 1/3, achene x 4, other details x 1). (Ma, Mi endemic) FE IV 351

5. *Crepis foetida* L. subsp. *foetida*. Stinking Hawk's-beard. Annual, usually up to about 60cm. Stem branched from base. Upper leaves sessile, auriculate. Heads usually numerous. **Outer involucral bracts linear-lanceolate.** Ligules yellow, reddish-purple on the outside. **Achenes of 2 kinds**, the outer stout, with or without a short beak, the inner with a long slender beak. **NS.** Seen by Duvigneaud. (Specimen from Spanish mainland). (Ma, I) FE IV 354

6. *Crepis pusilla* (Sommier) Merxm. **Stemless annual.** Heads in a sessile cluster. Achenes of 2 kinds, the outer enclosed by the inner involucral bracts. **NS.** (From Greek specimen: upper details x 3 show, from left to right, outer involucral bract, bract enclosing outer achene from outside and from inside). (Ma) Not BI in FE IV 355

7. *Crepis vesicaria* L. subsp. *vesicaria* Beaked Hawk's-beard. Usually biennial or perennial. Stems up to nearly 1m, usually much-branched, often reddish below. Basal leaves very variable: upper auriculate-amplexicaul. **Outer involucral bracts broadly ovate. All achenes with a beak as long as the body.** Mar.-May. Common. (Plant x 1/10, details x 1). (Ma, I) FE IV 356

ANDRYALA

8. *Andryala integrifolia* L. Annual to perennial. **Leaves soft and silvery.** Whole plant covered in stellate and simple hairs, upper part, especially **involucral bracts, with long yellowish glandular hairs** too. Ligules pale yellow. Probably garden escape, but occasional in wild situations in Pollensa area. (x 1/10, details x 1). (Ma) Not BI in FE IV 358

HIERACIUM

Hieracium species. Hawkweed. Apomixis is common in this genus, as with *Taraxacum*. However *Hieracium* species are not common here, though several species have been recorded. They are perennial herbs with yellow ligules and involucral bracts in several overlapping rows. The achenes are never beaked, and have a pappus of 1-2 rows of brittle usually brownish hairs (occasionally white).

9. *Hieracium amplexicaule* L. Whole plant with numerous stellate hairs and sticky brown glandular hairs, also sometimes simple hairs. Stem leaves auriculate-amplexicaul, sometimes cordate. Ligules yellow, with dense, simple eglandular hairs at apex. **NS.** Not seen by Duvigneaud. (Specimen from Spanish mainland x about 1/3, head x 1). Llorens lists. (Ma) BI in FE IV 396

Other species recorded from Mallorca:
Crepis bellidifolia Loisel. Llorens lists. (Ma) ?BI in FE IV 357
Crepis vesicaria subsp. *haensleri* (Boiss. ex DC.) P.D.Sell. FE IV 356
Hieracium several species including *H. pilosella* L. FE IV 368

In other islands:
Other species of *Taraxacum* and *Hieracium*.
Andryala ragusina L. Ibiza. FE IV 358

Plate 75

ALISMATACEAE: *ALISMA, (BALDIELLA), DAMASONIUM*
JUNCAGINACEAE: *TRIGLOCHIN*
POTAMOGETONACEAE: *POTAMOGETON*

ALISMATACEAE
ALISMA

1. *Alisma plantago-aquatica* L. Water Plantain. Hairless perennial up to about 1m. Leaves mostly subcordate or truncate at base, occasionally wedge-shaped. Flowers with 3 white or pale lilac petals, usually opening after midday. Style arising about half way up fruit. Carpels numerous in a single whorl. May. Rooted in mud in shallow water. **NS**. Seen by Duvigneaud. (From British specimen x 1/4, flower x 2). (Ma) BI excluded in FE V 2

2. *Alisma lanceolatum* With. Narrow-leaved Water plantain. As above, but leaves always wedge-shaped at base. Flowers pink, opening in the morning. Style arising near top of fruit. May. Very occasional in mud or shallow water. (Terminal part of inflorescence x 1, leaf x 1/4). (Ma, Mi, I) FE V 2

DAMASONIUM

3. *Damasonium alisma* Miller. Star-fruit. Hairless annual or perennial usually less than 10cm. Flowers rather like those of 1, usually in whorls along the erect or procumbent stems. Carpels usually 6 in one whorl, gradually contracted into a beak, producing a star-shaped fruit. Apr. In water or mud, rare. (Main illustration from Mallorcan specimen, flower x 2 from British specimen). (Ma) FE V 3

JUNCAGINACEAE
TRIGLOCHIN

4. *Triglochin bulbosa* L. subsp. *barrelieri* (Loisel.) Rouy. Arrow-grass. Bulbous perennial, usually less than 20cm. Flowers in racemes with 6 greenish sepal-like perianth segments. Carpels 6, of which only 3 are fertile. Mar.-May. Locally common in saline mud. (x 1/2, details enlarged). (Ma, Mi) FE V 6

POTAMOGETONACEAE
POTAMOGETON

Aquatic herbs with elongated stems and alternate leaves. Flowers in pedunculate spikes with a perianth of 4 sepal-like segments. Carpels 1-4, more or less free.

5. *Potamogeton coloratus* Hornem. Fen Pondweed. Floating leaves up to 10 x 5cm, ovate to lanceolate, translucent, slightly cordate to wedge-shaped at base. Submerged leaves up to 18cm, similar to floating leaves but narrower. Fruit about 1.5mm, greenish. Fairly common, mostly in mountain areas. (Fruit x 4). (Ma, Mi, I) FE V 9

6. *Potamogeton crispus* L. Curled Pondweed. Leaves all submerged, broad linear, wavy-edged. Fruit 4-5mm, long-beaked. Occasional in ponds and streams. **NS**. Seen by Duvigneaud. (From British specimen, fruit x 4). (Ma, Mi) FE V 10

7. *Potamogeton pectinatus* L. Fennel-leaved Pondweed. Leaves all submerged, narrow linear, usually less than 2mm wide. Spikes dense, becoming interrupted in fruit. Fruit 3-5mm with a short beak. Common in brackish water. (Fruit x 4). (Ma, Mi, I) FE V 11

Other species recorded for Mallorca:
Baldiella ranunculoides (L.) Par. Lesser Water Plantain. Resembles *alisma*, but smaller. Carpels numerous, spirally arranged in a globular head. Possibly not seen since Garcia's collection 1905. Llorens lists. (Ma, Mi) Not BI in FE V 2

Potamogeton species: key to those occurring here:
1. Floating leaves present.
2. Petiole of floating leaves with discoloured flexible joint just below the lamina. *P. natans* L. (Ma, ?I) BI excluded in FE V 9
2. Petiole of floating leaves without joint below lamina.
3. Floating leaves translucent. *P. coloratus* Hornem. (Ma, Mi, I) FE V 9
3. Floating leaves opaque. *P. nodosus* Poiret. (Ma, Mi) Not BI in FE V 9
1. Floating leaves absent.
4. Leaves linear.
5. Leaves narrow linear (usually less than 2mm wide), not undulate: beak of carpel much shorter than body
6. Leaf-sheaths adnate to the leaf base: fruit 3-5mm. *P. pectinatus* L. (Ma, Mi, I) FE V 11
6. Leaf-sheaths free or almost so from leaf-base, but closed, forming a tubular stipule: fruit 2mm. *P. pusillus* L. (Ma, Mi) FE V 10
5. Leaves broad linear (3-15mm wide), usually with undulate margin: beak of carpel as long as body or longer. *P. crispus* L. (Ma, Mi)
4. Leaves elliptical or ovate-elliptical. *P. lucens* L. (Ma) FE V 9

In Minorca only:
Triglochin bulbosa L. subsp. *laxiflora* (Guss.) Rouy. FE V 7

Plate 76

RUPPIACEAE: *RUPPIA*
POSIDONIACEAE: *POSIDONIA*
(ZOSTERACEAE: *ZOSTERA*)
ZANNICHELLIACEAE: *(ALTHENIA), ZANNICHELLIA,*
    CYMODOCEA
NAJADACEAE: *NAJAS*

RUPPIACEAE
RUPPIA

Hairless submerged perennial herbs of saline water, rooted in mud. Stems leafy. Leaves linear, 1mm or less in width, minutely denticulate at apex. Flowers small, hermaphrodite in 2-flowered pedunculate spikes subtended by 2 almost opposite leaves with inflated sheaths. Perianth absent. Stamens 2. Carpels 4 or more, sessile in flower but becoming long stipitate in fruit.

1. *Ruppia maritima* L. Beaked Tasselweed. Peduncles less than 6cm, curved or flexuous in fruit, but not spirally coiled. Common in saline water. **NS.** Seen by Duvigneaud. (Ma, Mi, I) FE V 11
2. *Ruppia cirrhosa* (Pentagna) Grande. Spiral Tasselweed. Peduncles more than 8cm, spirally coiled in fruit. Common in saline water. (Ma, Mi) FE V 11

POSIDONIACEAE
POSIDONIA

3. *Posidonia oceanica* (L.) Delile. Submerged marine perennial, more conspicuous in death than in life! Rhizomes stout. Base of plant densely covered in remains of old leaf-sheaths. Leaves long linear with rounded apex. Peduncles up to 25cm with 3-6 flowers without a perianth. Most of the flowers hermaphrodite, some with vestigial carpels only. Common in off-shore waters. Remains very common on shores: leaves as dry silvery coils or piles of brown rotting debris at the water's edge. Base of plant, sometimes with shining ovoid fruit also common on beaches, and balls about 8cm diameter formed by fibrous matter that becomes matted together by action of sea. (Inflorescence and uncoloured enlarged detail of flower after Hutchinson 1959). (Ma, Mi, I) FE V 12

ZANNICHELLIACEAE
ZANNICHELLIA

4. *Zannichellia palustris* L. Horned Pondweed. Submerged perennial, with male and female flowers separate on the same plant. Stems slender, pale brown, leaves long linear, up to 2mm wide with pointed tip. Male flower without a perianth, the peduncle simulating a filament for 1-3 stamens. Female flower with a cup-like perianth. Fruitlets 3-6mm, subsessile, crenate, curved with a short beak. Locally common in fresh or brackish water. (Enlarged detail of flower below main illustration after Hutchinson 1959). (Ma, Mi, I) FE V 13

CYMODOCEA

5. *Cymodocea nodosa* (Ucria) Ascherson. Submerged perennial with male and female flowers on separate plants. Creeping stems have scars at nodes left by fallen leaves. Leaves 2-7 together on short shoots, up to 40 x 4mm, rounded at tip. Sheaths shining, auriculate. Fruit 8mm, semicircular, compressed with short beak. **NS.** Seen by Duvigneaud. (From Cretan specimen). (Ma, Mi, I) FE V 13

NAJADACEAE
NAJAS

6. *Najas marina* L. Holly-leaved Naiad. Brittle submerged annual, with male and female flowers on different plants. Leaves prickly-toothed on margins and back of midrib. Fresh or brackish water, not marine in spite of name. **NS.** Seen by Duvigneaud. (Main illustration slightly enlarged from British specimen, detail of male flower above and fruit below after drawing in Hutchinson 1959). (Ma) FE V 13

Also recorded from Mallorca:

Zostera noltii Hornem. Dwarf Eelgrass. and *Zostera marina* L. Eelgrass. Perennial submerged marine herbs with creeping stems rooting at the nodes, often exposed at low tide. There is a leaf with a shoot in the axil at each node. Flowering stems are lateral and simple or sparingly branched (in *Z. noltii*), or terminal and much branched (in *Z. marina*). Inflorescence a cyme with a basal spathe. Male flowers with one stamen and female flowers with one ovary with two thread-like stigmas on one style, both without a perianth. In sand or mud, *Z. marina* in rather deeper water. Neither seen by Duvigneaud. Llorens lists both. (Ma, Mi, I) FE V 12

Althenia filiformis Petit. Submerged perennial of brackish water, stems slender, leaves less than 0.5mm wide. Flowers axillary, solitary, male with 3-toothed perianth with one stamen, female with 3 perianth segments and 3 carpels, both on one plant. Seen by Duvigneaud. Llorens queries. (?Ma) Not BI in FE V 13

Plate 77

LILIACEAE (1): *ASPHODELUS, (COLCHICUM), MEREN-DERA, GAGEA, (LILIUM), ORNITHOGALUM, URGINEA*

ASPHODELUS

1. *Asphodelus aestivus* Brot. Asphodel. Robust perennial, often more than 1m. Leaves flat. (x 1/10, detail x 1). Stem solid. Mar.-May. Cultivated areas, often a serious weed. Common. (Ma, Mi, I) FE V 17

2. *Asphodelus fistulosus* L. Onion weed. Annual or short-lived perennial, usually about 50cm. Leaves and stem hollow. (x 1/10, detail x 1). Apr.-May. Waste places, common. (Ma, Mi, I) FE V 17

MERENDERA

3. *Merendera filifolia* Camb. Perennial corm, flowers solitary. Leaves flat, often absent at time of flowering. Sept. Local in rocky places. (Ma, Mi, I) FE V 25

GAGEA

4. *Gagea mauritanica* Durieu. Perennial bulb. Perianth segments 13mm or more. Feb.-Mar. Very rare. (See Rita et al. 1985). (Ma, I) Not in FE (not recorded in Europe at time of publication). From own photo of Ma plant.

5. *Gagea nevadensis* Boiss. (*Gagea iberica* Terrac.). Bulbous perennial. Perianth segments 10mm or less. Feb.-Mar. Rare (this one growing round an informal football pitch!). (Ma, I) FE V 27

ORNITHOGALUM

6. *Ornithogalum narbonense* L. Bath Asparagus. Bulbous perennial. Leaves without white stripe. Flowers in elongated leafless raceme (50cm or so). Perianth milky-white, with green stripe on back of each segment. Apr.-May. Common in grassy places. (Ma, Mi, I) FE V 37

7. *Ornithogalum umbellatum* L. Star of Bethlehem. Leaves with white-stripe on upper surface. Flowers usually less than 20, in a compact raceme suggesting an umbel. Apr.-May. Occasional. (Ma, I) FE V 39

8. *Ornithogalum arabicum* L. Leaves with white stripe. Flowers large (3cm or more across) in elongated raceme, creamy white, with black ovary. Apr.-May. Locally common. (Ma, Mi) FE V 40

URGINEA

9. *Urginea maritima* (L.) Baker. Perennial with large (up to 15cm) bulb, most of it above ground. Flowers small, very numerous, on stems up to 1.5m. Aug.-Oct. Common near sea in rocky places (including abandoned building sites). (flowering bulb and one in leaf x 1/10, detail x 1). (Ma, Mi, I) FE V 41

Also recorded from Mallorca:

Gagea arvensis (Pers.) Dumort. Knoche doubts. Llorens omits. ?BI in FE V 27

Lilium candidum L. Introduced, occasionally seen in wild situations. (Ma) BI not mentioned in FE V 34

Colchicum species: Knoche saw a specimen of Bianor's purporting to be *C. bivonae* Guss. (FE V 24) from near Deyà, but doubted its actual provenance, and thought it was *C. lusitanicum* Brot. (FE V 24) in any case. *C. lusitanicum* ?BI in FE

In other islands:

Asphodelus ramosus L. Ibiza. (Not BI in FE V 17)

Aphyllanthes monspeliensis L. ?Ibiza. BI in FE V 19

Ornithogalum collinum Guss. Ibiza. Not BI in FE V 38

Ornithogalum orthophyllum Ten. subsp. *baeticum* (Boiss.) Zaher. Ibiza. Not BI in FE V 39

Urginea fugax (Moris) Steinh. Ibiza. Not BI in FE V 40

Plate 78

LILIACEAE (2): *SCILLA, BRIMEURA, MUSCARI, ASPARAGUS, RUSCUS, SMILAX*

SCILLA

1. *Scilla autumnalis* L. Autumn Squill. Bulbous perennial. Leaves very short or absent at time of flowering. Sept. Local in dry rocky places. (Ma, Mi, I) FE V 43

BRIMEURA

2. *Brimeura amethystina* (L.) Chouard. Bulbous perennial. Very like *Hyacinthoides non-scripta* (L.) Chouard (Bluebell), but bracts are solitary, not paired, and the flowers are paler and smaller, with stamens all inserted at base of perianth. **NS**. Rare. (Specimen from Spanish mainland). Llorens lists for Ma. Not BI in FE V 44

MUSCARI

3. *Muscari comosum* (L.) Miller. Tassel Hyacinth. Bulbous perennial. Fertile flowers (lower part of inflorescence) brownish, sterile flowers forming tassel, violet. Apr.-May. Dry grassland, common. (Ma, Mi, I) FE V 47
4. *Muscari neglectum* Guss. Fertile flowers blackish-blue, strongly constricted at mouth, with recurved white teeth. Sterile flowers paler without white teeth. Mar.-Apr. Common. (Ma, I) FE V 48
5. *Muscari parviflorum* Desf. Raceme very lax. Flowers pale blue, fertile 3-5mm, sterile very small or absent. Oct. **NS**. (Illustration x 1 1/2, specimen from Rhodes). (Ma) FE V 48

ASPARAGUS

Shrubby scrambling perennials, often with male and female flowers on different plants. Cladodes in bundles or solitary in the axils of reduced leaves, which often have a spiny basal spur. Perianth with 6 segments, slightly connate at base. Fruit a black (here) berry.

6. *Asparagus albus* L. Stems white, with bundles of 10-20 unarmed cladodes (up to 25mm long, less than 2mm wide, and soon falling) in axils of straight spreading spines up to 12mm long. Perianth segments 2-3mm, white. Aug. Fairly common. (Ma, Mi) FE V 72
7. *Asparagus acutifolius* L. Cladodes spiny, 2-8mm long and up to 0.5mm wide, in bundles of 10-30. Perianth segments 3-4mm, creamish. Common in bushy places. (x 1, detail x 2). (Ma, Mi, I) FE V 72
8. *Asparagus stipularis* Forskål. Cladodes usually solitary, 15-30mm, strongly spiny. Perianth segments 3.5-4mm, white, often with purplish tips. Common. (Ma, Mi, I) FE V 72

RUSCUS

9. *Ruscus aculeatus* L. Butcher's Broom. Evergreen shrubby rhizomatous perennial. Leaves small, scarious. Cladodes leaf-like, ovate or broadly lanceolate with spine at tip, dark green and leathery. Minute white flowers and red berries borne in axil of a small bract on cladode. Common in dry scrub. (Ma, Mi, I) FE V 73

SMILAX

10. *Smilax aspera* L. Sarsaparilla. Scrambling or climbing spiny and woody perennial with male and female flowers on different plants. Variable: plants in exposed places often intricately branched, exceedingly prickly, and almost leafless (endemic var. *balearica*). Flowers white or reddish in umbels on stems. Fruit a shining red to blackish berry. Common in scrub and in exposed rocky situations. (Specimens from 4 different plants x 1, and single flower x 2). (Ma, Mi, I) FE V 74

Also recorded from Mallorca:

Brimeura fastigiata (Viv.) Chouard. This resembles 2, but racemes are subcorymbose, and the flowers lilac or white with the segments longer than the tube. (See Rita J. et al. 1985). (Ma, Mi) FE V 44

Recorded from Ibiza:

Scilla obtusifolia Poiret. FE V 43
Scilla numidica Poiret. (Not described in FE)
Dipcadi serotinum (L.) Medicus. FE V 46
Asparagus tenuifolius Lam. Not BI in FE V 73

Plate 79

LILIACEAE (3): *ALLIUM*

(Illustrations all approximately x 1/2-3/4. Leaves included even if actually withered at time of flowering)

Note: Filaments in this genus are often important in distinguishing species. The filaments may be simple and separately inserted at base of the petals, or connate at base into a ring or *annulus*. Some have a basal lamina supporting 3 cusps, with only the central cusp bearing an anther. (See details of illustrations 10 and 11). Other important distinguishing features of this rather difficult genus in **Bold** lettering below:

1. *Allium roseum* L. Rosy Garlic. Not usually much more than 30cm. Umbels usually lax, with few flowers (5-30) on long pedicels, with or without bulbils. Colour rose pink, rarely white. **The only pink-flowered garlic here with simple filaments not united into an annulus.** Mar.-June. Common. FE V 56
2. *Allium neapolitanum* Cyr. Neapolitan Garlic. Easily distinguished by the **stem**, usually about 35cm, **triangular in section with narrow wings on two edges.** Flowers always white. Filaments simple, not united at base. (Ma, Mi, I) Not BI in FE V 57
3. *Allium subhirsutum* L. Hairy Garlic. **Leaves nearly basal, linear, ciliate on margins.** (Only 3 and 4 here combine these features). Flowers white. Filaments simple, free, 1/2 to 3/4 length of perianth. **Anthers brown or pale yellow.** Mar.-May. **NS.** (From garden specimen). Seen by Knoche and Duvigneaud. (Ma, Mi) FE V 57
4. *Allium subvillosum* Salzm. Very like 3, including the **linear, nearly basal, ciliate leaves,** but **anthers are bright orange-yellow** and usually well-exserted. Common, often growing through bushes. (Ma, ?Mi) FE V 57
5. *Allium triquetrum* L. Three-cornered Garlic. Easily recognised by the **three-cornered stem** (but see 2). Flowers white, pendent. Very common, especially in damp places. (Ma, Mi) FE V 58
6. *Allium chamaemoly* L. **Stem very short, umbel in rosette of leaves which spread out on the ground.** Umbel with 2-20 white stellate flowers. Dec.-Mar. Local. **NS.** (From herbarium specimen, collected Ma). (Ma, Mi, I) FE V 58
7. *Allium paniculatum* L. Leaves sheathing lower 1/3-1/2 stem. Umbel usually ovoid in outline, with upper pedicels erect and much longer than curved lower ones. **Spathe with 2 unequal valves, both long-beaked the longer one 5-14cm, greatly exceeding pedicels.** (Like no 8) Perianth pinkish-lilac or white. Stamens all simple, filaments connate into an annulus. Apr.-June. Locally common. Seen by Duvigneaud. (Ma, I) Not BI in FE V 60
8. *Allium pallens* L. Resembles 7, but umbel usually hemispherical in outline and smaller than in 7. Pedicels almost equal in length. **NS.** (Specimen from Spanish mainland). (Ma) FE V 61
9. *Allium ampeloprasum* L. Wild Leek. Stem usually about 1m. Leaves sheathing lower 1/3-1/2 stem, **margins of upper leaves scabrid** (use lens or feel). Head dense (up to 500 flowers: many less if bulbils are present)). Flowers white, pink or dark red (2 illustrations here). **Spathe single with a beak which soon falls,** long or short (sometimes beak falls leaving the base of the spathe – look around for fallen bits). This feature shared with 10. Filaments of inner three stamens tricuspidate. Apr.-June. Very common. (Ma, Mi, I) FE V 63
10. *Allium polyanthum* Schultes & Schultes fil. Like 9, but leaves sheathing basal 1/4 stem: margins of upper leaves smooth (leaves often withered at time of flowering, but margins can still be examined under lens). Umbels more lax than in 9. Common. (Ma, Mi, I) FE V 64
11. *Allium commutatum* Guss. Leaves sheathe basal 1/4-2/3 stem. **Spathe with ovoid base,** about 2cm, **abruptly contracted into a 2-edged beak,** 16-30mm. Perianth segments whitish pink or dull magenta with green or purple keel. Filaments usually all tricuspidate, though inner 3 sometimes simple. Apr.-June. **NS.** (From Italian specimen). Llorens lists. (Ma, Mi, I) Not BI in FE V 64
12. *Allium sphaerocephalon* L. Round-headed Leek. **Leaves semicircular in section, hollow,** a feature shared with 13 only here), sheathing up to 1/3 of stem. Spathe 2-valved, shortly beaked, persistent. Heads globose to broad ovate, pink to dark reddish-purple or white, sometimes with bulbils. Anthers **reddish** until ripe. Stamens exserted, outer 3 usually tricuspidate as well as inner. Apr.-June. Not common. **NS.** (From garden specimen). Seen by Duvigneaud. (Ma, I) ?BI in FE V 66
13. *A. vineale* L. Crow Garlic. Usually rather smaller and more slender than 12, but also has hollow semicircular leaves, in this species sheathing 1/3-2/3 stem. Other differences: spathe with 1-valve with a short beak, soon falling: umbel may have very few flowers and variable number of bulbils, or it may be many-flowered. Outer 3 filaments always simple, anthers exserted or just not. Anthers **yellow.** May-June. Local. (Ma, Mi, I) FE V 67

Also recorded from Mallorca:

Allium oleraceum L. Field Garlic. **Leaves 2-4, hollow below, flat and channelled above.** Umbels with bulbils only or up to 40 flowers, whitish or pinkish, variably tinged with green or brown. Stamens simple, connate into annulus. Llorens lists. Not BI in FE V 61

In other islands:

Allium cupani Rafin. subsp. *hirtovaginatum*. Cabrera FE V 59
Allium senescens L. Cabrera, not BI in FE V 53
Allium victorialis L. Cabrera, not BI in FE V 56
Allium grosii Font Quer. (Ibiza, endemic) FE V 59
Allium eivissanum Garbari & Miceli. (Endemic Ibiza, not described in FE)
Allium ebusitanum Font Quer. (Endemic Ibiza) : see under *A. vineale* L. FE V 67

Plate 80

AMARYLLIDACEAE: *STERNBERGIA, LEUCOJUM, NARCISSUS, PANCRATIUM*
DIOSCOREACEAE: *TAMUS*
IRIDACEAE (1): *IRIS, GYNANDIRIS, CROCUS, (FREESIA)*

AMARYLLIDACEAE
STERNBERGIA
1. *Sternbergia lutea* (L.) Ker-Gawler. Solitary flower superficially like a large Crocus. Oct. **NS.** Listed by several authors. Llorens treats as alien. (Specimen from Rhodes). (Ma) FE V 76

LEUCOJUM
2. *Leucojum aestivum* L. subsp. *pulchellum* (Salisb.) Briq. Summer Snowflake. Scape up to about 60cm, hollow, compressed, 2-winged. Flowers usually 2-4. June-July. Rather local by streams. (Ma, Mi) FE V 77

NARCISSUS
3. *Narcissus serotinus* L. Leaves appear in spring and are absent in Sept. when the flowers appear, 1-3 together. Locally common, roadsides and dry hills. (Ma, Mi, I) FE V 79
4. *Narcissus tazetta* L. Leaves present at time of flowering in March. Flowers in umbels of 3-15 (usually 6 or 7), fragrant. Corona orange. Locally common, in some areas pushing through tarmac at roadsides. (Ma, Mi) FE V 79

PANCRATIUM
5. *Pancratium maritimum* L. Sea Daffodil. Scape stout, with umbel of 3-15 flowers 10-15cm. Leaves appearing before flowers. Aug.-Sept. Sandy or stony beaches and dunes, where locally common. (Ma, Mi) FE V 84

DIOSCOREACEAE
TAMUS
6. *Tamus communis* L. Black Bryony. Climbing perennial with male and female flowers on separate plants. Flowers tiny in long axillary racemes. Fruit a red berry. Apr.-May. Common. (Ma, Mi, I) FE V 85

IRIDACEAE
IRIS
7. *Iris pseudacorus* L. Yellow Flag. Apr.-May. Wet places. Occasional. (Ma, Mi, I) FE V 91
8. *Iris pallida* Lam. Pale Iris. Spathes below inflorescence entirely scarious. May-June. Introduced, occasionally established. (Ma, Mi, I) FE V 91

GYNANDIRIS
9. *Gynandiris sisyrinchium* (L.) Parl. Barbary Nut. Slender perennial growing from a corm. Flowers usually solitary here. Widespread, especially in coastal situations (including at least one area of salt-marsh). (Ma, Mi, I) FE V 92

CROCUS
10. *Crocus cambessedesii* Gay. Flowers 1-2, usually white, sometimes lilac, conspicuously striped and veined on the outside with deep purple. Nov.-Mar. Rocky hillsides and mountains. (Endemic Ma, Mi) FE V 94

Also recorded from Mallorca:

The pure white *Iris albicans* Lange, which has scarious spathes, and bluish-purple *Iris germanica* L. with its white var. *florentina*, with spathes scarious in the distal 1/2 to 2/3, are naturalised here, though not widely. FE V 90-91.

Narcissus elegans (Haw.) Spach, resembling 3, but with flowers in larger umbels and leaves present at time of flowering, is established in several places. (Native in Italy and Sicily). (Ma, I) FE V 80

Freesia refracta (Jacq.) Ecklon, turns up on tips and in fields quite frequently. Flowers are very fragrant, creamish-yellow with orange markings, much brighter on one petal. (Native of S. Africa). Not BI in FE V 92

Plate 81

IRIDACEAE (2): *ROMULEA, GLADIOLUS*
JUNCACEAE: *JUNCUS*

IRIDACEAE
ROMULEA

Small perennial plants, usually with an asymmetrical corm. Basal leaves 2, narrow, often twisted or curved. Stem leaves similar, usually shorter. Pedicels from the axils of stem leaves, semicircular in section, recurved after flowering. Bracts herbaceous or with a hyaline margin, bracteole herbaceous or scarious. Perianth of 6 segments. Style thread-like with 3 bifid branches.

1. *Romulea ramiflora* Ten. Bracteole entirely herbaceous or almost so. Scape usually below ground at flowering time, later elongating and up to 30cm. Flowers lilac-blue with darker veins, yellow-green outside. Feb.-Mar. **NS.** (Side and top view of Portuguese plant x 1). The presence of this plant in Mallorca has recently been questioned: see Rita (1990). (I have a painting done from a specimen collected near Cala Bona that seems to conform to description of *R. ramiflora* – but in absence of specimen this cannot be confirmed). Llorens queries. FE V 100

2. *Romulea columnae* Sebastiani & Mauri. Bract herbaceous, bracteole almost entirely scarious. Perianth 1-3cm. (Flower not from Mallorcan specimen, but fruit beside illustration of *R. ramiflora* is from Mallorca (x about 2/3), and was originally identified as this species. However Dr Rita of the Universitat de les Illes Balears has studied this genus here, and finds that flowering plants seem to be *R. columnae*, but the form and size of fruiting stems varies very much with the habitat, and is often not as described in FE in damp situations (personal communication). Common, especially in seasonally damp situations. (Ma, Mi, I) FE V 100

3. *Romulea assumptionis* Font-Quer & Garc. As 2, but perianth pure white with yellow and violet markings in the throat, about 6mm. Mar.-Apr. Locally common in mountain area. Not described in FE: there is good reason to raise this as a new species and Balearic endemic). (x 2). (Ma, Mi, I)

GLADIOLUS

The three species are very similar. Seeds seem to be distinctive here.

4. *Gladiolus illyricus* Koch. Generally small (but up to 30cm), with few **leaves** that **hardly reach flowering spike. Spike with 3-10 flowers,** very rarely branched. **Anthers equalling filaments or shorter. Seed winged.** Apr.-May. Common in dry scrubby ground and as field weed. (All x 1 except small plant below to show habit). (Ma, Mi, I) FE V 101

5. *Gladiolus communis* L. More robust than 4, commonly 60-80cm. **Leaves reach bottom of 10-30-flowered spike,** which is often branched. **Anthers as 4, seed winged.** Mar.-Apr. Very local, abundant in one site. (Part of spike and branch showing dark-veined sheaths, also seed, all x 1). (Ma, Mi, I) Not BI in FE V 101

6. *Gladiolus italicus* Miller. Robust plant, commonly up to 80cm. Leaves usually reach well above bottom of spike. Spike with 6-16 flowers, often branched. **Anthers always longer than filaments or aborted. Seeds unwinged.** Mar.-Apr. Fairly common as a field weed. (Lateral view of flower x 1, with petal removed to show filaments. Much reduced plant to show habit). Introduced. (Ma, Mi, I) FE V 101

JUNCACEAE
JUNCUS

Hairless herbs, usually of damp places. Leaves narrow with sheathing base. Flowers with 6 perianth segments, (recognisably a flower of similar form to those of Liliaceae), variously arranged in bracteate inflorescences. Ovary superior, becoming a 3-valved capsule (whose form is important in distinguishing between species).

7. *Juncus maritimus* Lam. Sea Rush. Creeping perennial. Stems up to 1m. Leaves basal, 2-4, sharp tipped. Lowest bract sharply pointed, exceeding inflorescence, second much shorter. Inflorescence lax. **Flowers yellowish brown.** Capsule as long or slightly longer than perianth, ovoid, mucronate. Mar.-Oct. Common in saltmarshes and damp places near the sea. (Upper part flowering stem x 1, detail of capsule x 2). (Ma, Mi, I) FE V 104

8. *Juncus acutus* L. Sharp rush. Densely tufted perennial, up to 150cm or more. Leaves basal, 2-5, ending in very sharp spine. Lowest 2 bracts sharply pointed, the longer exceeding the inflorescence. Flowers red-brown. **Capsule 4-6mm, much exceeding perianth,** ovoid, with a conical apex, mucronate. Mar.-Oct. Common in sandy places near the sea. (Top of small fruiting stem x 1, capsule and flower x 2). (Ma, Mi, I) FE V 104

9. *Juncus inflexus* L. Hard Rush. Tufted perennial. **Stem** slender, up to 1m, **with 10-20 prominent ridges and interrupted pith,** leafless apart from brown basal sheaths. Lower bract long, much exceeding inflorescence, appearing as continuation of stem. Flowers brown with narrow acuminate segments in lax cluster. Apr.-June. Damp places, occasional. (Upper part flowering and fruiting stems slightly reduced, details enlarged). (Ma) FE V 104

10. *Juncus subulatus* Forskål. Fine-leaved Rush. Rhizomatous perennial up to about 1m, **with 2-4 leaves on stems (no basal leaves). Pith continuous** in stem. May-July. Common in saltmarshes. (Inflorescence x 1, details enlarged). (Ma, Mi, ?I) FE V 105

11. *Juncus bufonius* L. Toad Rush. **Tufted annual,** usually less than 20cm, up to 50cm. Stems leafy. Inflorescence a spreading cluster, with **most flowers solitary.** Capsule exceeded by narrow acute perianth segments, the outer herbaceous with scarious margin, inner 3 mostly scarious. Seed narrowly elliptical. Apr.-May. Very common in wet places. (x 1, detail of capsule x 2, seed x 10). (Ma) FE V 107

12. *Juncus hybridus* Brot. Annual, resembling 11, but with **flowers in clusters.** Inner perianth segments shorter than outer and less acute. Seed barrel-shaped. (See Cope T.A. and Stace C.A. 1980) Apr.-May. Occasional in damp saline habitats. (Ma, Mi, I) FE V 107

13. *Juncus subnodulosus* Schrank. Blunt-flowered Rush. Rhizomatous perennial, 1m or more. Stems with basal sheaths and 1-2 leaves, bright green with longitudinal and transverse septa. Bracts at base of inflorescence short. **Perianth segments blunt,** the outer boat-shaped. May-July. Wet places. Occasional. (Inflorescence slightly reduced, details enlarged). (Ma, Mi, I) FE V 109

14. *Juncus articulatus* L. Jointed Rush. Tufted or creeping perennial up to about 80cm. Stems with 3-6 leaves. **Leaves and longer bracts with transverse septa,** visible from outside. Inflorescence spreading, with **clustered heads of 5 or more flowers.** Apr.-May. Common in damp places. (Ma, Mi, I) FE V 111

Others recorded for Mallorca:

Juncus effusus L. Soft Rush. Inflorescence a small tight cluster apparently lateral on stem (because a long bract appears to be continuation of stem). Duvigneaud lists. Llorens lists. (Ma, Mi) BI specifically excluded in FE V 105

Juncus capitatus Weigel. Dwarf Rush. Annual. Stems up to 20cm, leafless. Flowers in heads of 5-10 greenish flowers, subtended by two bracts, one at least longer than the inflorescence. Duvigneaud and Llorens list. (Ma, Mi) BI not excluded in FE V 108

Juncus bulbosus L. Resembles 11. Leaves with a bulbous base when submerged. Perianth segments often replaced by adventitious shoots. Duvigneaud lists with query. (Llorens lists *J. mutabilis* Lam., which could be this species). BI not excluded in FE V 109

Juncus fontanesii Gay. Stoloniferous perennial. Leaves septate, on flowering stems arising from nodes. Flowers in heads. Duvigneaud and Llorens list for (Ma, Mi) BI in FE V 110

In Minorca:
Juncus littoralis C.A.Meyer. FE V 104

Plate 82

GRAMINEAE (1): *FESTUCA, LOLIUM, VULPIA, DESMAZE-RIA, CUTANDIA, (MICROPYRUM), (NARDUROIDES)*

FESTUCA

Perennial grasses. Inflorescence usually a panicle. Leaves plicate, involute or flat, ligule membranous. Spikelets pedicellate, usually with 4-7 florets, laterally compressed. Glumes 2, the lower usually 1-veined, the upper 3-veined. Lemma with rounded back, sometimes awned.

1. *Festuca arundinacea* Schreber. Tall Fescue. Up to 200cm in flower, tussock forming. Leaves 5-10mm wide. Inflorescence much branched. Spikelets 10-12mm with 4-5 florets. Lemmas awned or not. May-June. Common in damp places. (Terminal part of inflorescence, slightly reduced. Spikelet with awned lemma x 2). (Ma, Mi, I) FE V 132

LOLIUM

Annual, biennial or perennial grasses. Inflorescence a simple spike with laterally compressed spikelets arranged edgeways to concavities in the rhachis. Lateral spikelets without a lower glume, terminal one with 2 glumes. (Illustrations approx. x 1).

2. *Lolium perenne* L. Perennial Rye-grass. Young leaves flat or folded. Spikelets with 2-10 florets. Glumes usually shorter than spikelet. Lemma usually unawned. Apr.-June. Common. Recent introduction. (Ma, I) FE V 154
3. *Lolium multiflorum* Lam. Italian Rye-grass. Usually annual. Spikelets usually with 11-22 florets. Lemmas usually awned. (Ma, Mi, I) FE V 154
4. *Lolium rigidum* Gaudin. Annual. Spikelets usually with 5-8 florets, often more or less concealed by glumes, which are 3/4 length of floret at least, often exceeding floret. Lemma usually unawned. Common. Duvigneaud and Llorens list. (Ma, Mi, I) Not BI in FE V 154
5. *Lolium temulentum* L. Darnel. Annual. Lemma usually long-awned, very swollen at maturity. (Ma, Mi) FE V 154

VULPIA

Annual grasses (here). Panicles (occasionally racemes) often secund. Spikelets with 3-12 florets, sometimes with a distal group of sterile florets. Glumes very unequal, the upper often awned. Lemma narrow, rounded dorsally, tapering to a long, straight awn. (Main illustration slightly reduced, details enlarged).

6. *Vulpia geniculata* (L.) Link. Diffuse panicle, not secund, branches erect to erecto-patent. Florets open normally with anthers 2-5mm (all other species here are cleistogamous, with anthers 2mm or less). Lower glume 2/5-3/5 length of upper. Apr.-June. Rather uncommon. (Ma, Mi) FE V 155
7. *Vulpia fasciculata* (Forskål) Samp. Typically the inflorescence is partly included in the uppermost leaf-sheath, though not in this robust specimen, which at first glance was taken for a *Bromus* species. Inflorescence a sparingly branched panicle: pedicels 3-7mm, dilated distally. Proximal, fertile florets 2-5. Distal, reduced and sterile florets 3-6. Lower glume less than 1/6 upper. Lemma awn up to 2 x length lemma. Ovary hairy at apex. Mar.-May. Occasional. (Ma, Mi, I) FE V 155
8. *Vulpia membranacea* (L.) Dumort. Dune Fescue. Resembles 7, including distally dilated pedicels. Inflorescence usually well exserted from uppermost leaf-sheath. Ovary hairless at apex. Mar.-May. Local on sandy beaches. (Ma, I) FE V 155
9. *Vulpia bromoides* (L.) S.F.Gray. Squirrel-tail Fescue. Panicle usually smaller and less dense than other species here. Pedicels not dilated distally. Most florets fertile: distally 2-3 gradually reduced and male or sterile. Lower glume 1/2-3/4 length upper. Awn of lemma usually about equalling lemma. Mar.-June. Possibly rare NS. (Illustration from British specimen). (Ma, Mi) FE V 157
10. *Vulpia muralis* (Kunth) Nees. Most florets fertile: distally 2-3 gradually reduced and male or sterile. Lower glume 1/4 - 1/2 length upper. Lemma with awn 2-3 x length lemma. Mar.-June NS. (Illustration from specimen from Spanish mainland). (Ma, Mi, I) FE V 156
11. *Vulpia myuros* (L.) C.C.Gmelin. Rat's Tail Fescue. Resembles 10, but panicle usually partly included in uppermost leaf-sheath. Lower glume 1/10-2/5 length upper. Lemma with awn 1-2 x length. (Ma) FE V 156
12. *Vulpia ciliata* Dumort. Proximal 1-3 florets fertile: distal 3-7 sterile, usually with longer and wider lemmas and shorter awns, densely ciliate. Mar.-May. Common. (Ma, Mi, I) FE V 156

DESMAZERIA

Rather rigid annual grasses. Inflorescence a raceme or panicle. Spikelets with up to 25 florets. Glumes subequal, sometimes keeled. In dry conditions whole plant often turns red.

13. *Desmazeria marina* (L.) Druce. Stiff Sand-grass. Flowering plant up to 25cm, more usually 10cm or so. Inflorescence usually unbranched, sometimes with short branches below. Spikelets in two rows. Pedicels short and stout. Spikelets with 5-14 florets. Lower glume 2-3mm. Mar.-June. Common near sea. (Ma, Mi, I) FE V 158
14. *Desmazeria rigida* (L.) Tutin. Fern Grass. Similar to 13, but usually branched below, with rather narrower spikelets. Lower glume 1.3-2mm. Mar.-June. Common. (Ma, Mi, I) FE V 158
15. *Desmazeria balearica* Willk. (FE index equates with 14) seems to be a particularly well-branched robust form of 14, often with axillary inflorescences. (Ma, Mi, I)

CUTANDIA

16. *Cutandia maritima* (L.) W. Barbey. Resembles *Desmazeria,* but spikelets much larger. Inflorescence branches divaricate. Often prostrate, turning a deep blackish-purple in dry conditions. Mar.-June. Occasional, maritime sands. (Ma, Mi, I) FE V 158

Other species occurring in Mallorca:

Festuca ovina L. Sheep's Fescue. Densely tufted. Stems rarely exceeding 45cm. Leaves 0.7mm wide or less, scabrid towards apex. Panicle dense. Spikelets usually less than 7mm with 3-8 florets. Lemma awned. Llorens lists for Ma. Not BI in FE V 145

Vulpia unilateralis (L.) Stace. Inflorescence a rigid, secund raceme, sometimes with short branches at lower nodes. Llorens lists for (Ma, Mi, I) Not BI in FE V 156

Micropyrum tenellum (L.) Link. Llorens lists for Ma. Not BI in FE V 157

Narduroides salzmannii (Boiss.) Rouy. Llorens lists for Ma. Not BI in FE V 158

Recorded from Ibiza:
Festuca heterophylla Lam. FE V 139

Plate 83

GRAMINEAE (2): *SPHENOPUS, (VULPIELLA), POA, PUCCINELLIA, DACTYLIS, (SCLEROCHLOA), CYNOSURUS, LAMARCKIA, PSILURUS, BRIZA*

SPHENOPUS

1. *Sphenopus divaricatus* (Gouan) Reichenb. Hairless annual. Inflorescence a much-branched panicle, divaricate after flowering. Pedicels slender, mostly in pairs, but distinctive in being gradually thickened distally. (Looks rather like *Aira* species, which sometimes have pedicels thickening distally: this much more marked in *Sphenopus*). Spikelets with 2-5 florets. Lemma unawned (some florets in each spikelet awned in *Aira*). Apr.-May. Rather local in saltmarshes. (Ma, Mi, I) FE V 159

POA

Annuals or perennials. Flowers in more or less pyramidal branched panicles. Spikelets compressed. Glumes and lemmas keeled, lemma usually without an awn. The membranous ligule at the junction of leaf with stem sometimes important for identification.

2. *Poa annua* L. Usually annual, commonly up to 15cm. **Branches of panicle smooth, in pairs**, at least at lower nodes, deflexed after lowering. Spikelets with 3-5 florets. Lemma sparsely hairy on veins, not woolly at base. All year. Very common. (Ma, Mi, I) FE V 161

3. *Poa trivialis* L. Tufted perennial, often 30cm or more. **Leaves 2.5-4mm wide**, thin and soft. **Ligule 3.5-10mm**, pointed. **Panicle branches 3-5 together** at lower nodes, not deflexed after flowering. Spikelets with 3 or more florets. Lemma shortly hairy on keel, woolly at base. Apr.-May. Common in damp places.

4. *Poa angustifolia* L. Densely tufted greyish-green perennial. **Leaves rarely exceed 1.5mm wide**, the basal wiry, strongly folded. **Ligule 1-3mm. Lower panicle branches 3-5 together**, not deflexed after flowering. **NS.** Seen by Duvigneaud. (Ligule only here, from British specimen). Llorens lists (Ma) FE V 162

5. *Poa flaccidula* Boiss. & Reuter. Loosely tufted perennial. **Branches of panicle scabrid, in pairs** at lower nodes, not deflexed after flowering. Lemma appressed hairy on outer surface, sparsely woolly at base. May-June. Occasional in NW mountains. (Ma) FE V 164

6. *Poa bulbosa* L. Tufted perennial, **bulbous at base**, usually around 25cm. Panicle 2-6cm, compact, ovoid. Branches scabrid, in pairs at lower nodes. **Spikelets sometimes purple-tinged and often proliferating**, with 2-6 florets. Common in dry places. (Ma, Mi, I) FE V 165

PUCCINELLIA

7. *Puccinellia fasciculata* (Torrey) E.P.Bicknell. More or less tufted perennial. Leaves bluish. Panicle like that of *Poa*, with 2-4 branches at each node. Some branches, especially short ones, have spikelets right to the base. Spikelets rounded on back (unlike *Poa*). Lemma minutely hairy at base. Apr.-May. Common in saltmarshes – previously identified as *P. distans* (L.) Parl. (BI in FE), though this species does not occur here. (Ma, I) Not BI in FE V 168

DACTYLIS

8. *Dactylis glomerata* Cock's Foot. Coarse tufted perennial. Panicle with spikelets in tight more or less ovate clusters on patent to erect branches. The familiar plant of Northern Europe is less common here than subsp. *hispanica* (Roth) Nyman, with branches mainly erect (illustrated here). May. Common in cultivated areas. (Ma, Mi, I) FE V 171

CYNOSURUS

Annuals here. Panicles lobed, one-sided. Spikelets either fertile, and laterally compressed with 1-5 florets, or sterile, with only narrow glumes and lemmas. Lemmas with apical awn.

9. *Cynosurus echinatus* L. Rough Dog's Tail. Leaves 3-4mm wide. Panicle fairly dense. Upper lemmas of sterile spikelets much the same as lower. Apr.-May. Common in dry grassy places. (Ma, Mi) FE V 171

10. *Cynosurus elegans* Desf. Like 8, but smaller and much less dense. Upper lemmas of sterile spikes much shorter and wider than lower, like the lemmas of fertile spikes. May. Not common. (Specimen from Spanish mainland, but also seen in Mallorca in mountain pasture). (Ma) FE V 172

LAMARCKIA

11. *Lamarckia aurea* (L.) Moench. Golden Dog's Tail. Annual. Fertile spikelets, with one floret and a sterile rudiment, surrounded by 2-4 sterile spikelets with many florets – all fall together. Lemma of fertile floret with a long awn from the sinus. The whole panicle turns golden at maturity. Apr.-May. Common in cultivated areas. (Ma, Mi) FE V 172

PSILURUS

12. *Psilurus incurvus* (Gouan) Schinz & Thell. Annual. Leaves and stems thread-like. Spikelets with one hermaphrodite floret widely spaced in joints of angular rhachis. Terminal spikelet with 2 glumes, others with one. Lemma linear-lanceolate, exceeding spikelet, with apical awn. **NS.** Seen by Duvigneaud. Rare, or overlooked. (From Cretan specimen). (Ma, I) FE V 173

BRIZA

Annual. Spikelets broader than long, pendent on long slender pedicels.

13. *Briza maxima* L. Quaking or Totty Grass. Usually 5 or fewer spikelets (but occasionally up to 12), 14-25mm, often purplish brown. Apr.-May. Common. (Ma, Mi, I) FE V 173

14. *Briza minor* L. Spikelets numerous, 3-5mm, usually greenish. Apr.-May. Common, but less so than 13. (Ma, Mi, I) FE V 173

In Minorca:
Poa infirma Kunth. Not BI in FE V 161
Sclerochloa dura (L.) Beauv. Not BI in FE V 170

Plate 84

GRAMINEAE (3): *SESLERIA, MELICA, BROMUS*

SESLERIA

Tufted perennial grasses. Inflorescence a spike-like panicle with well-developed toothed bracts at the base. Spikelets laterally compressed with 2-5 florets. Glumes unequal, membranous.

1. *Sesleria insularis* Sommier subsp. *insularis.* Glumes 4-6mm, ciliate, with 2-3mm awn. (x 1, with lowest spikelet subtended by toothed bract x 3). (Ma) FE V 177

MELICA

Perennials. Inflorescence a panicle. Spikelets with terminal club-like structure formed by sterile lemmas.

2. *Melica minuta* L. Lax inflorescence, more or less branched, usually purplish. Spikelets 5-9mm, with 2 fertile florets. Mar.-May. Common. (x 1/2, details slightly enlarged). (Ma, I) FE V 178
3. *Melica ciliata* L. Panicle rather dense, spike-like at least above. Spikelets 4-8mm. Fertile lemmas with long hairs on margins and veins, inflorescence softly hairy at time of flowering. Mar.-May. Common. (x 1/2, spikelet x 2). (Ma, MI) FE V 178
4. *Melica bauhinii* All. Resembles 3, but panicle (or raceme, as here), is lax. Spikelets 8-10mm. Lemma hairless in distal 1/3. Not common. **NS.** (From garden specimen, reduced). Llorens omits. Duvigneaud lists. (Ma) FE V 179

BROMUS

Annual or (rarely) biennial. Inflorescence a panicle with long many-flowered spikelets, drooping or erect, often on long pedicels. Illustrations offer only a rough guide to identification, and keys in the FE or elsewhere do not seem to help in distinguishing 8, 9 and 10. General habit seems more significant (Fatima Sales, private communication.).
(Main illustrations x 1/3-1/2, details x 1).

5. *Bromus diandrus* Roth. Great Brome. Panicle branches long, spreading, usually with a single spikelet. Lemma 20-35mm, lanceolate, tapering to deeply notched apex with 35-65mm awn, which is flat and scabrid. Mar.-May. Common. (Ma, Mi, I) FE V 183
6. *Bromus rigidus* Roth. Panicle branches short, held stiffly erect. Spikelets resemble those of 5. Occasional. (Ma, Mi, I) FE V 183
7. *Bromus sterilis* L. Barren Brome. Like 5, but spikelets usually smaller, awn only 15-30mm. Very dubious here. **NS.** Llorens omits. Knoche includes many 'forms', now recognised as other species. (From British specimen). BI not excluded in FE V 183
8. *Bromus madritensis* L. Panicle erect, lax. Branches 10mm or more. Spikelets wedge-shaped. (Panicle often more dense than here, but peripheral spikelets at least usually distinct, not concealed among other spikelets as usual in no 10). Mar.-May. Common. (Ma, Mi, I) FE V 184
9. *Bromus fasciculatus* C.Presl. Small plant. Panicle 4-5cm, with rigid branches. Occasional. **NS.** (Specimen from Spanish mainland). (Ma, Mi, I) FE V 184
10. *Bromus rubens* L. Panicle dense with rigid branches. Mar.-May. **NS.** (Specimen from Spanish mainland). (MA, Mi, I) FE V 184
11. *Bromus hordeaceus* L. Soft Brome. Spikelets ovate, softly hairy. Awn of lemma straight, erect. Mar.-May. Common. (Ma, Mi, I) FE V 187
12. *Bromus lanceolatus* Roth. Spikelets elongated, up to 5cm with as many as 20 florets with long awns, flattened at base. Mar.-May Rare. **NS.** (From garden specimen). Could perhaps be confused with *Avenula bromoides* (Plate 86), which is a tufted perennial. (Ma, Mi) FE V 188

Also recorded from Mallorca:
Bromus squarrosus L. Barceló recorded as very rare. Llorens lists for Ma, Mi. BI in FE V 188
Bromus wildenowii Kunth. Specimen recently collected in Mallorca by R. Palmer. Llorens lists for Ibiza. FE V 189

In Minorca:
Bromus arvensis L. FE V 186

Plate 85

GRAMINEAE (4): *BRACHYPODIUM, ELYMUS, AEGILOPS, TRITICUM, (DASYPYRUM)*

BRACHYPODIUM

Inflorescence a raceme of long many-flowered spikelets, inserted edgeways to rhachis.

1. *Brachypodium sylvaticum* (Hudson) Beauv. False Brome. Tufted **perennial** with lax stems. Leaves hairy. Spikelets rather widely spaced, with 8-22 florets with **lemmas awned to at least 7mm**. Apr.-June. Local. (Ma, Mi, I) FE V 189

2. *Brachypodium retusum* (Pers.) Beauv. Wiry, stiff creeping perennial. Leaves bluish, appearing linear because convolute. Raceme usually of less than 5 widely spaced stiff **spikelets 20-30mm**, lemmas **usually unawned**, sometimes with awn up to 4mm. Apr.-June. Common in dry places, usually in the mountain area. (Ma, Mi, I) FE V 190

3. *Brachypodium phoenicoides* (L.) Roemer & Schultes. Resembles 2, but larger and less stiff. Leaves flat and flaccid, or convolute and stiff. Raceme of 6-13 long **spikelets 30-60mm**, often curved, and usually overlap one another. **Awns up to 2.5mm or (usually) absent.** Common in dry places. (Ma, Mi, I) FE V 190

4. *Brachypodium distachyon* (L.) Beauv. **Annual. Upper leaf with characteristic twist.** Spikelets few, with up to about 16 florets, lemma with straight **awn 7-15mm**. Mar.-May. Common. (Ma, Mi, I) FE V 190

ELYMUS

Inflorescence a spike, with spikelets on alternate sides of rhachis. Flattened side towards rhachis.

5. *Elymus elongatus* (Host) Runemark. Tufted perennial, not creeping. Rhachis usually with **spiny hairs** on angles, **not disarticulating** when ripe. June-July. Local, saltmarshes and higher parts of beaches. **NS.** Seen by Duvigneaud. (Specimen from Spanish mainland). (Ma, Mi, I) FE V 194

6. *Elymus repens* (L.) Gould. Couch Grass. Creeping perennial. Leaf-blades finely pointed, but not hard and sharp. Rhachis **not disarticulating**. June-July. Common agricultural weed. (Green and bluish forms shown). (Ma, Mi, I) FE V 196

7. *Elymus pungens* (Pers.) Melderis. Sea Couch. Creeping perennial. **Leaf-blades with sharp and hard-pointed tips.** Rhachis not disarticulating. Uncommon. Dry soils, usually near the sea. NS. Seen by Duvigneaud. (Specimen from Spanish mainland). (Ma, Mi, I) FE V 196

8. *Elymus farctus* (Viv.) Runemark ex Melderis. Sand Couch. Creeping perennial. **Rhachis disarticulating** just above each spikelet (places where this occurs clearly visible before maturity). May-Sept. Common on beaches. (Ma, Mi, I) FE V 197

AEGILOPS

Annuals. Inflorescence a spike. Lower spikelets often vestigial, upper sometimes sterile. Glumes swollen and leathery, with several teeth or awns.

9. *Aegilops ventricosa* Tausch. **Spike cylindrical, more than 10 x as long as wide.** Glumes with teeth or very short awns. Lemmas usually with one awn. Common. Apr.-June. (Ma, Mi) FE V 201

10. *Aegilops triuncialis* L. **Spike up to 5 x as long as wide,** gradually tapering upwards. Awns of lemmas shorter than awns of glumes, which are 7-10mm on lowest spikelet, 30-60mm on terminal spikelet. May-June. Rare. (From garden specimen, but seen in Mallorca). (Ma) Not BI in FE V 201

11. *Aegilops geniculata* Roth. **Spike about 2 x as long as wide.** Awns of glumes about equalling awns of lemmas. Apr.-May. Common. (Ma, Mi, I) FE V 201

TRITICUM

Cultivated wheat. Several species and varieties are cultivated. They are annuals, usually with large spikes with awned or unawned glumes.

12. *Triticum aestivum* L. is illustrated here as an example, sometimes found as a casual, commonly cultivated. Ma, Mi, I) FE V 203

Also recorded from Mallorca:

Aegilops neglecta Req. ex Bertol. Resembles 10, but top of spike abruptly contracted, upper 1 or 2 spikelets sterile. Llorens lists. (Ma) Not BI in FE V 202

In Minorca only:

Elymus pycnanthus (Godron) Melderis. FE V 196
Dasypyrum villosum (L.) P.Candargy. FE V 203

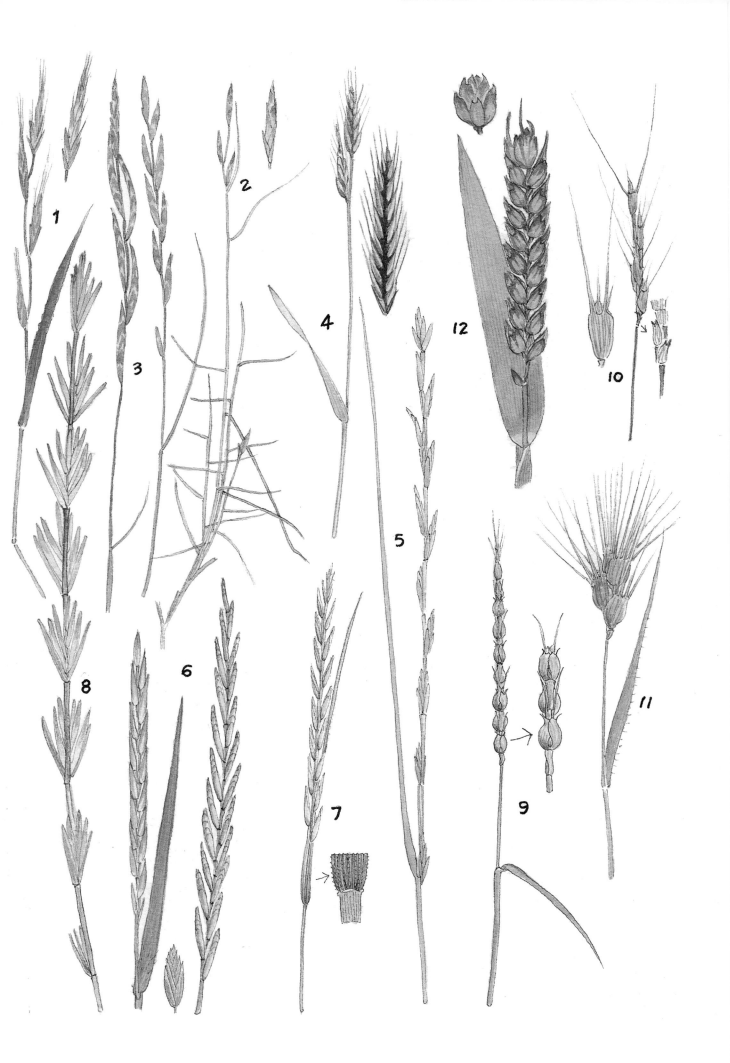

Plate 86

GRAMINEAE (5): *HORDEUM, AVENA, AVENULA, ARRHENATHERUM, GAUDINIA, (KOELERIA), LOPHOCHLOA, TRISETUM, LAGURUS, AIRA*

HORDEUM

Annuals here. Inflorescence a dense spike with spikelets arranged in two rows of triplets, a central hermaphrodite spikelet between 2 vestigial or male spikelets. The glumes and lemmas have long awns.

1. *Hordeum murinum* L. Wall Barley. Glumes of central spikelet in each trio long-ciliate. Mar.-May. Common in disturbed ground. (Ma, Mi, I) FE V 204
2. *Hordeum marinum* Hudson. Sea Barley. Glumes of central spikelet slightly rough, not ciliate. Inner glume of lateral spikelets winged at base. Apr.-June. Fairly common near the sea. (Ma, Mi) FE V 205

AVENA

Annuals. Inflorescence a branched panicle of drooping spikelets. Lemmas with long geniculate awns. In addition to the two given below, are cultivated species with spikelets falling entire above the glumes.

3. *Avena barbata* Pott ex Link. Bearded Oat. Spikelets 18-30mm. Lemma with woolly hairs up to the insertion of awn, apex with 2 bristles 3-12mm long. Spikelets fall apart above the glumes and between the florets when mature. Apr.-May. Common. (x 2/3, details x 1: smaller detail shows back of lemma without awn). (Ma, Mi, I) FE V 206
4. *Avena sterilis* L. Winter Wild Oat. Like 3, but generally more robust. Spikelets 25-45mm without awns. Lemma with rigid hairs in lower 2/3, apex with teeth up to 1.5mm. Spikelets fall entire above the glumes. (MA, Mi, I) FE V 208

AVENULA

5. *Avenula bromoides* (Gouan) H.Scholz. Tufted rather bluish green perennial. Inflorescence a loose panicle. Spikelets 12-20mm with 7-8 florets. Lemmas with divaricate awns. Apr.-May. Common. (Plants here differ from FE description in some respects. Panicles frequently have more than 20 spikelets. Glumes are acute, lemmas regularly bifid at apex). (Ma, Mi, I) FE V 215

ARRHENATHERUM

6. *Arrhenatherum elatius* (L.) Beauv. ex J. & C. Presl. False Oat-Grass. Tufted perennial. Inflorescence a panicle of erect or spreading spikelets with 2 florets. Lower lemma with geniculate awn arising from lower 1/3, upper with a fine short bristle from near tip. Not common. Apr.-May. NS. Seen by Duvigneaud. (Specimen from Spanish mainland). (Ma, I) FE V 216

GAUDINIA

7. *Gaudinia fragilis* (L.) Beauv. Annual. Inflorescence a spike with spikelets appressed to rhachis in 2 opposite rows. Glumes unequal, lower short, narrow and acute, upper nearly as long as spikelet, broad and blunt with 7 strong veins. Lemmas with dorsal awns, geniculate and twisted when dry. Apr.-May. Occasional. (Ma, Mi, I) FE V 217

LOPHOCHLOA

8. *Lophochloa cristata* (L.) Hyl. Annual. Inflorescence a spike-like panicle, usually dense, cylindrical to ovoid. Spikelets 3-7.5mm, with 2-5 florets. Lemma shortly bifid with 5 veins and a short straight awn from near apex. Mar.-May. Very common. (Ma, Mi, I) FE V 220

TRISETUM

(Not numbered). *Trisetum paniceum* (Lam.) Pers. Tufted annual, looking like a lobed version of 8 (indeed painted originally in the supposition that it was this) appears to the left of the three (unlobed) *Lophochloa cristata* (no 8). Spikelets 3-5.5mm, with 2 or more florets slightly exceeding the glumes. Lemma acute or bicuspidate with a 1.5-4mm awn. Mar.-May. Fairly common. (Ma, Mi) FE V 224

9. *Trisetum aureum* Ten. Golden Oat-grass. Tufted annual. Spikelets about 3mm in fairly dense pyramidal to ovoid panicle. Lemma with bent awn inserted slightly above middle. Palea silvery, not enclosed by lemma at maturity. Apr.-May. Fairly common in sandy places. (Ma) FE V 224

LAGURUS

10. *Lagurus ovatus* L. Hare's Tail. Annual with soft woolly ovoid panicle. Mar.-May. Common. (Ma, Mi, I) FE V 225

AIRA

11. *Aira cupaniana* Guss. Annual. Inflorescence a wiry branched panicle of small spikelets (2-3.5mm) with 2 florets and pedicels thickened at apex. Glumes more or less obtuse, often mucronate, exceeding lemmas. Upper floret with lemma awned below the middle, lower often unawned. Apr.-May. Rather local in sandy places. (Ma, Mi, I) FE V 227

Other species recorded for Mallorca:

Hordeum hystrix Roth. Resembles 2, but glumes of lateral spikelets similar, unwinged. Seen by Duvigneaud. Llorens lists. (Ma, Mi) FE V 205

Avena fatua L. Wild Oat. Resembles 4, but spikelets fall apart above the glumes and between the florets, and spikelets 18-25mm. Duvigneaud queries. Llorens lists. (Ma) BI not excluded in FE V 207

Koeleria macrantha (Ledeb.) Schultes. Knoche's synonyms ambiguous. Duvigneaud lists. Llorens omits. BI in FE V 219

Aira caryophyllea L. Resembles 12, but pedicels not thickened at apex and glumes acute to acuminate. Llorens lists. Not BI in FE V 227

In other islands:

Avenula crassifolia (Font Quer) J.Holub. Ibiza, endemic. FE V 215

Arrhenatherum album (Vahl) W.D.Clayton. Ibiza. Not BI in FE V 216

Aira elegantissima Schur. Minorca. FE V 227

Aira tenorii Guss. Minorca. FE V 228

Plate 87

GRAMINEAE: *ANTHOXANTHUM, HOLCUS, AVELLINIA, TRIPLACHNE, AGROSTIS, GASTRIDIUM, POLYPOGON, AMMOPHILA, PHLEUM, ALOPECURUS*

ANTHOXANTHUM

1. *Anthoxanthum odoratum* L. Sweet Vernal-grass. Coumarin-scented tufted perennial. Inflorescence spike-like usually (right illustration). Spikelets 7-9mm, with 2 basal sterile, and a terminal hermaphrodite floret. Glumes very unequal, upper enfolding floret. Lemmas shortly awned. Apr.-May. Scattered in mountain areas. (Ma, Mi) FE V 230

HOLCUS

2. *Holcus lanatus* L. Yorkshire Fog. Softly hairy perennial. Panicle lax, greenish, whitish or purple. Spikelets 4-6mm, with 2-3 florets, lower hermaphrodite, terminal male. Upper glume longer and broader than lower, usually shortly awned. Lemma of at least upper floret with hooked awn. May-June. Not common. (From British specimen). (Ma, Mi, I) FE V 230

AVELLINIA

3. *Avellinia michelii* (Savi) Parl. Panicle 2-7cm, elongated ovoid, often lobed. Stems numerous, puberulent. Spikelets 3-5mm, with very unequal glumes, the upper mucronate and nearly as long as spikelet. Lower glume 1/4 length of upper or less. Apr.-May. Common. (From Duvigneaud's Mallorcan specimen). (Ma, Mi, I) FE V 232

TRIPLACHNE

4. *Triplachne nitens* (Guss.) Link. Annual. Panicle densely cylindrical to long-ovoid. Spikelets 3.5-4mm, glumes both exceeding the single floret. Lemma (L) brown, with geniculate awn from near base. Two veins run out to form setae on the truncate apex. **NS.** (Resembles *Lophochloa cristata* and could be overlooked). (Specimen from Spanish mainland). Seen by Duvigneaud. (Ma, Mi, I) FE V 232

AGROSTIS

Inflorescence lax, more or less pyramidal, much-branched. Spikelets small, the one floret enclosed by glumes which persist when the spikelet falls.

5. *Agrostis pourretii* Willd. Annual. Lemma less than 1/2 length lower glume, with lateral veins which run out beyond the tip and a 3mm awn. Rare. **NS.** (Specimen from Spanish mainland.). Listed by Duvigneaud and Llorens. Not BI in FE V 234

6. *Agrostis stolonifera* L. Creeping Bent. Tufted perennial with leafy stolons. Panicle open only at time of flowering, otherwise spike-like. Spikelets 2-3mm. Lemma at least 2/3 length glumes, usually unawned. Apr.-May. Common. (Ma, Mi, I) FE V 234

GASTRIDIUM

7. *Gastridium ventricosum* (Gouan) Schinz & Thell. Nit Grass. Annual, panicle spreading in flower, contracted before and after. Spikelets with one floret usually 3-4mm, glumes longer than the floret, shiny, swollen and coriaceous below, constricted immediately above swelling, with long subulate apex. Apr.-May. Occasional. (Ma, Mi, I) FE V 235

POLYPOGON

Resembles *Agrostis*, but inflorescence generally more dense, and spikelets fall entire with glumes.

8. *Polypogon monspeliensis* (L.) Desf. Annual Beard-grass. Panicle, dense, silky, often lobed. Glumes shortly ciliate in the proximal part, awn 5-7mm arising from apical sinus. Lemma with short apical awn. Apr.-May. Common in damp places. (Ma, MI, I) FE V 235

9. *Polypogon maritimus* Willd. Panicle smaller and less silky than in 8, often partly included in inflated sheath of upper leaf. Glumes long-ciliate and awned, lemma unawned. Local in damp places near the sea. (Ma, Mi, I) FE V 235

10. *Polypogon viridis* (Gouan.) Breistr. Water Bent. Stoloniferous perennial. Panicle dense, deeply lobed, not silky. Glumes and lemma unawned. Local. (Ma, Mi, I) FE V 235

AMMOPHILA

11. *Ammophila arenaria* (L.) Link subsp. *arundinacea* H.Lindberg fil. Marram Grass (subsp. *arenaria* in NW Europe only). Robust rhizomatous perennial. Leaves convolute. Panicle cylindrical, rigid. Spikelets with one floret only, 12-14mm. Glumes and lemma about equal, lemma with short awn from near apex. May-June. Common on coastal dunes. (Main illustration x 3/4). FE V 236

PHLEUM

12. *Phleum arenarium* L. Sand Cat's tail. Annual. Panicle dense cylindrical to ovoid up to 5.5cm, usually less. Spikelets 2.2-4.4mm, strongly compressed, with one floret. Glumes with stiff spreading hairs on keel. Lemma truncated, about 1/3 length glumes. Local in sandy places. Seen by Duvigneaud. (From Mallorcan specimen). (Ma) Not BI in FE V 240

ALOPECURUS

13. *Alopecurus myosuroides* Hudson. Slender Fox-tail, or Black Twitch. Panicle spike-like. Spikelets of one floret. Glumes connate for up to half length. Margins of lemma united below, with long slightly bent awn from near base. Rather rare. **NS.** (From British specimen). Duvigneaud and Llorens list. (Ma) Not BI IN FE V 242

In other islands:
Anthoxanthum aristatum Boiss. Minorca. FE V 230
Corynephorus divaricatus (Pourret) Breistr. Formentera. Not BI IN FE V 231

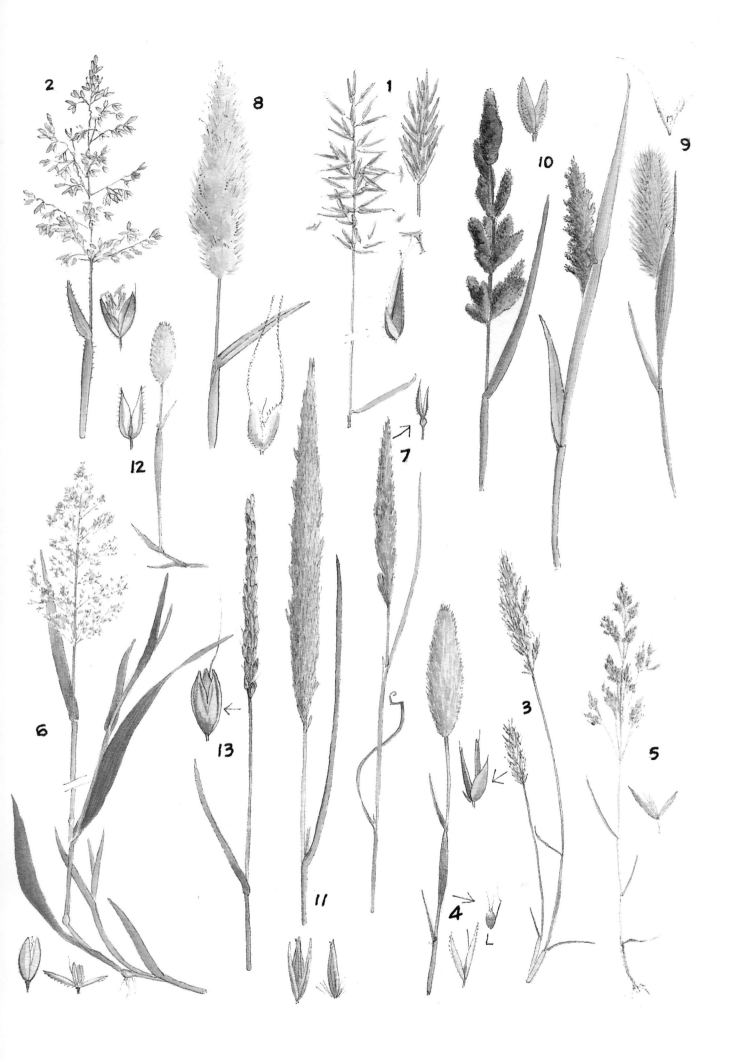

Plate 88

GRAMINEAE (7): *PARAPHOLIS, HAINARDIA, PHALARIS, PIPTATHERUM*

PARAPHOLIS

Annuals. Spikelets with one floret embedded in cavities of the rhachis (1, fig. ii left). Glumes 2, side by side, covering cavity (1, fig. i and fig. ii right). Scarious outer margin of glumes (fig. i M) abruptly inflexed, so that keel (K) seems from outside to be outer margin. Keel may be winged (2, fig. i K) or not. Rhachis breaks when mature beneath each spikelet. Main illustration x 1 except where stated otherwise.

1. *Parapholis incurva* (L.) C.E.Hubbard. **Spikes** often strongly **curved**, with 10-20 spikelets, rather longer than internodes. **Glumes unwinged. Anthers less than 1mm.** Apr.-June. Common, drier parts of saltmarshes and sandy and rocky places near the sea (including Palma airport, where it resists much trampling). (Ma, Mi, I) FE V 243

2. *Parapholis filiformis* (Roth) C.E.Hubbard. Sea Hard-grass. Much like 1, but stems more slender and not curved. **Glumes with narrowly winged keels.** June-July. Local, saltmarshes. (Spike x 3. L is lemma appressed to rhachis after flowering). (Ma, Mi, I) FE V 243

3. *Parapholis pycnantha* (Hackel) C.E.Hubbard. Straggling plant up to 60cm. Spikes straight. **Keel of glumes unwinged. Anthers 3-4mm.** Seen by Duvigneaud and listed by Llorens. Not BI in FE V 244

HAINARDIA

4. *Hainardia cylindrica* (Willd.) W.Greuter. Very like *Parapholis*, but **only the terminal spikelet has 2 glumes.** When in flower the glumes of *Parapholis* separate a little, but otherwise it can be difficult to distinguish from *Hainardia*. **NS.** Not seen by Duvigneaud, but has been recently collected in Mallorca. (Ma, Mi, I) FE V 244

PHALARIS

Annual or perennial grasses. Panicle dense, ovoid or cylindrical, rarely lobed. Spikelets strongly compressed, usually with three florets. Only one is fully developed, the other 1 or 2 are represented by small lemmas. Glumes large, flattened and papery with prominent green veins. The characteristics of the glumes and relative sizes of fertile and sterile lemmas are much more important in identification than general shape of spike, which varies quite a lot.

5. *Phalaris aquatica* L. Creeping perennial usually about 1m. Spikelets all hermaphrodite. **Glumes** acute, **with untoothed wings tapering to apex. Lowest lemma minute or absent.** Panicle normally unlobed. (2 specimens, both from Mallorca, illustrated here. The one on the right is typical of this species, the one on the left untypical. It might possibly be *Phalaris arundinacea* L., though this has not previously been recorded here). (Ma, Mi, I) FE V 244

6. *Phalaris canariensis* L. Canary Grass. Annual. Panicle ovoid. Spikelets 7-9mm, mostly hermaphrodite. **Glumes with untoothed wing. Sterile lemmas at least half length fertile lemmas.** Apr.-May. Common casual. (Ma, Mi) FE V 244

7. *Phalaris minor* Retz. Lesser Canary Grass. Very like 6, but spikelets 4.5-5.5mm, and **glumes with a toothed wing. Sterile lemmas less than 1/5 x fertile.** Apr.-May. Common, usually a field weed. (Name is misleading, panicles 15x70mm are not uncommon). (Ma, Mi, I) FE V 244

8. *Phalaris brachystachys* Link. Very like 6, but **sterile lemmas both less than 1mm**, the lower with hairs on the margin, the second hairless. **Wing of glume untoothed.** Apr.-May. Common, field weed and ruderal. (Ma, Mi, I) FE V 245

9. *Phalaris paradoxa* L. Annual. Panicle often partly enclosed in the inflated sheath of top leaf. **Spikelets in groups of 5-7**, central sessile and hermaphrodite, 6-8mm, others male or abortive. **Glumes narrow with scabrid margin and single tooth near apex.** Spikes fall together as a group, leaving bare rhachis at top of panicle. Apr.-May. Occasional field weed. (Ma, Mi) FE V 245

10. *Phalaris coerulescens* Desf. Much like 9, but perennial, with swollen stem-base. **Margin of glume wings not scabrid: several teeth near apex.** Apr.-May. **NS.** Seen by Duvigneaud. (Specimen from Spanish mainland). (Ma, Mi) FE V 245

PIPTATHERUM

Perennial grasses. Inflorescence a lax panicle. Spikelets with 1 floret. Glumes equal, the lower 5-veined, the upper 3-5-veined.

11. *Piptatherum miliaceum* (L.) Cosson. Up to about 1m. Panicle diffuse with hundreds of spikelets. Branches 4-8 or more at each node. **Spikelets 3-4mm**, in distal half of branches. Lemma with 3-5mm awn. Apr.-May. (Panicle x 1/2, details x 1 and x 4). (Ma, Mi, I) FE V 246

12. *Piptatherum coerulescens* (Desf.) Beauv. Smaller plant than 11. Panicle branches 1-3 at each node. **Spikelets 6-8mm**, twice the size of those of 11, but much less numerous. Apr.-May. Common in dry places in the mountains. (Ma, Mi, I) FE V 246

Also in Mallorca:

Parapholis marginata Runemark. Resembles 1, but with spikes not curved, glumes with winged keel, and (usually) inflated reddish leaf-sheaths. Listed by Duvigneaud and Llorens. (Ma, I) FE V 243

Piptatherum thomasii (Duby) Kunth. Resembles 11, but has 20-50 short branches at lowest node which are sterile, or bear only a single spikelet. Llorens lists. (Ma) see FE V 246

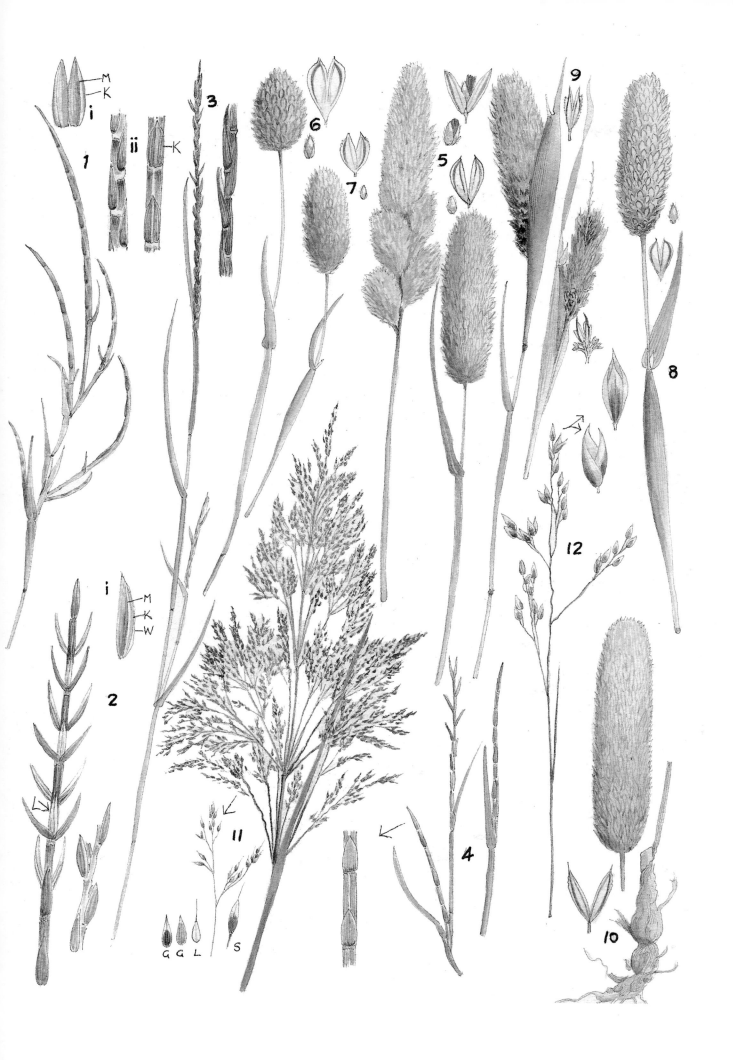

Plate 89

GRAMINEAE (8): *STIPA, AMPELODESMOS, ARUNDO, PHRAGMITES, (CORTADERIA), AELUROPUS, ERAGROSTIS*

STIPA

Leaves convolute at least when dry. Inflorescence a slender panicle. Spikelets with one floret, the lemma with a very long awn.

1. *Stipa capensis* Thunb. Annual or biennial. Mature lemma straw-coloured with awn 7-10cm, awns lying parallel to one another until ripe, so that dense, straw-coloured panicle resembles brushed hair. When ripe lemma becomes 2-geniculate. The part above the upper bend (the seta) remains straight, and the rest (the column) becomes twisted, often round adjacent spikelets (unbrushed hair!). Apr.-June. Common. (Ma, Mi, I) FE V 250

2. *Stipa offneri* Breistr. Tufted perennial. Brownish elongated panicle is few-flowered. Mature lemma brownish, with awn 9-11cm, becoming twisted as in 1. Apr.-June. Locally common, mainly in the South. **NS.** Seen by Duvigneaud. (Specimen from Spanish mainland. Seta of awn is more or less straight, shown curved in enlargement here to indicate relative length). (Ma, Mi, I) FE V 251

3. *Stipa bromoides* (L.) Dörfler. Tufted perennial, resembling 2, but with awn 1.5-2.5cm, also straight. Apr.-June. Occasional. (Specimen from Spanish mainland, though seen subsequently in Mallorca). Seen by Duvigneaud. Llorens lists. (Ma) ?BI in FE V 252

AMPELODESMOS

4. *Ampelodesmos mauritanica* (Poiret) T.Durand & Schinz. Robust tufted perennial, commonly up to 2m or more in flower. Inflorescence a panicle, up to 50cm. Mar.-May. Commonly dominant in open rocky scrub. (Much reduced, detail x 3). (Ma, Mi, I) FE V 252

ARUNDO

5. *Arundo donax* L. Giant Reed. Creeping perennial grass, flowering stems up to 6m. Inflorescence a more or less erect much-branched panicle. Spikelets 12-18mm with 3 florets. Lemma shortly awned, with long soft hairs from the lower part. July-Oct. Wet places, planted for shelter; used formerly for manufacture of paper and baskets, and as roofing. (x 1/20, detail x 1). Introduced from SE Asia. (Ma, I) FE V 253

PHRAGMITES

6. *Phragmites australis* (Cav.) Trin. ex Steudel. Common Reed. Similar to 5, but smaller. Panicle more or less drooping to one side. Spikelets with up to 10 florets. Lemma without hairs. Rhachilla with numerous long silvery hairs. July-Oct. Common in wet places. (Much reduced; detail of spikelet x 2). (Ma, Mi, I) FE V 253

AELUROPUS

7. *Aeluropus littoralis* (Gouan.) Parl. Perennial with creeping rhizomes. Leaves stiffly spreading in 2 rows (beware confusion with *Sporobolus pungens* on Plate 90). Inflorescence narrowly ovoid, 2-sided, with almost sessile short spikes, each with about 20 spikelets, arranged broadside to rhachis. Spikelets usually with 4-8 florets. April. Sandy places, usually maritime. **NS.** Not seen by Duvigneaud. (Specimen from Spanish mainland: detail of spikelet x 4; spike, front and side view, and arrangement of spikes also shown). Llorens lists. (Ma, I) FE V 256

ERAGROSTIS

Annual. Ligule a row of hairs. Panicle loosely branched, of elongated many-flowered spikelets without awns. Glumes keeled, almost equal.

8. *Eragrostis cilianensis* (All.) F.T.Hubbard. Leaves glandular on the margin and midrib. Spikelets with up to 40 florets. June-Sept. **NS.** Not seen by Duvigneaud. (From Cretan specimen). Llorens lists. (Ma, Mi, I) FE V 257

9. *Eragrostis barrelieri* Daveau. Similar to 8, but leaves without glands and spikelets generally smaller, with 10-20 florets. June-Sept. Fairly common. (Ma) FE V 257

Also recorded from Mallorca:

Arundo plinii Turra. Resembles 5, but smaller. Spikelets 8-10mm with 1-2 florets. Duvigneaud omits. Llorens lists. (Ma) BI in FE V 252

Cortaderia selloana (Schultes & Schultes fil.) Ascherson & Graebner. Pampas Grass. Large tufted perennial with blue-green leaves 1-3m long. Panicle with erecto-patent branches in male plant, patent in female. Native of S. America, well established in Alcudia area. (Ma) FE V 253

In Ibiza only:

Stipa tenacissima L. FE V 251

Schismus barbatus (L.) Thell. FE V 254

Lygeum spartum L. FE V 255

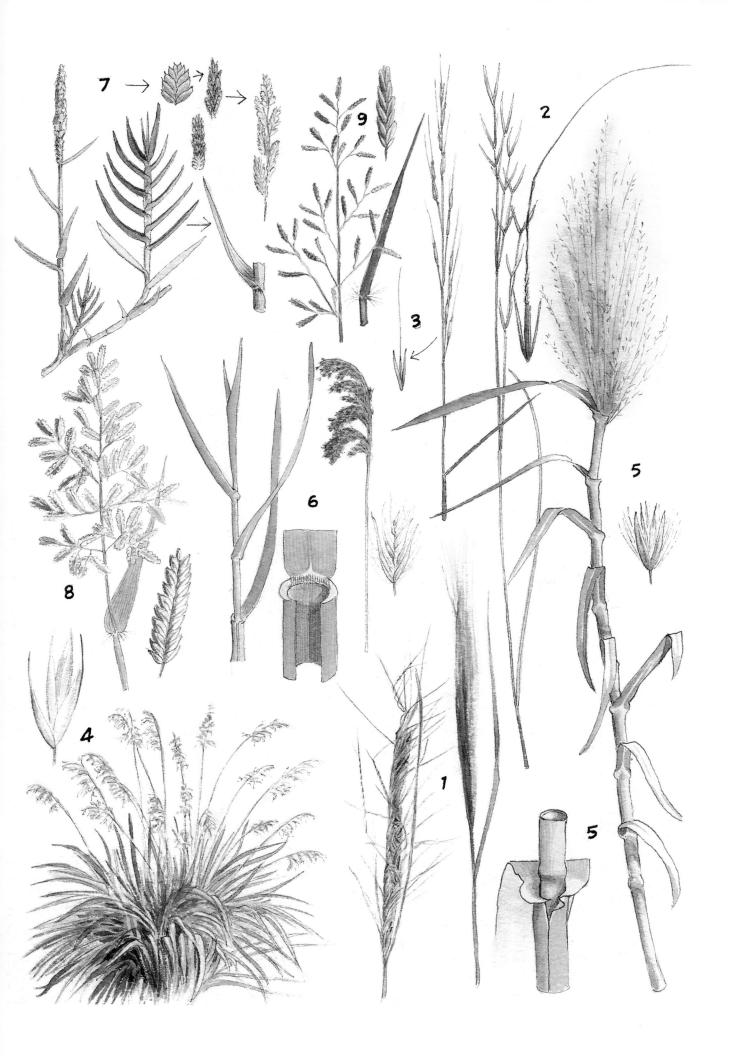

Plate 90

GRAMINEAE (9): *SPOROBOLUS, (CRYPSIS), CYNODON, (TRAGUS), PANICUM, ECHINOCHLOA, DIGITARIA, PASPALUM, STENOTAPHRUM, SETARIA, PENNISETUM, IMPERATA, (SACCHARUM), SORGHUM, (DICHANTHIUM), HYPARRHENIA, HETEROPOGON, (HEMARTHRIA)*

SPOROBOLUS
1. *Sporobolus pungens* (Schreber) Kunth. Creeping, hairless perennial. Leaf sheaths overlapping, distichous. Ligule a row of short hairs. Spikelet a single floret. May-August. Common on sandy beaches. (Small specimen x 1, spikelet x 4). (Ma, Mi, I) FE V 258

CYNODON
2. *Cynodon dactylon* (L.) Pers. Bermuda Grass. Creeping perennial. Ligule a ring of hairs. Inflorescence of 3-5 spikes arising from top of stem. Spikelets in opposite rows on spikes. July-Sept. Common. (Small specimen x 1, spikelet x 4, other details x 2). (Ma, Mi, I) FE V 259

PANICUM
3. *Panicum miliaceum* L. Millet. Robust annual with branched and eventually drooping inflorescence. Ligule membranous with a dense fringe of hairs peripherally. Spikelets flattened, with 2 florets, the upper fertile, lower sterile. June-July. Cutivated for fodder, sometimes naturalised. (Upper part small specimen x 1, spikelets x 4). Native of China and SE Asia, introduced Ma. FE V 261
4. *Panicum repens* L. Creeping Millet. Rhizomatous perennial. Inflorescence an erect panicle of numerous tiny spikelets resembling those of no 3. Stamens bright orange, anthers purple. July-Sept. Common, grassy places near sea. (Upper part small specimen x1, spikelet x 4). (Ma, Mi, I) FE V 261

ECHINOCHLOA
5. *Echinochloa colonum* (L.) Link. Shama Millet. Tufted annual. Leaf without a ligule. Inflorescence of several dense 4-rowed unilateral racemes arranged along a central axis. Racemes up to 3cm, unbranched. Spikelets in pairs, unawned. Lower glume much smaller than upper, which is as long as the spikelet. Sept.-Oct. Occasional. (Inflorescence of small specimen slightly reduced: detail x 2). (Introduced Ma). ?BI in FE V 262

DIGITARIA
6. *Digitaria sanguinalis* (L.) Scop. Crab-grass. Hairy annual. Ligule membranous. Spikelets in pairs, one longer than the other, on axes which are triangular in section. Fairly common in cultivated areas. (Ma, Mi, I) FE V 262

PASPALUM
7. *Paspalum paspalodes* (Michx) Scribner. Creeping stoloniferous perennial, superficially resembling 2. Leaf-sheaths ciliate on margin. Ligule membranous. Inflorescence with 2 (rarely -4) terminal spikes, the spikelets in one row but directed to alternate sides of the axis so that they appear to be in 2 rows. Lower glume minute, upper herbaceous with a distinct mid-vein. Lower floret a sterile lemma equalling spikelet, upper hermaphrodite, with a hardened lemma and an exposed palea. Sept. Local in damp places. (x 1, spikelet x 3). (Ma, Mi, I, introduced from tropics). Not BI in FE V 263

STENOTAPHRUM
8. *Stenotaphrum secundatum* (Walter) O.Kuntze. Creeping stoloniferous perennial, rooting at the nodes. Leaves green even in very dry situations, with broad linear abruptly tipped leaf-blades. Inflorescence spike-like, with spikelets 1-3 together, embedded in a narrow, flattened rhachis. Native of tropics, frequently planted to form a coarse, drought-resistant lawn, and sometimes naturalized on the coast. (Ma, I) FE V 263

SETARIA
Annuals (usually) or perennials. Ligule a dense fringe of hairs. Inflorescence a spike-like panicle, with the spikelets subtended by bristles, which persist after spikelets fall.
9. *Setaria pumila* (Poiret) Schultes Yellow Bristle-grass. Bristles 3-8mm, usually 4-12 per floret. Upper glume 1/2-1/3 length spikelet, exposing the rugose upper lemma. Bristles usually pinkish to gingery. June-Sept. Roadsides, waste places. (x 1, and below it, spikelet x 5, showing upper glume and transversely wrinkled upper lemma). (Ma, Mi, I) FE V 263
10. *Setaria verticillata* (L.) Beauv. Rough Bristle-grass. Resembles 9, but panicle usually interrupted. Upper glume about equalling spikelet. Bristles 1 or 2 to each spikelet, retrorsely barbed, usually green. June-Sept. Common. (Small specimen x 1, spikelet x 4). (Ma, Mi, I) FE V 263
11. *Setaria viridis* (L.) Beauv. Green Bristle-grass. Resembles 10, but panicle very dense, not interrupted, and bristles antrorsely barbed. June-Sept. Not common. **NS.** (Details from small Cretan specimen x 1 and x 4). (Ma, Mi) FE V 263

12. *Setaria italica* (L.) Beauv. Foxtail Bristle-grass. Robust annual up to 1m or more. Panicle usually lobed. Bristles antrorsely barbed, 2-5 in each cluster of spikelets, not all of which have bristles. Occasional. Cultivated for bird-seed and fodder. **NS.** (From robust garden specimen: spike often narrower and less lobed. Inflorescence x 1/2, detail x 3). (Probably arisen in cultivation, introduced Ma, I) FE V 264

PENNISETUM
13. *Pennisetum villosum* R. Br. Tufted perennial. Inflorescence a cylindrical panicle with long feathery bristles arising below each spikelet and falling with it. Aug.-Sept. Locally naturalised. (Native Ethiopia) (Ma, I) Not BI in FE V 264

IMPERATA
14. *Imperata cylindrica* (L.) Raeuschel. Robust rhizomatous perennial, up to 120cm. Panicle elongated, shining, silvery. Spikelets in pairs, each surrounded by long silky hairs. Very local. (Specimen from Spanish mainland, subsequently found in Ma: x 1, detail x 2). (Ma, I) FE V 265

SORGHUM
15. *Sorghum halepense* (L.) Pers. Johnson Grass. Robust perennial. Leaves broad with conspicuous white dorsal vein. Inflorescence a panicle 10-30cm, terminal branches racemose with up to 5 pairs of dissimilar spikelets, one sessile and ellipsoid, sometimes awned, the other narrow-lanceolate with a short pedicel, often purple. July-Sept. Common. (Introduced from N. Africa or Asia). (Ma, Mi, I) FE V 265

HYPARRHENIA
16. *Hyparrhenia hirta* (L.) Stapf. Tufted perennial. Inflorescence with paired racemes at the tip of branches arising in the axils of leaf-like bracts. Racemes bear up to 7 pairs of spikelets, one pedicellate and unawned, one sessile and awned. Apr.-Sept. Very common. (Inflorescence x 1/2, detail x 1). (Ma, Mi, I) FE V 266

HETEROPOGON
17. *Heteropogon contortus* (L.) Beauv. Tufted perennial. Inflorescence a raceme (usually solitary) with paired dissimilar spikelets, one sessile, one pedicellate in upper part of raceme. The sessile spikelets have thick, hairy awns which form a spiral twist. In the lower part of the raceme spikelets are similar and unawned. Rare. **NS.** (Specimen from Spanish mainland) (Ma) FE V 266

Also recorded from Mallorca:
Crypsis aculeata (L.) Aiton. Annual, up to 30cm. Leaves flat, villous on both sides, sheaths with tuberculate-based hairs. Ligule a row of hairs. Inflorescence a spike-like panicle. Spikelets 4mm, of one hermaphrodite floret only, strongly laterally compressed. Glumes subequal, slightly shorter than lemma. Glumes and lemma with stout mucro or short awn. Llorens lists for Ma, Not BI in FE V 258
Tragus racemosus (L.) All. Annual up to 40cm, decumbent or procumbent, rooting at nodes. Glumes very unequal, the upper 7-veined, exceeding spikelet, with large hooked spines on the veins. Recorded by Barceló (1867-1877), listed by Duvigneaud and Llorens. (Ma) FE V 260
Panicum capillare L. Dubious. Llorens omits. Included by Bonafè. Not BI in FE V 261
Echinochloa crus-gallii (L.) Beauv. Cockspur Grass. Resembles 5, but longest racemes up to 10cm, usually branched at the base, Some spikelets usually long-awned. (Ma, Mi) FE V 262
Paspalum vaginatum Swartz. Very like 7, but leaf-sheaths are hairless at apex except on back of ligule. Lower glume usually absent. Llorens lists for Ma and I. Not BI in FE V 263
Setaria geniculata (Lam.) Beauv. Resembling 9, but perennial. Recorded from near Sóller. (A.A.Butcher, personal communication 1990). Not BI in FE V 263
Saccharum ravennae (L.) Murray. Tufted perennial. Stems up to 3m. Panicle 25-60cm, plumose and lobed. Spikelets with 2 florets, dorsally compressed, enveloped in long hairs arising from the callus. Formerly cultivated. Llorens lists. (Ma, I) FE V 264
Sorghum bicolor (L.) Moench. Great Millet. Resembles 15, but annual. Llorens lists (Ma, Mi). Not BI in FE V 265
Dichanthium ischaemum (L.) Roberty. Perennial, up to 100cm, subdigitate with 3-15 terminal racemes. Racemes bear paired dissimilar spikelets one sessile with a lower sterile lemma and an upper lemma with a 10-15mm geniculate awn, one stalked and awnless. Llorens lists. Not BI in FE V 266
Hemarthria altissima (Poiret) Stapf & C.E.Hubbard. Not included by Llorens or Duvigneaud. BI in FE V 266

In Ibiza:
Setaria adhaerans (Forskål) Chiov. (See FE V 263)

Plate 91

PALMAE: *CHAMAEROPS*
ARACEAE: *ARUM, ARISARUM, DRACUNCULUS,*
LEMNACEAE: *LEMNA*
SPARGANIACEAE: *SPARGANIUM*
TYPHACEAE: *TYPHA*

PALMAE
CHAMAEROPS
1. *Chamaerops humilis* L. Dwarf Fan Palm. Shrub or small tree up to 2m. Leaves fan-like, the stem spiny. Flowers numerous at leaf bases, yellowish. Fruits like small dates. (Both illustrations reduced). Locally common in hilly places. (Ma, Mi, I) FE V 267

ARACEAE
ARUM
Tuberous rooted fleshy perennials. Flowers very small on a broad spike (*spadix*) often with a fleshy coloured extension above the flowers (*appendix*), all enfolded by a large bract (*spathe*), with overlapping margins.

2. *Arum italicum* Miller. Arum. Leaves appear in autumn. Spathe pale green, drooping forward at tip. Appendix yellow. Flowers Mar.-Apr. Common in shady places. (x 1/2). (Ma, Mi, I) FE V 270

3. *Arum pictum* L. fil. Painted Arum. Leaves appearing shortly after flowers. Spathe purple. Appendix blackish-purple. Locally common in stony scrub, but much less common than 2. Aug.-Oct. (Ma, MI) FE V 270

ARISARUM
4. *Arisarum vulgare* Targ.-Tozz. Friar's Cowl. Similar to *Arum*, but spathe with proportionately longer tube without overlapping margins. Tube of spathe variously striped with green or purple, limb dark green or purplish. Appendix usually purple or ochre. Mar.-June. Common. (Ma, Mi, I) FE V 271

DRACUNCULUS
5. *Dracunculus muscivorus* (L. fil.) Parl. Resembles *Arum* but leaf compound, with a large terminal segment and two narrower lateral segments at right angles, with a reduced repeat of this in the angles on each side. Free part of spathe bent sideways on the base, all dull ochre with purplish blotches. Appendix of spadix covered in yellowish hair-like processes. Foul-smelling in flower. Apr.-May. Fairly rare. (Ma, Mi) FE V 272

LEMNACEAE
LEMNA
6. *Lemna gibba* L. Gibbous Duckweed. Floating aquatic herb. Fronds often swollen below, like a kettle-drum, the surface reticulate to the naked eye. Flowers minute, in cavity on lower surface, stamen protruding above. **NS.** Seen by Duvigneaud. (From British specimen, smaller illustration x 1). (Ma, Mi, I) FE V 273

7. *Lemna minor* L. As above, but nearly flat on both surfaces, reticulation invisible to the naked eye. **NS.** Seen by Duvigneaud. (From British specimen, smaller illustration x 1). (Ma, Mi, I) FE V 273

SPARGANIACEAE
SPARGANIUM
8. *Sparganium erectum* L. Bur-reed. Tall aquatic perennial. Flowers in globose unisexual heads, sessile along axillary stems, male smaller above female. **NS.** Seen by Duvigneaud. (From British specimen). (Ma, Mi) FE V 274

TYPHACEAE
TYPHA
9. *Typha domingensis* (Pers.) Steudel. Southern Reedmace. Flowers packed tightly in a dense cylindrical inflorescence, the female part pale brown, 15-25cm long about 10 x as long as wide. Male part much narrower, separated from the female by up to 6cm of bare stem. May-June. Occasional in marshy places. (x 1/4). (Ma, Mi, I) FE V 276

10. *Typha latifolia* L. Reedmace (also, incorrectly but commonly, Bulrush). Female part of spike about 6 x as long as wide, deep chocolate brown, usually immediately below male, occasionally with a small gap. Female flowers without scales. May-June. Fairly common. (Ma, Mi, I) FE V 276

Another possible species for Mallorca:
Typha angustifolia L. Female part of spike coloured as 10, 6-10 x as long as wide, separated by 3-8cm from male. Female flowers with dark brown opaque scales. Llorens lists. (Ma, Mi, I) FE V 275

Plate 92

CYPERACEAE (1): *SCIRPUS, ELEOCHARIS, CYPERUS, CLADIUM, SCHOENUS*

CYPERACEAE

Herbs with grass-like leaves, sometimes reduced to sheaths. Perianth absent or represented by fine bristles. Flowers are each enclosed by a glume, and consist of two or three stamens (male flower), an ovary with two or three styles (female flower) or both (hermaphrodite flower). The fruit is a small nut (hardened ovary), and the base of the styles sometimes persist in the nut.

SCIRPUS

Spikes of flowers are one-to many-flowered. The glumes are spirally arranged in the spikelet. Flowers are all hermaphrodite, sometimes with a perianth of up to 6 bristles. **Style bases not persistent.**

1. *Scirpus maritimus* L. Sea Club-rush. Creeping perennial. **Stems sharply triangular in section, leafy**, up to 1m or more. Longer bracts leaf-like the **lowest much exceeding the inflorescence**, the shorter ones more or less bristle-like. Inflorescence of clusters of sessile spikelets or rays up to 5cm bearing spikelets at their tips. May. Common in (usually) saline mud. (Ma, Mi, I) FE V 278

2. *Scirpus lacustris* L. subsp. *tabernaemontani* (C.C.Gmelin) Syme. Bulrush. Creeping perennial. **Stems circular in section**, up to 2m or more, **leaves usually represented by sheaths at the base of the stem**, the upper one sometimes with a short blade. Bracts 2-4, leaf-or bristle-like, the **lower bract usually shorter than the inflorescence.** Inflorescence of clusters of spikelets on unequal rays or sessile. Common in water. (Ma, Mi, I) FE V 278

3. *Scirpus litoralis* Schrader. Very like 2, but **stems triangular in section. Leaves represented by sheaths at the base of the stem**, the upper one usually with a short blade. Bracts leaf- or bristle-like, the lowest longer or shorter than inflorescence. Damp places. (Ma, Mi, I) Not BI in FE V 278

4. *Scirpus holoschoenus* L. Round-headed Club-rush. Creeping perennial, very variable in height, usually less than 1m. Stems circular in section with leaf-sheaths at base, upper sheaths sometimes with a short blade. Bracts semicircular in section, the lowest erect, continuing line of stem so that inflorescence appears lateral. Inflorescence of **globular heads,** one at least sessile, the others on simple or compound rays. Common in damp places. (Ma, Mi, I) FE V 279

5. *Scirpus cernuus* Vahl. Slender Club-rush. Tufted **annual up to 30cm.** Bract continuing delicate stem, more or less leafy below. Inflorescence usually of one sessile spikelet (occasionally 2 or 3). Apr.-Aug. Common in damp places. (Ma, Mi, I) FE V 279

ELEOCHARIS

Stems leafless apart from basal sheaths. Inflorescence a single terminal spike. Glumes spirally arranged. **Style base persistent** and usually swollen.

6. *Eleocharis palustris* (L.) Roemer & Schultes. Common Spike-rush. Creeping perennial. Stems up to 1m, usually much less. Common in marshy places. (Ma, Mi, I) FE V 283

CYPERUS

Annuals or perennials. Inflorescence of spikelets arranged in clusters or umbels. Glumes (here) always arranged in two rows.

7. *Cyperus longus* L. Galingale. Creeping perennial, with rhizomes 3-10mm wide, covered in broad scales. Stems solitary, 3-sided, up to more than 1m. Inflorescence a compound umbel of 4-25 x 1-2mm spikelets with dark or reddish-brown glumes with a greenish keel. Rays up to 35mm. **Spikelets tend to radiate to form more or less globular clusters.** May-Oct. Very local. (Ma, Mi, I) FE V 286

8. *Cyperus rotundus* L. Very much like 7, but rhizomes 1mm wide with narrow scales rather widely spaced, and sometimes with tubers. Stems not more than 60cm, rays not more than 10cm. **Spikelets usually more or less erect.** June-Oct. Common. (Ma, Mi, I) FE V 286

9. *Cyperus laevigatus* L. subsp. *distachyos* (All.) Maire & Weller. Creeping perennial, often leafless. Stems up to 50cm, tufted or solitary. Bracts 2, the lower erect and exceeding inflorescence, which appears lateral, the upper spreading. **Inflorescence a sessile cluster** of up to 40 spreading spikelets, 5-23 x 2mm, often curved upwards. May-July. Occasional. (Ma, Mi, I) FE V 287

CLADIUM

10. *Cladium mariscus* (L.) Pohl. Great Fen Sedge. Creeping perennial forming patches of hollow stems up to 2.5m, leafy. Blades of leaves rigid, keeled, with saw-like cutting margins. Inflorescence a terminal panicle, with 1-3-flowered spikelets in dense short stemmed clusters with sheathing bracts. Glumes spirally arranged. Apr.-May. Local in base-rich water. (Ma, Mi, I) FE V 288

SCHOENUS

11. *Schoenus nigricans* L. Black Bog-rush. Tufted round-stemmed perennial, stems up to 60cm. Inflorescence a head of 5-10 blackish-brown spikelets with 2 dark bracts, the lower with a sheathing base and a brown lamina exceeding the inflorescence. Common in wet base-rich habitats and dune slacks. (Ma, Me, Ei) FE V 289

Other records for Mallorca:

Cyperus fuscus L. Brown Galingale. **Tufted annual**, with 3-sided stems up to 30cm. Inflorescence a simple or compound umbel of 3-8 rays, each with a dense head of reddish-brown spikelets. Listed but not seen by Duvigneaud. Llorens lists. (Ma, Mi, I) FE V 286

Cyperus capitatus Vandelli Creeping perennial with solitary stems up to 50cm. Bracts 3-6, conspicuously dilated and often reddish at the base, with revolute margins, exceeding the dense inflorescence. Inflorescence hemispherical to globose head of 8-20 x 3-4mm spikelets. Glumes reddish or purplish below with yellowish-green apex. Listed but not seen by Duvigneaud. Llorens lists (this has been listed in the Ma flora since Marès and Vigineix 1850-1880). (Ma, Mi, I) FE V 287

Also, more or less cultivated: *Cyperus esculentus* L., *Cyperus eragrostis* Lam., *Cyperus alternifolius* L.

In other islands:

Eleocharis geniculata (L.) Roemer & Schultes. Ibiza Not BI in FE V 282

Eleocharis uniglumis (Link) Schultes. Minorca. Not BI in FE 283

Plate 93

CYPERACEAE (2): *CAREX*

CAREX

Perennials. Stems unbranched (except sometimes in the inflorescence), solid, without nodes, often triangular in section. Leaf base sheathing. Leaves grass-like. Inflorescence of spike-like panicles (called spikes here for convenience) in the axils of more or less leaf-like bracts. Flowers without perianth, but each have a scale at the base (glume). Male and female flowers distinct, but usually in the same spike. Flowering time here March or April until June, when anthers of male flowers are conspicuous. Female flowers are enclosed in a utricle, from which the stigmas project, and which eventually hardens to form the 2 or 3-sided nut, often very important for identification.

Unless otherwise stated, main illustration approximately x 1, nuts and female glumes x 6.

1. *Carex distachya* Desf. Densely tufted perennial. Stems sharply triangular in section. **Spikes lax, 2-4, widely spaced**, with male flowers above and 2-5 female flowers below. **Lower bracts leaf-like, exceeding inflorescence.** Female glumes exceed the nut, the lower sometimes leaf-like and up to as long as the spike. Nut 4-6mm, ellipsoid, abruptly contracted above into a short smooth beak, greenish-brown with one prominent vein on each face. Occasional in dry places. (Ma, Mi, I) FE V 296

2. *Carex otrubae* Podp. False Fox Sedge. Tussock-forming perennial. Stem triangular in section with almost flat faces. Inflorescence branched with **5-10 dense contiguous ovoid spikes (lowest one sometimes slightly apart) all similar in appearance.** Nut ovate, 5-6mm, greenish or orange-brown. (Nut and female glume x 6). (Ma, Mi) FE V 297

3. *Carex divulsa* Stokes. Grey Sedge. Inflorescence elongated. **Spikes 5 or more**, male and female together, **few-flowered and not or hardly elongated.** Spikes usually close together but not overlapping, the lowest well-separated, often on short branches. Nut pale yellowish-brown. 3.5-5mm. Common, often as a street weed in dryish situations. (Ma, Mi) FE V 298

4. *Carex divisa* Hudson. Salt Meadow Sedge. Creeping plant. Stems triangular in section, rather rough at the top. **Spikes small, 3-8 in a short inflorescence (usually shorter than shown here).** Upper spikes often entirely male. Nut 2.5-4mm, yellowish to dark reddish-brown, with prominent slender veins, gradually narrowed into short beak. Female glumes equalling or slightly exceeding nuts, with scarious border. Common in saline soils. (Inflorescence from two specimens). (Ma, Mi, I) FE V 299

5. *Carex flacca* Schreber. Glaucous Sedge. Creeping perennial. **Leaves bluish beneath, dark green above.** Spikes dense, elongated, the upper 2-3 male, the female spikes 1-5, with lowest sometimes pendent. Lowest bract exceeds spike and often the inflorescence. Nut broadly ellipsoid, rounded at the apex with a very short beak. Common in damp places. (Ma, Mi, I) FE V 306

6. *Carex hispida* Willd. **Robust** tufted perennial, often 1m or more. Leaves blue-green. Male spikes 3-5, **female spikes 40-120 x 7-12mm, dense**, overlapping, the **upper often male above.** Nuts flattened, 4-5mm, pale yellowish or greenish-brown, with small teeth on margin. Occasional in marshy places. (Inflorescence only: this specimen had upper 3 male spikes aborted). (Ma, Mi, I) FE V 306

7. *Carex distans* L. Densely tufted. **Male spike usually solitary, female spikes 2-3, widely spaced**, the lower with peduncles 1-4cm. Nut pale greenish-brown, prominently veined, contracted into a bifid beak. (Ma, Mi, I) FE V 308

8. *Carex extensa* Good. Long-bracted Sedge. Tufted perennial. **Male spike usually solitary.** Female spikes dense, short, globular to long ovoid, **mostly sessile around or immediately below the male spike**, sometimes one stalked and well below the others. Lowest bract greatly exceeding the inflorescence. Nut greyish or greenish-brown, gradually narrowed to a bifid beak. Common in damp places. (Ma, Mi, I) FE V 308

9. *Carex hallerana* Asso. Slender tufted perennial, usually less than 20cm. Male spike solitary, 10-20mm, **female spikes** much smaller, mostly sessile or shortly pedunculate immediately below the male spike, **1-3 on a long peduncle arising from the bottom of the stem.** Nut greenish **abruptly contracted into a rather short beak.** Common, usually in dry shady places. (Ma, Mi, I) FE V 311

10. *Carex rorulenta* Porta. Resembles 9, but **creeping**, not tufted, and much slenderer, with a **fine thread-like stem. Nut gradually narrowed into a longer beak** than that of 9. (Ma, Mi, I, endemic) FE V 311

Possibly in Mallorca:

Carex acuta L. Slender Tufted Sedge. Tufted and creeping perennial often up to 1m. Spikes dense, male 2-4, up to 60mm long, female 2-4 up to 100mm. Rather dubious. Queried by both Duvigneaud and Llorens. BI in FE V 322

In Minorca:
Carex oedipostyla Duval-Jouve. FE V 313

Plate 94

ORCHIDACEAE (1): *EPIPACTIS, CEPHALANTHERA, LIMODORUM, NEOTTIA, SPIRANTHES, (PLATANTHERA), (GYMNADENIA), (DACTYLORHIZA), NEOTINEA*

EPIPACTIS

1. *Epipactis microphylla* (Ehrh.) Swartz. Small-leaved Helleborine. May-July. Fairly common under *Quercus ilex*, but slender, greyish and inconspicuous. (Ma) FE V 328

CEPHALANTHERA

2. *Cephalanthera damasonium* (Miller) Druce. White Helleborine. Leaves broad ovate, bracts characteristically exceeding ovary (but not in this specimen). Apr.-May. Occasional in woods. (x 1/2). (Ma) FE V 328
3. *Cephalanthera longifolia* (L.) Fritsch. Long-leaved Helleborine. As 2, but at least lower leaves lanceolate, bracts much shorter than ovary. Uncommon in woods. (x 1/2). FE V 328

LIMODORUM

4. *Limodorum abortivum* (L.) Swartz (including *L. trabutianum* (Batt.) Rouy). Violet Limodore. Mar.-May. Fairly common in woods. (x 1/5, details x 1). (Ma, Mi) FE V 329

NEOTTIA

5. *Neottia nidus-avis* (L.) L.C.M.Richard. Bird's Nest Orchid. Apr.-May. Shady woodland, locally common and increasing. The flowering stem persists for a long time, and dead yellowish flowers with brown edges (detail x 1/2) are more commonly encountered than the greenish-ochre fresh plant. (Main illustration x 1/2) (Ma) FE V 329

SPIRANTHES

6. *Spiranthes spiralis* (L.) Chevall. Autumn Lady's Tresses. September. **NS.** (But reported to be abundant in at least one area 1989). (From British specimen. Details slightly enlarged). (Ma, Mi, I) FE V 330

NEOTINEA

7. *Neotinea maculata* (Desf.) Stearn. Dense-flowered Orchid. Flowers very small. Plants with slightly pinkish flowers have spotted leaves, those with greenish-white flowers lack spots on leaves. April. Occasional in woods, much commoner in some years than others. (x 3/4, details x 3). (Ma, I) FE V 337

The following species have also been recorded from Mallorca, or are listed as BI in FE (illustrations, flowers only, are not from Ma specimens):

Epipactis palustris (L.) Crantz. Marsh Helleborine. (Not illustrated). Not listed by Knoche, Duvigneaud, Bonafè, Hansen or Llorens. ?BI in FE V 327.

i. *Epipactis helleborine* (L.) Crantz. Broad-leaved Helleborine. Knoche quotes Bourgeau (collecting 1813-1877). Duvigneaud lists with ?. Llorens lists without query. ?BI in FE V 327

ii. *Cephalanthera rubra* (L.) L.C.M.Richard. Red Helleborine. Resembles 3, but petals bright pinkish-purple. Knoche quotes Barceló, who quotes Richard (collecting 1761). Duvigneaud and Llorens list without query. Not BI in FE V 329

iii. *Platanthera bifolia* (L.) L.C.M.Richard. Lesser Butterfly Orchid. Knoche quotes Barceló. Duvigneaud lists with query, Llorens without query. BI included in FE V 331

iv. *Gymnadenia conopsea* (L.) R.Br. Fragrant Orchid. Duvigneaud and Llorens record without query. Not BI in FE V 332

Dactylorhiza sulphurea (Link) Franco. Llorens omits. ?BI in FE V 334 (Not illustrated).

Dactylorhiza maculata (L.) Soó. Spotted Orchid. Duvigneaud, Hansen list with query, and other *Dactylorhiza* species. Llorens lists *D. maculata* without query. ?BI in FE V 336

Recorded for Ibiza:
Gennaria diphylla (Link) Parl. Not BI in FE V 330

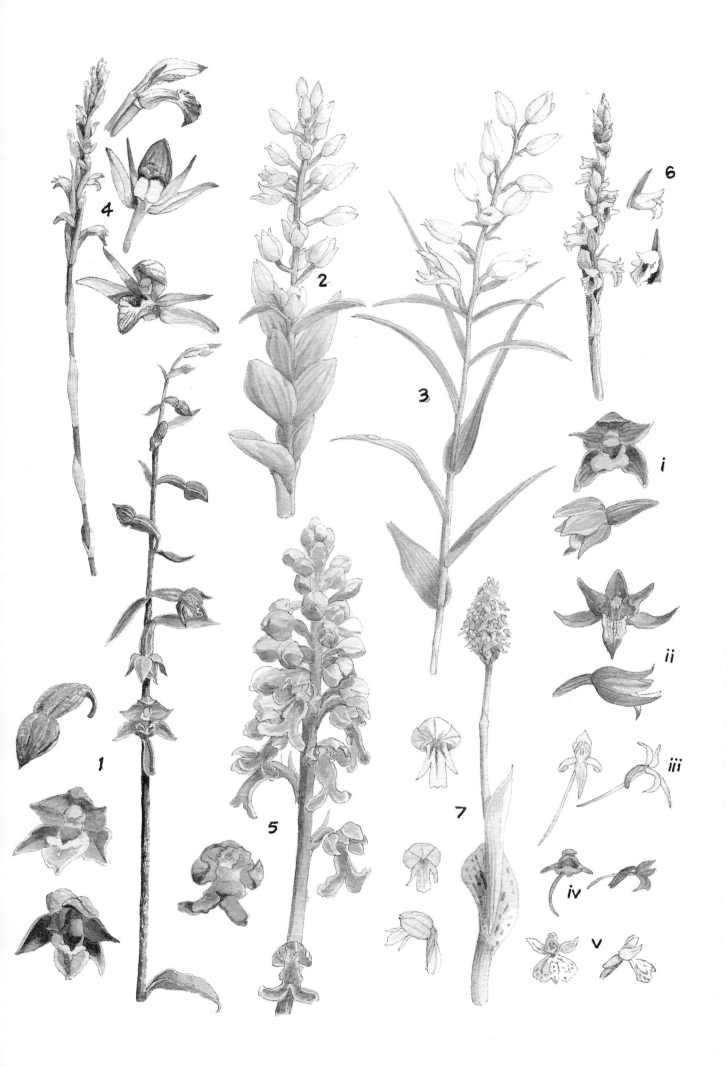

Plate 95

ORCHIDACEAE (2): *ORCHIS, ACERAS, BARLIA, HIMANTOGLOSSUM*

(Colour not described: this should be apparent from illustrations).

ORCHIS
Perianth segments free, but some convergent to form a hood. Lips are entire or 3-lobed with a basal spur.

1. *Orchis longicornu* Poiret. Long-spurred Orchid. Stem with basal rosette of leaves and 2 or 3 stem leaves. Spike fairly lax. All perianth segments except lip convergent to form a helmet. Lip 3-lobed, with lateral lobes longer than median and edges recurved. Spur about 16mm, widened at tip, horizontal or curved upwards. Mar.-Apr. Very local, but often in large numbers. (Ma, Mi) FE V 339

2. *Orchis coriophora* L. subsp. *fragrans* (Pollini) Sudre. Fragrant Orchid. Stem with 4-7 leaves below and sheaths higher up. Spike dense, more or less cylindrical. All perianth segments except lip convergent to form a helmet. Lip 3-lobed. Spur half length of ovary, conical and downward pointing. Fairly common. Apr.-May. (Ma, Mi, I) FE V 339

3. *Orchis tridentata* Scop. Toothed Orchid and/or *Orchis lactea* Poiret. Milky Orchid. Stem with 3-4 leaves near base and sheaths above. Inflorescence fairly dense, more or less cylindrical. All perianth segments except lip convergent to form a helmet. Sepals tapering into long points. Lip 3-lobed, the lateral lobes smaller, the central lobe triangular with the apex just below insertion of lateral lobes. Mar.-Apr. Locally common, but not always clearly distinguishable. Two specimens illustrated here seem to be *O. lactea* on basis of spur length. Llorens queries *O. tridentata* for Ma and Mi, gives (Ma, Mi) for *O. lactea*. BI in FE for *O. tridentata*, not BI for *O. lactea* FE V 339

Differences given in FE:

	O. tridentata	*O. lactea*
Stem:	15-45cm	7-20cm
Flower colour:	Pale violet-lilac	White or greenish pink
Shape of middle lobe labellum:	Notched with or without point in notch	Usually not notched
Spur:	Half as long as ovary	Sometimes longer than ovary

4. *Orchis italica* Poiret. Naked Man Orchid. Stem with 5-8 leaves, some at least wavy-edged, some in basal rosette, with sheaths above. Inflorescence fairly dense, conical at first, becoming ovoid. All perianth segments except lip convergent to form a helmet, the lip is shaped like a man's body. Occasional, not common. (Ma, I) FE V 339

5. *Orchis mascula* (L.) L. subsp. *olbiensis* (Reuter ex Grenier) Ascherson & Graebner (Northern European Early Purple Orchid is another subspecies). Slender orchid with 3-15

flowers. Middle sepals and lateral petals form a helmet, lateral sepals are erect. Middle lobe of lip is widest, and up to 1 1/2 x as long as wide as lateral lobes, spur longer than ovary. Apr.-May. Occasional in hilly areas, nowhere common. (Ma) FE V 340

6. *Orchis laxiflora* Lam. subsp. *palustris* (Jacq.) Bonnier & Layens. Lax-flowered Orchid. Tall plant (I saw an 80cm specimen in Mallorca in 1982 with many approaching this height. They became both rarer and smaller). Spike cylindrical. Upper sepal and lateral petals form a loose, forward pointed helmet. Lateral sepals erect and turned outwards. Lip 3-lobed with the middle lobe notched. (Ma) FE V 341

ACERAS
7. *Aceras anthropophorum* (L.) Aiton fil. Man Orchid. Spike narrow cylindrical (illustration not typical in this respect), usually fairly dense with very many flowers. All perianth segments except labellum connivent to form a helmet. Labellum like a rather slender man. Spur absent. Apr.-May. Locally common in scrubby places. (Ma, I) FE V 342

BARLIA
8. *Barlia robertiana* (Loisel.) W.Greuter. Giant Orchid. Stems tall (commonly 40cm, sometimes more) and stout. Inflorescence more or less conical to cylindrical, many-flowered. Flowers large, with labellum up to 20cm. All perianth segments except labellum connivent to form a loose helmet, labellum man-like with rather a long body and short limbs. Jan.-Mar. Fairly common. (Ma, Mi) FE V 342

Other species recorded from Mallorca, all very rare and possibly not seen recently (flowers only illustrated, not from Mallorcan specimens)

i. *Orchis papilionacea* L. Not seen by Duvigneaud. Llorens lists. (Ma) FE V 338

ii. *Orchis militaris* L. Hansen records as seen 1983. Llorens omits. Not BI in FE V 340

iii. *Orchis saccata* Ten. Not seen by Duvigneaud. Llorens lists without query. (Ma) FE V 340

iv. *Orchis patens* Desf. Duvigneaud lists 'groupe de *O. patens*'. Llorens lists without query. (Ma) FE V 340

v. *Himantoglossum hircinum* (L.) Sprengel. Hansen records as seen in 1982. Llorens omits. Not BI in FE V 342

vi. *Orchis morio* L. subsp. *champagneuxii* (Barn.) Camus. Llorens lists. (Ma, Mi) FE V 338

On other islands:
Orchis simia Lam. Cabrera. Not BI in FE V 339
Orchis mascula (L.) L. subsp. *mascula* Minorca. FE V 340

Plate 96

ORCHIDACEAE (3): *ANACAMPTIS, SERAPIAS, OPHRYS*

ANACAMPTIS

1. *Anacamptis pyramidalis* (L.) L.C.M.Richard. Stem slender, with narrow leaves below and sheaths above. Inflorescence a dense pyramidal to ovoid spike of numerous flowers (usually pink as illustrated, white not infrequent). Upper three perianth segments connivent to form a helmet, lateral 2 sepals spreading, labellum about the same length, deeply divided into 3 more or less equal lobes. Fairly common in scrubby places. (Ma, Mi, I) FE V 343

SERAPIAS

2. *Serapias lingua* L. Tongue Orchid. Sepals partially connate, connivent with upper two petals to form a pointed helmet. Labellum large, constricted in the middle to form a basal hypochile, which has a solitary dark ridge at the base and two dark purple lateral lobes, all largely hidden by the helmet, and a prominent epichile, in this species like a long pointed tongue, white or pink. Mar.-May. Occasional near the sea. (Ma, Mi, I) FE V 344

3. *Serapias parviflora* Parl. Small-flowered Serapias. Much like 2, only flowers smaller. Helmet as above. Labellum not much longer than other segments, with two brownish red ridges at the base and dark lateral lobes, the epichile short, brownish-red, commonly with the tip turned inward towards the stem. Fairly common in scrubby places. (Ma, Mi, I) FE V 344

OPHRYS

Leaves in a basal rosette, often with stem leaves too. Sepals large, coloured and spreading, upper two petals relatively small. Labellum distinctive, often resembling an insect, with a central hairless area, the speculum (= mirror in Latin, particularly appropriate in 4).

4. *Ophrys speculum* Link. Mirror Orchid. Sepals green, upper petals dark or light brown, labellum fringed with dark purplish-brown hairs, including the two short lateral lobes, the speculum shining bluish, outlined in yellow or reddish brown. Mar.-June. Common. (Ma, Mi, I) FE V 345

5. *Ophrys lutea* (Gouan.) Cav. subsp. *murbeckii* (Fleischm.) Soó. Yellow Bee Orchid. Sepals large, greenish-yellow. Lateral petals small, deep yellow. Labellum strongly 3-lobed, with the middle lobe indented at the apex. The margin of the labellum is yellow. The speculum is W-shaped and bluish on a brownish-red background with an inverted V at the tip. Local. Feb.-Mar. (Ma, Mi, I) FE V 345

6. *Ophrys fusca* Link. Sombre Bee Orchid. A very variable species. Sepals green or yellowish-green. Petals narrow, half length of sepals, green or reddish-green. Labellum varies greatly. Brown velvety, often with narrow white or yellow margin incurved, usually notched at tip. Mar.-June. (Ma, Mi, I) FE V 346

There are many subspecies here, themselves variable

a. subsp. *fusca*. Labellum 13-15 x 9-12mm, dark brown with greyish-blue 2-lobed speculum. Size of lobes vary. Median lobe indentedat apex, sometimes with thin yellowish or white margin, By far the most common, very widespread.

b. subsp. *iricolor* (Desf.) O. Schwarz. Large plant with large flowers. Labellum up to 21x 25mm, very dark rich purplish-brown. Speculum iridescent blue. Occasional.

c. subsp. *dyris* (Maire) Soó, has labellum reddish <14mm. Dark colour of basal part of labellum continues as narrow line between two paler basal markings which are outlined in cream. A subsp. o*megaifera* (Fleischm.) E.Nelson seems to be similar without the narrow line.

d. (which was large) and e. are other distinctive variants painted from Mallorcan specimens.

7. *Ophrys sphegodes* Miller subsp. *atrata* (Lindley) E.Mayer. Early Spider Orchid. Sepals and upper petals (half length of sepals and often wavy-edged) pale greenish, straw-coloured or (rarely) pinkish. The labellum is broad blackish or brownish with hairy margins and reduced side lobes, often with a small forward-pointing appendage at the tip. The speculum (spider) is bluish or pinkish, with two long 'legs' extending downwards, two shorter ones extending into the side lobes, and two very short legs upwards. (Total 6 – real spiders have 8!). This species is also rather variable. (Ma, I) FE V 346

8. *Ophrys bertolonii* Moretti. Bertoloni's Bee Orchid. Petals and sepals pink, the petals shorter, narrower and more deeply coloured. Labellum is large, with inconspicuous or absent side-lobes and the lower part directed forwards. Colour dark velvety brown, with a yellow appendage at the tip and a narrow reddish or yellow border. The speculum is small and variable in shape, compact and angular. Apr.-May. Fairly common. (Ma, Mi, I) FE V 347

9. *Ophrys tenthredinifera* Willd. Sawfly Orchid. Sepals and upper petals pink, the sepals broad, the petals about one third length of sepals, linear and more deeply coloured. Labellum more or less square with a forward pointing basal appendage. Marginal zone wide yellow or orange and hairy. Central part of labellum dark purplish-brown and velvety with a small bilobed bluish speculum. Common. (Ma, Mi, I) FE V 349

10. *Ophrys apifera* Hudson. Bee Orchid. Sepals pink to lilac or greenish-white. Petals narrow, greenish, pink or pinkish-yellow. Labellum brownish or blackish purple, usually with a deflexed basal appendage. Speculum reddish-brown or violet, bilobed, with a yellow margin: yellow spots lower on the labellum may be connected to the speculum by yellow lines, or lines may be present without spots. Again variable. May-June.Widespread. (Ma, Mi, I) FE V 349

11. *Ophrys bombyliflora* Link. Bumble-bee Orchid. A small orchid with green sepals: upper petals usually paler green. Labellum deeply 3-lobed, with very hairy lateral pointed lobes, and rounded middle lobe looking plump like a small bumble-bee. Speculum small, bilobed or with 2 separate parts. Common, but inconspicuous. (Ma, Mi, I) FE V 349

12. *Ophrys hybrid*. Demonstrates the difficulties! Hybridization is fairly common in this genus. Mr J.J.Wood of the Herbarium at the Royal Botanic Gardens, Kew suggests that this one could be *O. speculum* x *O. fuciflora* (F.W.Schmidt) Moench, in which case *O. fuciflora* is probably about somewhere (though Duvigneaud and Llorens only list it for Minorca). However there are also puzzling plants here which suggest a hybrid between *O. apifera* and *O. fuciflora*.

Also recorded for Mallorca:

Ophrys insectifera L. Fly Orchid. Flowers very slender. Sepals green, petals linear, brownish and antenna-like, nearly as long as sepals. Labellum blackish-violet with a blue bilobed speculum. Hansen lists as first recorded 1982. Llorens also lists. Not BI in FE V 345

In Minorca:

Serapias cordigera L. FE V 343
Serapias vomeracea (Burm.) Briq. FE V 343
Ophrys fuciflora FE V 348

INDEX TO LATIN NAMES OF FAMILIES AND GENERA

Where a family or genus occupies more than one plate, it is indexed only to the first.
If a family is represented in Mallorca by only one genus, from which the name of the family is derived, only the genus is given here.